AMERICA'S BEST FEMALE
SHARPSHOOTER

The

William F. Cody

Series on the History and
Culture of the American West

AMERICA'S BEST FEMALE SHARPSHOOTER

The Rise and Fall of LILLIAN FRANCES SMITH

Julia Bricklin

UNIVERSITY OF OKLAHOMA PRESS : NORMAN

Frontispiece: Lillian in her trademark hat and dress, 1887.
Buffalo Bill Center of the West, Cody, Wyoming, P.69.1588.

Buffalo Bill Center of the West sponsorship of
The William F. Cody Series on the History and
Culture of the American West is generously
funded by the Geraldine W. & Robert J. Dellenback
Foundation, Inc.

LIBRARY OF CONGRESS CATALOGING-IN-PUBLICATION DATA

Name: Bricklin, Julia, 1970– author.
Title: America's best female sharpshooter : the rise and fall of Lillian
    Frances Smith / Julia Bricklin
Other titles: Rise and fall of Lillian Frances Smith
Description: First edition. | Norman, OK : University of Oklahoma Press,
    [2017] | Series: William F. Cody series on the history and culture of the
    American West ; volume 2 | Includes bibliographical references and index.
Identifiers: LCCN 2016043288 | ISBN 978-0-8061-5633-0 (hardcover : alk. paper)
Subjects: LCSH: Smith, Lillian Frances. | Shooters of firearms—United
    States—Biography. | Entertainers—United States—Biography. | Buffalo
    Bill's Wild West Show. | Women—West (U.S.)—Biography.
Classification: LCC GV1157.S65 B75 2016 | DDC 799.3/1092 [B] —dc23
LC record available at https://lccn.loc.gov/2016043288

America's Best Female Sharpshooter: The Rise and Fall of Lillian Frances Smith is Volume 2 in the William F. Cody Series on the History and Culture of the American West.

The paper in this book meets the guidelines for permanence and durability of the Committee on Production Guidelines for Book Longevity of the Council on Library Resources, Inc. ∞

1 2 3 4 5 6 7 8 9 10

To my family:
Kevin, Andrew, and Jane

And to
Nannette Lindemann Clark, a true California girl

CONTENTS

ILLUSTRATIONS

SERIES EDITORS' FOREWORD

On May 11, 1887, two female sharpshooters with Buffalo Bill's Wild West show performed before Queen Victoria. The first performer, billed as "California Girl" Lillian Smith, shot nearly fifty glass balls thrown in the air and missed only twice. Summoned to the royal box, Smith bowed before the queen, who bowed in return. On May 13 the *Washington Post* reported that Annie Oakley, "who followed [Smith], was equally successful." The article noted, "both of the young women bowed in a matter-of-fact way and then walked off as if they were not at all overcome by the situation."

Performing before Queen Victoria that day, Annie Oakley and Lillian Smith stood as equals, yet after their command performances, these two sharpshooters followed very different career paths. Annie Oakley's route led to iconic status within the mythic American West. After her death, numerous publications and documentaries highlighted Oakley as a leading female sharpshooter and significant international spokesperson for women in shooting sports. Oakley, who was featured in a popular Broadway musical, films, and a television series, secured a beloved place within American popular culture well into the twentieth century.

Although Lillian Smith proved herself equal to Oakley before Queen Victoria that day in 1887, Smith seemed to fade away, obscured by the popularity of her peer. Eventually she dropped her moniker "The California Girl" and reinvented herself as Princess Wenona, a sharpshooting Indian princess. Within the conventional history, Smith emerges as the foil to Annie Oakley's traditional American girl image. No television series or smash Broadway hit transformed Smith into an iconic western legend admired by countless fans.

The William F. Cody Series on the History and Culture of the American West is pleased to reintroduce Lillian Smith through Julia Bricklin's biography *America's Best Female Sharpshooter*. The series features scholarship on that phase of the American past, exemplified in Cody's life and the Buffalo Bill phenomenon, which foregrounds the relationship between material history and its popular mythologies. This work takes us back to 1887, offering a more nuanced account of the well-publicized feud with Annie Oakley from her less-famed rival's perspective. Bricklin's recovery of Lillian Smith contributes to this broader history as it pieces together the fragmented record of Smith's life and career and uncovers the gendered history of sharpshooting, market hunting, and popular depictions of Western womanhood. We also learn how Smith dramatized the complex identity politics of "playing Indian," as Philip J. Deloria has termed it.

Julia Bricklin's *America's Best Female Sharpshooter* affords a fresh account of the Wild West show phenomenon with its depictions of the American Western experience as well as its transnational appeal. Lillian Smith's career as the California Girl and Princess Wenona provides a unique perspective on the relationship between western expansion and mass culture, as well as on representations of American Indians in popular culture. Through the life and times of Lillian Smith, carefully documented within this work, readers will find a better understanding of the social and cultural means that shaped a key moment in the popularization of the American West.

Jeremy Johnston
Frank Christianson
Douglas Seefeldt

ACKNOWLEDGMENTS

This book would not be possible without the enthusiasm and graciousness of the following people: Tom Shelton, Helen Shelton, Ann Alley, Patricia Sayre, Sara Hodge, Martha Small, Philip Sheldon, Paul Webb, Kenli Hill, and Glenda Grigsby. All of these people generously offered so much of their family lore so that I could have a better understanding of Lillian Smith.

I am deeply grateful to Josh Sides, who encouraged me mightily to write this book and took so much time to help shape it. I am also indebted to Tom Devine and Merry Ovnick, who have always supported my research and my enthusiasm for lost histories; to the two anonymous reviewers of my manuscript; and to Jay Fultz for whipping it into shape.

Thank you to Julie Moring, Michelle Maxwell, Brian Moore, John Benson, Heather Benson Stricker, Melissa Rosen, Kristina Barunas Jepsen, Dan Nelson, Clark Gray, Sue Mueller, Tristan Traviolia, Clementine Oliver, Marilyn Robbins, Eileen Litchfield, Michael Devall, Beth Freeman, Raymond "Littlewolf" Spendley, Tom Lindemann, Adam Kane, Sarah C. Smith, Fran E. Greenberg, Jacqueline Reese, Mette Flynt, Dennis Hagen, Jen Duvally, and Kristina Clark Ost.

Special thanks to the Whitsett Committee for its generous support.

AMERICA'S BEST FEMALE
SHARPSHOOTER

INTRODUCTION

Molly Bawn tells us the stars twinkle all night because
they have nothing else to do. So we suppose little Lilly
shoots because she cannot help it.

Breeder and Sportsman, 1884

In the midst of the temperate California winter of 1879, a man named
Levi Smith placed twenty-five glass balls in a basket of sawdust,
walked out to his field, and called for his daughter. Lillian, seven years
old and clad in cowboy boots and a dirty plaid dress, sauntered out to
the field and turned her back on him. But this was no sign of disrespect;
instead, it was her signature move. She hoisted a Ballard .22 rifle up
to her shoulder and signaled for her father to throw the balls in the air
one at a time. When he did, Lillian sited them with a mirror and blasted
each one out of the sky.

The girl who made it rain glass that day would grow up to be
Princess Wenona, billed by promoters as the best pistol- and riflewoman to perform in the Miller Brothers' 101 Ranch Wild West, a
traveling extravaganza that rivaled Buffalo Bill's Wild West show.
What few people acknowledged was that she was actually the best
female shot in America, better even than legendary Annie Oakley.
A preponderance of anecdotal evidence suggests that although both
were extraordinarily capable with all weaponry, Lillian could probably have claimed top prize for rifle expertise. She thrilled millions
on the Wild West shows and the vaudeville circuit, she was one of
Buffalo Bills' top billing acts, and she ultimately transformed herself
into a faux Sioux Indian princess, believed and beloved by millions.
And yet Lillian Smith has been almost entirely forgotten. Why?

The answer is that Lillian bucked convention in almost every part of her already unconventional life and failed to adopt acceptable gender and racial roles in the ways that her rival did, leaving no place for historians to compartmentalize her. She was not a prim and thrifty Victorian woman who chose her words carefully, like Oakley. Nor was she a blood member of any Native American tribe, and therefore could never be an authentic actor like Luther Standing Bear, who appeared in Wild West shows and film. She certainly was not quite like the many cowgirls she performed with and lived around on the 101 Ranch, her home later in life—cowgirls who were described as beautiful composites of "a perfect woman reared in the lap of nature, whose rough edges have been smoothed down by a college education."[1]

As a result, surprisingly little has been written about Lillian.[2] Most biographies of William "Buffalo Bill" Cody briefly mention the identity-shifting Lillian, if only because it was at his 1886 Wild West outfit that she met Annie Oakley. Almost all of the discussions refer to Smith's lack of self-control, her appearance, and her inability to keep a husband. "Although Smith's sharpshooting rivaled Oakley's, the latter's display of petite domesticity outshone Smith, who was heavy and single," wrote Louis S. Warren in *Buffalo Bill's America*, his landmark work about Cody's influence upon the culture of the American West.[3] "Wonderful as she was, the girl never made the impact on the public, nor on history that Annie Oakley did," Nellie Yost wrote of Lillian in 1976 in *Buffalo Bill*.[4]

Despite the shortage of writing on Lillian, several myths surround her career.[5] One of the most common rumors about Smith was that she was a flirtatious, brash, uncouth woman, who did not work well with others and was dismissed by showrunners as soon as the novelty of her pluck wore off. "She was outspoken, brassy, sexually intemperate and a frank braggart," summarized one historian, "much more the role that Ethel Merman should have played than the titular character of 'Annie Get Your Gun.'"[6] This may have been true when Lillian was a very young girl, but records indicate that by the time she was twenty, she was a literate, articulate, thoughtful woman who was very much aware of the machinations of the show business.

Smith may have stepped on some toes when she stepped into the ranks of professional shooters as a teen, leaving her familiar surroundings of Northern California behind. Who can blame a young girl for babbling, especially when out of the hawk-eyed sights of her parents for the first time? But many sources suggest that these derogatory descriptions stem largely from her first few awkward days at Buffalo Bill's Wild West Show in 1886, and that Oakley, who had every reason to be suspicious and jealous, grossly exaggerated these assessments.

The notion that Lillian took many lovers and husbands is often highlighted more than her rifle talents. These alternative partnerships did not allow Lillian to fit into the same romantic narrative as Oakley, who had found her one true love in her husband Frank. The couple even died within days of each other. In truth, Lillian was married only twice, and perhaps only once legally. She most certainly had some sort of "marital understanding" with an older cowboy at the Buffalo Bill show. Some years later, she married a man in Santa Cruz, but left him shortly thereafter. She and vaudeville king Charles "California Frank" Hafley lived as husband and wife for several years, though evidence implies that this was mostly a business arrangement with some genuine reciprocal affection. After Hafley, Smith was linked at least in the public eye to cowboy Wayne Beasley and Native American performer William Eagle Shirt.

During the last years of her life, Smith took up with Western painter Emil Lenders. She and the artist were intrigued by each other and were good roommates, but for the most part, it was a coupling of comfort, convenience, and the mutual enabling of bad habits. Mostly, Lillian's romances served some purpose for her, and while she may have unintentionally hurt one or two people, she was not the hapless, love-struck puppy dog who could not find true love when it suited her. But there is no escaping the fact that she was linked to many men romantically, and while thousands of women may have been silently jealous of her fluid love life, historians have often downgraded Lillian for it while they upheld Oakley as virtuously restrained.

Lillian's few chroniclers almost always give equal time to her vacillating weight and alleged drinking problem as they do to her shooting acumen. "Still she was gaining weight," notes one of her time with the 101 Ranch, "but still able to break glass balls. Her problem was with other glasses. Strong drink was taking its toll, and she had difficulty holding husbands."[7] When she took up with Lenders in Oklahoma, notes Michael Wallis, an expert on 101 Ranch history, the couple maintained a vineyard of five thousand grapevines, "mostly for quenching Lillian's thirst for alcohol."[8] This purported cloud of nonsobriety and slovenliness can be traced to remarks Annie Oakley's husband made in sporting magazines and newspapers late in the nineteenth century.

To find Lillian's story, we have to hunt broadly and deeply. She gave very few direct interviews, and did not leave any diaries behind. As Shirley once wrote: "Like many comparatively unknowns in real life, she gained her fame and fortune in the Wild West shows of the 1880s and 1890s and several years after the turn of the century. Pasts often were confused by the manufactured publicity so characteristic of show build-ups given star performers."[9] Worse, for historians, anyway, Lillian rarely dispelled anything written about her during her lifetime, and was happy to live out the last years of her life as a retired Native American princess.

Smith, like Oakley, had no children—at least none that she claimed. She left few documents in her own writing; thankfully, the ones she did leave speak volumes about her personality, her work ethic, and the grueling realities of earning a living by reenacting a frontier that no longer existed.

At age fourteen, Lillian stunned audiences in the East when she performed for Buffalo Bill Cody's Wild West show, receiving equal billing as Oakley but more press than her rival. To say that Smith was simply a crack rifle shot, argues Wallis, would have been as foolish as describing Lucille Mulhall as a "fair" horseback rider or calling Will Rogers merely "handy" with a lariat. No sharpshooter, Wallis writes, could compete with Smith.

When circumstances forced Smith off Cody's Wild West circuit, she reinvented herself as a multifaceted vaudeville star, then transformed herself into an entirely new person, "Princess Wenona," the "Winsome Wonder Shot of the World." She applied dark brown makeup to her face when weather did not permit natural tanning and chapping and wore Native American tunics and the occasional headdress. At the turn of the twentieth century, this supposed Sioux woman was billed as the only woman who had successfully incorporated shooting from the back of a galloping horse into her act.

Smith's successful metamorphosis was partly the cause of her obscurity. To be sure, employers like Cody, Gordon "Pawnee Bill" Lillie,

America's Best Female Sharpshooter

and Hafley offered, through their shows, a ready-made ethnic identity that an ambiguously dark performer could embrace. Shows by Buffalo Bill and his copycats, writes historian Laura Browder, "opened possibilities for dark-skinned people to redefine themselves by creating a visual icon of Indianness and an audience for Indian performance."[10] This is true, though more often than not, performers were actually Native American, black, or Mexican, and were forced to fit the mold of the prevalent stereotypes in their performances. Not many were Anglo American trying to pass as something else, like Smith.

By examining the events that led up to Lillian's identity shift and the events that followed, it becomes apparent that Smith not only used "Princess Wenona" as a professional passport of sorts, but also as a way to distance herself from her biological family and solidify ties to those who provided unconditional friendship and support for her. Often, these people were also untethered from their own biological families. The Miller 101 Ranch in Ponca City, Oklahoma, Lillian's home for the last third of her life, was also home to unattached Native American entertainers, black ranch hands and performers, up-and-coming silent film stars, and any number of ragtag immigrants from Canada, Ireland, Germany, England, and other states of the Union.

Annie Oakley was enormously talented and deserves every accolade ever given her. But unlike Lillian, Oakley gifted her biographers with plenty of direct interviews with legitimate press corps and left eight scrapbooks of her own. Also, she had an early, long, and successful marriage to a forceful man who not only loved her, but was also one of the best agents and managers of his time: Francis "Frank" Butler. Butler was also a gifted and prolific writer. In addition to writing his own accounts of the life and times of a female champion shooter, he got the press to write their own favorable stories about Oakley.

Most importantly, Oakley was exactly what American audiences wanted to see and what American storytellers wanted to talk about. For the most part, the West had been settled, and its Native inhabitants contained, in the 1880s and 1890s when Smith and Oakley were often compared. Oakley presented herself as a Victorian lady who also happened to be an expert markswoman. Her whiteness and ladylike behavior, Browder writes, clearly set her apart from the less savory examples of armed women that were floating around popular culture.

She also embodied a growing movement of elite sportsmanship that allowed husbands and wives to shoot together as a wholesome pastime.

By the time Oakley stepped into Buffalo Bill's Wild West Show as a replacement for Captain Adam Henry Bogardus, one of the most talented sharpshooters of the 1880s—she had perfected her image. It was, as Browder aptly describes—"far less bitten" than her pioneer foremothers like dime novel heroines Belle Starr and Martha "Calamity Jane" Canary. While Starr and Canary were still popular in the 1880s because of their gender-bending dress and stories of their violent behavior, they were not women a mother could encourage her daughter to emulate.

Lillian, later Wenona, was not as successful in this regard. Crowds went crazy for her, but her public image was less consistent than Oakley's. As a child, she was a novelty because of her raw talent and composure and, well, because she was a child. As a teen, Lillian was intriguing because of her young marriage to an older cowboy and their ensuing adventures with Buffalo Bill Cody. When her marriage and her association with Cody faltered, Lillian was left to a family that exploited her talent. All she had was pluck, nerve, and an insatiable desire to make a comfortable existence for herself whereby she could hone her craft.

To succeed, Lillian did what no one in the Wild West circuit had successfully done before: she completely reinvented herself as an Indian. This transformation allowed her to wipe clean her previous life, and it also served to intrigue audiences and the press. Of course, Smith, as Wenona, was a "rehabilitated" Indian—she was at least partially white, according to her new pedigree, and she was rescued by whites and anxious to live among them, if only tentatively. This was a departure from her entertainment forebears, like Belle Starr, who was the "unfortunate combination of a Cherokee squaw and a pale-face lady of the upper tendum."[11]

Considerable feeling existed among show people that Wenona was a much better shot than Annie Oakley but never received the credit and critical acclaim she deserved. At the time of her death in 1930, she still held several world records, such as breaking 300 swinging balls with a single .22 rifle in 14 minutes, 33 seconds. She kept the world record of shooting from the back of a horse and breaking 71 of 72 balls thrown in the air—as well as many other records.

To find the true story of Lillian, we are forced to look at others in the shooting and vaudeville world—those with whom she spent the most time, such as common-law husbands Charles Frank Hafley and Emil Lenders, and the men and women she worked with in the Wild West shows of William Cody, Gordon Lillie, and the Miller brothers. We must draw from those brief and rare occurrences where Lillian was neither prepared to nor encouraged to speak on the record. We can add to her story by pulling from newspaper records—including planted publicity pieces and unfiltered commentary—and letters and records left by those who knew her. Hunting and sport magazines from 1880 through 1925 provide technical commentary about Smith's shooting and equipment, as well as gossip about the circles in which she employed them. From these various sources, we can cobble together a biography of Smith's adventurous life and athletic prowess. With a fuller understanding of these shooting women and their time, we can credit Oakley as the woman who shot to make her living, and finally see Lillian Smith as the woman who lived to shoot.

Chapter One

NEVER ALONE, NEVER LONELY

The Smith girl that was such a good rifle shot was a fine looking girl. She would say: "Let me shoot your hat." You would throw it up and she would shoot it three or four times before it hit the ground. This Smith girl was way ahead of everything when it came to shooting with a rifle.

Joe Heacox, Merced pioneer, 1950

While sleeping off their all-night journey through the Pacheco Wagon pass, Lillian Smith's mother and father did not hear their nine-year-old wander off on her mustang. Exploring a tributary of the Pajaro River in Santa Cruz under the cool canopy of Monterey pines, the little girl heard her dog barking ahead. Later, she explained that she thought her pet had "treed a squirrel, sure," but instead found him shivering in the sights of a hissing and spitting mountain lion. Unflinchingly, the girl took aim with her 7.5-pound Ballard, pulled the trigger, and watched the cat flail as it fell from forty feet high. She let her dog bite the neck and finish off the animal, and then with some effort, slung it behind the saddle of her horse. Lillian's mother nearly fainted but her fellow campers cheered when she unceremoniously dumped the dead cougar at their feet.[1]

The other travelers encouraged little Lillian to write the local papers about her feat, which she did, though the newspaper people mistakenly assumed that this member of the Smith family was a boy.[2] No matter—by the time she turned ten in 1881, Smith was traveling up and down California on the Central Pacific Railroad, breaking records at gun clubs and exhibition halls, and there was no mistaking her gender, her age, or her mastery with a gun. Audiences flocked to see the "California Girl, Champion Rifle Shot of the World" and, later, an accomplished trick horse rider and trainer, too. In April 1885, *Sporting Life* magazine announced that efforts were being made to arrange a match between the "celebrated lady rifle shots" Lillian Smith and Annie Oakley, noting that both were equally adept in the use of shotgun or rifle, and that they thought newcomer Smith could hold her own against world-famous exhibition shooters Adam Bogardus and William Frank Carver.[3]

The press made much of the alleged rivalry between the two female sharpshooters. Smith, though, had little interest in specifically besting Oakley, even if many followers of shooting sports of their time believed Smith to be the better shooter. In 1887, William Cody himself offered a purse of ten thousand dollars to anyone who could outshoot Smith; no one ever claimed the prize.

While Cody was not able to get a formidable match for Lillian, he paved the way for something that may have been more beneficial to her. Buffalo Bill removed the requirement of ethnic authenticity, making it possible for Lillian to transform herself into Wenona, an "orphaned Sioux Indian Princess," and to distinguish herself from other shooters.[4] Her press biography was repeated often, though some papers made their own embellishments: "During the early struggles of the pioneers in the westward course Wenona's parents were members of an emigrant train which was attacked by the Sioux Indians. Nearly all of the members of the train were massacred. Wenona's mother was among the few who escaped alive but was later captured by the Indians who had attacked the train and was made prisoner. The chief of the tribe took a fancy to her and added her to his list of squaws against her will. Some years later a daughter was born and this was Wenona."[5] The biography also said that, at ten years old, she had become the most expert rifle shot of the tribe.

Conveniently, this story for Anglo readers claimed that her father, the chief, asked that she be adopted into a white family upon his death. After graduating with honors from the Carlisle Indian School in Pennsylvania, the story continues, Wenona found that she could not get a job, and so she cast aside the garments she had learned to wear "in civilization," and "once more donned the blanket of the Sioux and became active in the tribe's welfare."[6]

Because of her schooling, continues this fanciful biography, Wenona was the first woman permitted to sit among the Sioux councils, and her "word soon became a law" within the tribe. Her adoptive parents valiantly sought her return to her white family, but the life she knew in infancy was the one she wished to adhere to in adulthood. Thus, she became part of the 101 Ranch Wild West Show in 1910, and the other Sioux took their orders from her.

In truth, Lillian, later "Wenona," had not one drop of Native American blood. She was born to Quakers, and both sides of her family hailed from New England for at least five generations. Her sixth great-grandfather, John Smith, was an indentured servant on the Mayflower. Eventually, he won his release and purchased land in Dartmouth, Massachusetts, as did several Quaker families. These half dozen clans intermarried throughout the next two hundred years and every generation produced some of the finest boat crafters in New England.[7]

In 1856, Lillian's grandfather, Captain Levi Smith, famous among whaling agents for his abolitionist sentiment and his fish chowder, succumbed to an infected gall bladder and died writhing in pain. His job, a well-paying one as Dumpling Rock Lighthouse keeper, went to one of his older sons instead of his youngest, Levi Woodbury Smith. Nonetheless, at age twenty-two, Levi W. was already a fairly accomplished boat carpenter and engaged to Rebecca Robinson, the daughter of another boat builder.

A year after the couple married in 1857, Rebecca gave birth to a son, George, but like so many other children at that time, he died before his second birthday. For Levi's wife, it may have been small comfort that she was pregnant again. When Charles was born in October of 1859, Rebecca moved back in with her parents for support while her husband bunked in the Buzzard's Bay harbor for days at a time, sailing the custom houseboat.

Somehow, Lillian's father escaped the horrors of the Civil War battlefields, perhaps because his family had already provided two young men in the form of his brothers. He worked a few years as a boat builder in Bristol, Rhode Island, but found the lure of California too much to resist and moved there with Rebecca and Charles, right after the war ended.

The Smiths likely took the Great Western and Central railways to Bridger, Utah. From there, they joined an emigrant train, and forked southwest past the City of Rocks in Idaho toward Nevada, eventually stopping at the seat of the Sierra Nevadas in far eastern California.

This journey required Lillian's parents and her brother to become good shooters. Press reports told the Smiths that wagons were constantly besieged by Indians, who "fought different than that of white men," which was to rush in on the ponies for a little while, just to make their arrows fly, and then "run their horses for all they are worth and get out of gun shot as quickly as possible." It was not long before the Smiths realized it was more likely they could be harassed by desperate white drifters after the close of the states' conflict. Every able-bodied member of a family had to know how to shoot, and shoot often. They needed to hunt for food, and be at the ready in case of attack, whether it was by human or animal. A female contemporary of the Smiths who followed a similar path to the West and lived in Merced at the same time described their readiness training: "I'll bet our train threw a ton of bullets into the Platte river. We always camped about a hundred yards from the river in order to have water. It was the rule for everybody to take all his guns after supper and go down to the river and shoot. All guns were kept loaded. Some snag perhaps a couple of hundred yards away would be selected and everybody would shoot at it."

Emigrant train families took no chances. At that time, everybody used loose ammunition, and every man, woman, and child knew how to stuff a revolver—even a six-shooter—as well as a rifle and shotgun, which were muzzle-loading, cap and ball affairs. Powder had to be poured down the muzzle and then a ball "rammed home." To fire the gun, a cap was put on the tube to explode the charge. "This target practice every evening," recalled Lillian's friend, "was to make sure each gun was fresh loaded and that the cap would be sure to go off and not just snap."[8]

Levi stopped his westward travels in Mono County. Bodie Gold Mine and its ancillary businesses had long declined to a trickle, but neighboring Bridgeport and Coleville—also in Mono County, on the Nevada-California border—were rich in alluvial soil and could produce boom crops of hay, barley, potatoes, and especially wheat. In the 1870 U.S. Census, Levi listed himself as a farmer in Bridgeport, but he may also have hired himself out as a carpenter for silver mine framing. Daughter Lillian Frances Smith was born on August 4, 1871, in Coleville.

A couple of years later, Levi moved the family down to Merced County, which straddled a large segment of the San Joaquin River and constituted a large part of California's Central Valley. Farming apparently did not pan out for Smith in Mono, and the bitter Sierra winters were just too harsh, even for an easterner. Mark Twain observed of his time spent there, "There are only two seasons . . . and these are, the breaking up of one Winter and the beginning of the next. . . . Under favorable circumstances it snows at least once in every single month in the year, in the little town of Mono."[9] The family set out on Big Oak Flat Road, which at this time had become easily accessible from various outposts of the Yosemite Valley, and wound through the cool Sierra foothills. They headed toward Stockton, the San Joaquin County seat, passing wagonloads of prospectors coming from the other direction, and then continued south along the San Joaquin to a hamlet called Los Banos, which had just opened its first post office in 1873.[10]

Levi settled his family a few miles north of the main house of the Miller and Lux Ranch on the west side of the river.[11] If Levi had not heard of Miller and Lux before leaving Coleville, he certainly had by the time he reached Stockton. Henry Miller and Charles Lux, German immigrants and butchers by trade, had started acquiring vast tracts of land in the 1850s, eventually owning about a million and a half acres in California, Nevada, and Oregon.

Before this, few Californians had seriously considered permanent settlement in the San Joaquin Valley because of its isolation from centers of trade and population. Fear of Indian attack also kept rancheros from settling the interior valley.[12] Miller and Lux, however, saw its natural water sloughs and grasslands as a starting point for a massive cattle-grazing business. These capitalists spent nearly $1 million in the valley during the summer of 1871, building a canal forty miles long. It extended across the plains from the Fresno Slough to the Los Banos Creek. The canal water had two purposes: primarily, it was intended to bring water out on the plains in order to grow wheat. The canal itself was to be used again to float barges of grain down to Antioch on the San Francisco Bay, where ocean-going ships would take it to all parts of the world.[13]

No doubt, in 1873, Levi Smith read many of the pages-long proclamations printed in the *San Francisco Chronicle* and the *Sacramento Daily Union* about what this Miller and Lux enterprise planned to do in terms of irrigation to expand its grazing lands and also to farm on an unprecedented level. Essentially, Miller and Lux built an irrigation and barge system connecting the Tulare Lake Basin with the San Joaquin River at Mendota Pool. By the early 1880s, Henry Miller and Charles Lux controlled thousands of miles of irrigation ditches around the San Joaquin and Kern rivers, not to mention large portions of the main rivers.[14]

By now, these industrial barons were the biggest producers of beef cattle in California, and had forever changed the landscape of the state's Central Valley region, displacing the small rural farmer but creating new jobs for the influx of new residents.[15]

It would have been up to R. M. Brereton, chief of the canal engineering company, to hire some of these new residents who had the right skills—someone like Levi Smith—to help build the hundreds of locks and channels needed for the irrigation system, and also the watercraft necessary to monitor its progress. Although this irrigation system triggered plenty of litigation between Miller and Lux and the State of California for decades to come, all it meant for Levi was the chance to earn some consistent cash to feed his family.

With so many men flocking to the area for jobs, especially young, unattached ones, Miller and Lux could set relatively low wages across their work force, sometimes as low as sixty-six cents a day. This financial limit, and the fact that he had no formal degree or recommendation for an engineer's job, may have kept Levi within the ranks of those doing hard labor by digging ditches, building levees, running scrapers, constructing irrigation checks, and watering or draining the endless fields of alfalfa.[16]

So Lillian's father—strong and able-bodied but turning forty—shifted his attention to a phenomenon developing in this rapidly changing landscape of the San Joaquin Delta—to something that offered more autonomy and more money. Ducks and geese flocked to the artificial waterways by the hundreds of thousands, the destruction of their natural food and life cycles offset by the thick layers of alfalfa and wheat seed spread by farmers. Sarah Summers Clarke, a contemporary of Lillian's who lived near her in Los Banos, recalled, "Ducks and geese used to fill the sky in countless numbers in the early days. I have seen the ground covered with geese as far as the eye could see. A person would almost think the ground in the distance was covered with snow."[17]

Thus, Levi became one of the first, and certainly one of the best, commercial hunters of ducks and geese in the San Joaquin Valley. He was credited with inventing the "live blind," a method that used a trained animal to allow a hunter to stalk his prey.[18] Levi skiffed along the miles of irrigation canals and natural streams, experimenting with various boat and canoe shapes and sizes, depending on the size of the waterway. Lillian and Charles often went with him on these excursions. When on land, Charles drove the wagon for Levi while Lillian kept her dad's rifle full of cartridges. William T. White, the sheriff of Merced County, remembered that when he was a little boy in the late 1870s and early 1880s, market hunters could make a pretty good living while the geese and ducks were plentiful: "There was Kirby and Bill Browning and Old Man Smith. Browning had two or three outfits [but] all he did himself was to haul the game up to the shipping point. . . . [Mr.] Howard shot for Browning. [His] record was 224 ducks in two shots. With geese his record was 84 geese with two shots. . . . Old Man Smith lived at Smith's Ferry just a short distance down the river from the present San Joaquin Bridge. His daughter Lillian was a remarkable shot."[19] White was being derisive when he also remarked that "Howard's shots were the record," noting that Howard could only shoot this astounding number of birds because he was hiding behind oxen. The *Merced Express* gave the same impression of Lillian's father:

> Mr. Levy Smith, a gentleman who follows hunting for a living in this county, and who is at the present time engaged in that business on Miller & Lux's ranch, on the West Side, killed the other day 140 geese at two shots, discharging both barrels of his gun at each shot. Mr. Smith is the most successful buster of which we have any knowledge, having within the last five months killed and shipped to San Francisco over 9,000 head

of geese and ducks. He takes undue advantage, however, of his prey. He owns an ox [which] he trained to allow his master to walk in beat posture by his side to within easy range of the geese, when the shooting is done either over or under the animal, and without previous knowledge on the part of the geese of danger's proximity.[20]

The paper added that although this procedure was "rather an unfair advantage to take of the poor unsuspecting birds," it was of great advantage to the hunter and the farmer whose grain was being destroyed.

In deepest winter, when even the heartiest of duck hunters stayed away from the San Joaquin River basin, Levi found a way to make some cash while also saving on the cost of bird shot. After they harvested their crops, Miller-Lux farmers would stack the grain in high, conical bundles, which allowed them to dry some of it and thresh as needed or as market commanded the highest price. When a stack was entirely threshed, a pool of seed was left on the bottom, and water birds descended upon it by the thousands. This gave the enterprising Levi an idea.

Smith pounded two flexible poles into the ground on one side of the stack bottom, and then bent the poles clear down to the ground. Over the poles, he laid an old fishing net maybe thirty feet long and fastened one side of it securely to the bottom of the poles. He used rocks of two or three pounds to weigh down the other side of the net. Levi, Lillian, and Charles dug holes in the ground, climbed in, covered themselves with straw, and waited. Lillian usually had the pleasure and responsibility of holding the end of a rope Levi had fastened to the weighted side of poles. When the ducks and geese settled down and began to feed away greedily by the moonlight, Lillian pulled the rope, and up sprang the poles, casting the net over the birds, covering them before they had a chance to fly away. In their efforts to escape, the fowl stuck their heads up through the net. Levi and the kids rushed up to wring the birds' necks, taking just minutes to kill scores of them. Using this technique, the family could get at least five hundred heads for market in one fell swoop.[21]

Lillian's first encounters with real Native Americans—some twenty-five years before she "transformed" herself into one—were with the Yokuts. These people of the central California valley were already few in number, absorbed by missionization or killed by disease brought by the sudden influx of people when gold was discovered in 1848. Their population continued to decline when Lillian's family moved to Merced, because of the grazing of settlers' cows and horses. These livestock ate the native grasses around the San Joaquin River, depleting the natural environment for fox and deer, the Yokuts' main source of meat, and also their supply of basket fiber.

A childhood contemporary of Lillian's reported that when he camped out after a long day of hunting with his own father, he could peer out over a cliff at dusk to watch the Yokuts who had come to the river bottom to pick wild blackberries and shear sheep for Basque families. Beneath the bluff he could see forty or fifty campfires burning and the women cooking. There were several hundred of these Indians in this camp near Lillian's home.[22] Lillian was probably not aware of how few in number they were compared with just a generation prior, or how the Smiths' wholesale slaughter of waterfowl—a staple in the Yokuts' diet—was adding to their decline.

But the Smiths learned some things from the Natives in and around Santa Rita. Among the sensational stories about Lillian in her lifetime was her claim that she built a small boat of wood and tule reeds and floated down the San Joaquin River by herself for two weeks. If so, she and her father would have observed the Yokuts building watercraft from the tule reeds of the San Joaquin, watching how they hardened them in the baking sun, making them light and waterproof. Later, Levi incorporated some of these techniques into building lighter, yet stronger crafts to compete in high-stakes regattas.

Undoubtedly, Lillian was along for the ride when her father stalked prey that was a little more elusive than ducks, like black bears and beavers. He liked to combine watercraft with traditional hunting tricks. For example, he figured out a way to attach a rowboat to the side of a wagon's running gear, and when he was out hunting and came to a slough too deep to ford, he would nevertheless plunge right in with his team and wagon while he sat in the rowboat. When the water got too deep, his horses would swim and his rowboat mounted on the wagon wheels would float.

Levi's inventiveness became well known throughout the Delta. He was an inspiration to Henry Miller in regard to land claims. Ever since the United States claimed California from Mexico in 1848, government surveyors had been classifying swampy and flooded lands as "Swamp and Overflow." This was a problem for settlers like Miller, because such land was often just temporarily flooded, and then dry during California's long periods of drought. In order to claim or reclaim land, an owner or prospective buyer had to swear on oath that he had been all over it in a boat. This required meticulous land boundary records, which Miller paid handsomely to maintain. He had Smith attach a rowboat onto the running gear of a lumber wagon, and had his Italian navigator drive him all over lands he wished to possess, when flooding ebbed. He would then go to the land office, and confidently sign an affidavit that he had "been all over the land" in a boat.[23]

While Levi had a healthy reputation in his community for hunting and navigating waterways, he wanted to be known in sport circles outside the Central Valley. He wrote to the *San Francisco Chronicle:*

> To the Editor—Sir: I see that you pay considerable attention in shooting matters. Perhaps it may be of interest to some of your readers to see an account of a few days work that I did, which I call extraordinary. I arrived at my hunting grounds December 7th at 12 o'clock upon, and shot for three hours that afternoon, and the next morning, I commenced shooting at sunrise. At 8 o'clock that evening I had my game dressed and brung up on a fence, which made a long string. On counting I found I had 649 birds, thus: 26 honkers, 190 white geese, 108 mallards, 156 widgeons, 24 sprigs and 145 teal. The three and a half days shooting netted 1,190 birds.

Levi then positioned himself as worthy of challenging the world champion sharpshooter, Adam Henry Bogardus, who had also just invented the first practical glass ball trap: "I am satisfied that no other man can do the same amount of work in the same time. Captain A. H. Bogardus and others can smash glass balls, and so can I.—Levi W. Smith, Merced, December 29, 1877."[24] Determined to let the entire country know of his ability, Lillian's father also wrote to eastern papers. He managed to get a mention in New York City's *Evening Express,* summarizing his slaughter for the entire season: "Mr. L. W. Smith, of Merced county, Cal., killed between September 15, 1877, and April 21, 1878, 6,380 geese, 5,956 ducks, 367 sandhill crane, and 60 swan."[25]

Others noticed Levi's natural talents, too. The *Sacramento Daily Record-Union* repeated a story that appeared in the *Chico Union:*

> While hunting on the river bottom recently, Levi Smith jumped a couple of deer, both bucks. Checking his horse, he opened fire on one with a Henry rifle, killing it dead. The other ran into the brush, where it soon revealed its presence by its head peering over the top of some short brushes. Another shot from the Henry, and another deer. The distance from Levi to the first deershot was about 146 yards, and to the second 184 yards. Considering that both shots were made from a horse, and one of them while the deer was on the run, we consider it hard to beat.[26]

Lillian had a double advantage: she was born with Levi's talent for gunmanship and self-promotion, and she practiced with him nearly every day.

Food markets and farmers who suffered from pests paid Levi by the animal head, so it is not surprising that by age seven Lillian had killed "wildcats, squirrels, cotton-tail and jack rabbits by the score, and quails, red-heads, mallards, and young ducks by the thousand."[27] Later, when she was thirteen and had earned quite a few medals around the San Francisco Bay area, a reporter asked how her gunning skills came to be. "I really don't know," she said. "It came natural to me. I have a brother who is rather a good pigeon shot. Perhaps that induced me to emulate him, and that may be the reason."[28] Years later, Lillian reflected that she had very few friends, especially ones that were her age, and she shot out of boredom. Notably, as would be the case for the rest of her life, she did not give any credit to her father, at least not publicly.

Historians have often made particular note of the Smith family's whereabouts at the turn of the 1880s. This would not be very important, except for the fact that the census entry for 1880 put forth by many as the Smiths' plays into two misconceptions. One is that Lillian was of true Native American blood, and two, that Levi had already started grooming his family to appear Native American even before Lillian began to perform.

Lillian kept up this charade after somebody gave her a copy of her family's purported 1880 record. Michael Wallis writes, "Lillian was almost always billed as a Sioux Indian 'princess.' She might not have been a Sioux chieftain's daughter, but the questionable claim was hardly ever challenged. There is no doubt, however, that Lillian was in fact Indian; the 1880 California census records display an 'I,' which stood for Indian, and not a 'W' for white, in the personal-description column next to young Lillie Smith's name."[29] It is true that a copy of this census entry was found in Lillian's, or Wenona's, belongings, the bulk of which were eventually donated to the Thomas Gilcrease Museum in Tulsa, Oklahoma. But while the listing conveniently supports her later persona, it almost certainly is not Lillian's family. Nor are the given names a match. In 1876, her father registered to vote in Sandy Mush—a tiny outpost not far from Los Banos—and Charles was already working there. There was no reason for Levi and his family to backtrack to the harsher and less profitable terrain of Tuolumne County, which they may have passed through in leaving Mono County for more temperate Merced.[30]

In 1881, the first accounts of Lillian's shooting started to appear in Santa Cruz–area venues. Game hunters like Levi would often leave Los Banos in the summer, when waterways were dry, and head west to work on harvesting outfits in the Salinas Valley until the geese returned in the fall. Lillian's first formal appearance was at the Watsonville Opera House, then called the "Rink," where, on June 4, 1881, she sang "an original song," and then broke twelve glass balls, on pegs, in twelve shots.[31] The *Sacramento Record-Union* reported: "Santa Cruz county has a shooting prodigy in the person of Lillian F. Smith, a 10-year-old girl who lives near Corralitos. She recently gave an exhibition of her skill at Watsonville, and astonished the oldest sportsmen. . . . She repeatedly broke balls thrown by hand into the air, hit two ten cent pieces that were thrown up, and did other wonderful shooting."[32] Most people attended the Rink performance out of curiosity, not believing Levi's claims that Lillian could beat the champions. They were delighted to be proven wrong. After her twelve-peg feat, Lillian broke ten balls, on the same pegs, in a minute. She then broke twelve in fifty-six seconds, and did her own loading. This she followed with the famous Austin brothers' mirror feat. Smith stood about ten paces from the balls (twelve in a row), and held a very small hand glass in her left hand, steadied and shot the rifle, which rested on her right shoulder, with her left hand. She missed the third and fourth, but hit the remaining ten balls straight out, thus breaking twelve balls in fourteen shots.[33]

Levi took his daughter up and down the central coast of California, knowing that he had in her something the world had not yet seen. Onlookers were awed by the contrast between her stature and her feats. "When the size of the child, her hands, the glass, and the 7 1/2-pound rifle are considered, her performance is marvellous and is superior to the Austin brothers' act," wrote a local newspaperman. By all accounts, her calm composure was somewhat jarring in comparison with the violence of her performance. "She is perfectly cool before an audience, attends strictly to her work, and shows not the slightest nervousness."[34]

Lillian's age and her aloof stance, coupled with the quantity and quality of her shots, often made skeptics out of onlookers, such as the army officer who doubted that her shooting at a particular exhibition was genuine. He insisted on getting behind stage scenery to watch more closely, not realizing he was hemmed in until her last trick was finished. This last feat, her favorite, was to shoot a dozen glass balls filled with water that were suspended from a swinging board. When the show was over, he was a "thorough believer in Miss Smith's shooting abilities," but completely soaked, and lucky to have avoided glass shards in the eyes.

Within a couple of days, news of her Rink performance had reached the sporty West Virginia *Wheeling Register,* which described Lillian's composure under unfavorable light and space: "She broke balls swinging in a circle, part to a string, broke fifteen balls in a minute, and several other feats worthy the Austins or Dr. Carver. . . . [She] is about medium height for a ten [year] old child, bright as a dollar, artless and natural, and don't seem to think she can shoot much anyway."[35] Then, and for many years that followed, Lillian would always seem surprised at the hearty applause she received following her acts.

Father and daughter continued north. Levi approached Robert Woodward, owner of San Francisco's premiere amusement park, Woodward's Gardens. This entrepreneur, who made his money during the Gold Rush, had purchased the land underneath the Gardens from former senator John C. Frémont in 1866. It took up two city blocks, featured a zoo, roller skating rink and art gallery, and brought in performers and curiosities from all over the world, including the eight-foot, three-inch giant Chang Woo Gow.[36]

As one of those performers, Lillian did not disappoint. On July 23, 1881, just a few weeks shy of her tenth birthday, the little rifle artist made her debut at Woodward's.[37] The *San Francisco Chronicle* took some license when it said that she had never before appeared in public, but it was correct in that she showed no embarrassment as she proceeded to shatter glass balls in a businesslike way worthy of Dr. Carver, reloading her rifle like a veteran.[38] Anyone in San Francisco who had not seen her by August 7, when she gave her "positively last" performance, was out of luck, because it was the last before her "departure for the Eastern States and Europe," or more truthfully, before she went back to a schoolhouse in Merced.

Lillian earned most of her accolades with the rifle, but she appears to have been equally skilled with the shotgun. In late 1883, during a holiday turkey shoot in Hollister, a city between Los Banos and Santa Cruz, the young teen killed so many birds at a turkey shoot that she was set back to 200 yards from 150, and was finally told to "drop out and give the boys a chance at the turkeys, too!"[39]

In the spring of 1884, sportswriter Howard C. Bliss heard rumors about the California Girl, and decided to travel from Philadelphia to see for himself. The first shot she made for him was a double-shot, with a Winchester. For this trick, a ball was suspended a few inches from the ground, and another was put in a trap, which was set to only throw the ball up only three feet. At the holler "Ready!" she fired at the suspended ball, and at the same instant the trap was sprung. Both spheres were shattered before they hit the floor.

Lillian's eyesight was extraordinarily sharp, accounting for some of her natural coordination. Bliss was skeptical when she shot at the edge of an ordinary playing card attached to the nose of a swinging deer at thirty-two feet, and apparently missed three times, complaining that the card was "not set straight." But when he examined the card, he found that she had already hit it twice, and if the card had been straight she would have cut it in two either time. He straightened it, and on her first attempt, she "cut it clear through." Making this feat

America's Best Female Sharpshooter

even more noteworthy, wrote Bliss, was the fact that she did it by lamplight, ostensibly at night.[40] Lillian then repeatedly hit the edge of dimes placed on a piece of pine background, tearing them so they looked like a rabbit's foot and ankle. "Howard Carr, who is the best target shot on the Pacific Coast with a heavy rifle," wrote Bliss, "tried seven times to do the same thing and gave it up in disgust, and when Carr gets tired trying at steady shooting it is discouraging work to take up." Lillian gave Bliss one of these dimes as a charm for his time.[41]

At the opening of its season on February 23, 1885, the Alameda Gun Club did not allow Lillian to compete for prizes against its older, male contestants, but it did let her try out some new shotguns. She stood at eighteen yards, and with a dram and a half of powder and half an ounce of shot, killed ten out of twelve birds, a score that would have earned her a second-place had she been formally entered into the contest. The following month, she was the only female—the only contestant at all—at the San Bruno Wind Club's annual exhibition who killed twelve out of twelve birds. In this, she even beat Crittenden Robinson, and won a tidy sum of $120. Despite the fact that it was a windless day in this southern San Francisco town—great for fleeing pigeons, but not for shooters—Lillian made the "best shot of the day," according to the *Daily Alta California,* at a bird that "traveled like a flash of lightening [*sic*]," and brought him down at least sixty yards from her stand.[42]

In April, Lillian lost $250 to local trap champion John Kerrigan at San Bruno—by just two birds. But the *Daily Alta* conceded that both shooters lost out on some good scores because of a strong gale wind, which carried many of their dead fowl over the boundary fence, and thus they could not count them as kills.[43] Convinced she could beat Kerrigan, Lillian put up $150 at another match on May 31, also at San Bruno. At first, it seemed Kerrigan would win, since he led by four birds near the end of the contest. Lillian, however, "never lost courage, and gradually crept up until she tied him," and then beat him by one pigeon.[44]

News of Lillian's extraordinary skills reached the eastern papers before summer, and Levi's hometown paper proudly announced that she was probably "the best shot for a female in this country."[45] Levi issued a challenge of a "$1,000–5,000 purse" to anyone who would submit to a rifle competition with his daughter, but it seems no one took him up on this. To be sure, Lillian's reputation already scared off many great shooters, but anyone who knew the Smiths personally might have been skeptical that Levi had that amount of money to wager.

Four years later, when Lillian was drenched in attention as part of Buffalo Bill Cody's Wild West show, papers ran a story that, as a tiny girl, she used her skill to slaughter for meat until it was "notorious in California," a nod toward the state's growing conservation move-ment. The Smiths began to spend more time at shooting matches than game hunting.[46] Tellingly, Levi rarely stalked animals for a living after 1881, and in the quiet months of late 1881 and early 1882, he instead coached his daughter on how to take her "clever eye" to the next level: the contestant's purse.

Shirl Kasper summarizes the state of exhibition shooting—and prizewinning—when Lillian was a little girl. Exhibition shooting, she wrote, was a jealous, competitive business, and a man had to stay on top of his rivals, even if he suffered nights of pain. The physical effects would have been some tempered form of what William Frank "Doc" Carver experienced in order to claim his title of "Champion Rifle Shot of the World," in 1878: "As fast as Doc emptied one gun, he was handed another, freshly oiled and loaded. The empty guns, still smoking, were plunged into a tub of ice water to cool. By early evening the rifles were so fouled that a tongue of fire accompanied each shot. Doc's buckskin gloves were perfectly black, perspiration poured from his face, and his eyes were terribly inflamed from a combination of dirty water, glass dust, feathers, and sulphurous smoke." Despite his magnificent phy-sique and iron constitution and nerves, Doc took to his bed after this performance in San Francisco where he suffered all night, and the pain in his eyes was so great that "all the wealth in the world would not tempt him to try such a feat again."[47] But of course, he did, as did rivals Bogardus, John Ruth, Charley Austin, and Elmer E. Stubbs, to name a few of the more famous ones. Lillian suffered milder forms of these effects as Levi signed her up for more and more exhibitions.

Exhibition shooters were not a new phenomenon when Lillian was training. They dated to the early nineteenth century, when shooters performed with circuses. But by 1880, they were achieving the height of their popularity. "It was a time when the public liked a good show, and when guns were a familiar part of American life."[48] Glenda Riley elaborates a bit: "In a day when numerous people carried guns for protection or hunting or both, many wanted to see what the 'experts' could do with weapons."[49] Furthermore, notes Riley, theater audiences had long appreciated "Western" plays about Daniel Boone and Davy Crockett, and vaudeville-goers expected at least one act on the bill to include a trick shooter.

Lillian might have heard of some females in the exhibition-shooting world when she was little, in the late 1870s and early 1880s, but they probably were not featured acts. Ira Paine, a fancy pistol shooter from Rhode Island, would appear on stage in a simple suit of tight trousers, black coat, and a sports hat, assisted by his pretty wife. She would hold a cardboard target with a bull's-eye measuring about one inch—Paine would hit it from sixty-five feet.[50] But these appearances were few—Paine was more widely known as a trapshooter. Frank Howe, in the early 1880s, dressed himself in boots, a leopard-skin jacket, and a sombrero, and performed with a beautiful partner named Miss Russell. She could not shoot very well, but she provided a nice distraction while loading and cleaning Howe's weapons. And in 1880, John Ruth surprised everyone at Deerfoot Park, Coney Island, when he brought his wife and handed her a six-pound pistol. She proceeded to break glass balls while holding her pistol sideways and upside down. Unfortunately, John died the following year of a sudden-onset heart problem, and his wife faded into obscurity.

Almost all of these women were sidekicks or assistants, however. While they could certainly handle a gun safely and competently, there was not yet a female for whom an audience would come to see just for her raw shooting ability.

News of Lillian's remarkable talent spread so quickly that the press felt compelled to qualify it in some way. In the fall of 1884, the gossipy *New York Sun* ran an article that was quickly syndicated in every major city. It attempted to marry Lillian's talent with the perceived exoticism of the West: "Coleville, Cal.—A young girl, pretty and modest, with a rifle on her shoulder is not a strange sight in these parts. . . . The typical far Western girl would doubtless shock her more subdued sisters in the East in many things which here are considered within the bounds of propriety. She hunts, fishes, camps out, rides and tramps, with all the relish shown by the sterner sex." The article also poked fun at Lillian, and indirectly, at the coarseness and naïveté of her parents, explaining that one particular "plump young woman" from Coleville had her photograph taken in her "fresh-air costume" and sent to relatives back East: "The portrait exhibited a girl of eighteen, with a jaunty turban, her long hair done up tightly in a coil, her face full and fair and her eyes bright as dollars. Her dress was tight-fitting at the waist and sleeves, of dark serviceable material, and the skirt, coming just below the knees, failed to meet the tops of her high buttoned shoes by several inches." These eastern relatives, continued the all-knowing *Sun* reporter, were "profoundly shocked" at the receipt of this photograph, and would be even more horrified if they learned that she was seen on the streets almost daily in such attire.

Still, the *Sun* was compelled to report the specialness of this girl Lillian Smith, an expert with the rifle, who threatened to carry off the honors in any contest of skill: "She is only thirteen year of age, but she appears much older. She has a strong frame, abundant dark brown hair, and big brown eyes. Tanned by continued exposure to sun and wind, she is the picture of health and of far Western beauty." Her aim was so precise, the article continued, that "a failure to hit the mark" was considered almost out of the question.[51]

On February 25, 1884, the *Santa Cruz Surf* proudly repeated Lillian's accomplishments as listed in a recent issue of *American Field* magazine. It highlighted her acquisition of more difficult feats, and the correspondent thought they compared favorably with those of any expert who had appeared before the public.[52] Among many other physically taxing stunts, it said, Lillian shocked an audience in Vacaville by breaking 300 swinging glass balls in 14 minutes and 33 seconds, missing only 14. She made up for this by shooting 14 more on time.

Around this time, Lillian's father bought her a Winchester rifle. She was not quite as proficient with it as she was with the Ballard, but practiced until she was. Levi told the papers that—just like the year before—Lillian was going to head east with him, and that she hoped to meet some of the champions, as she was "confident that she can beat the world" with the rifle.[53]

Still, no champion took the bait. Lillian could hold her own against some of the most famous sharpshooters who were making headlines in the early 1880s, but many of these men were preoccupied with other matters. Carver, in his early thirties, was having a very publicized rivalry with Bogardus, whom the press often referred to as the "Champion Trap Shooter." In turn, Bogardus was more focused on perfecting the first practical glass ball trap, which he patented in 1879.[54] Elmer E. Stubbs billed himself the "Champion Combination Wing Shot," which meant he was expert at incorporating tricks with rifle, revolver, and shotgun in one program—he was not so much interested in besting others as he was in besting himself.

Levi wrote to *American Field* sports magazine. He remarked that he had not received a reply from anybody about going head-to-head with his twelve-year-old daughter: "I once more will say, I will match my daughter against Dr. Carver, Eugene Bogardus, E. E. Stubbs, or any other professional shot in the world, to shoot a bona fide match for speed and accuracy, using the rifle. I would like to hear from some of those parties."[55] No response.

Undeterred, Levi issued a more specific challenge through local and national newspapers: "I will wager five hundred dollars that Miss Lillian can break one thousand glass balls in fifty minutes with the rifle. I will wager one thousand dollars that she can beat anyone in the world as a gallery shot. I will also wager one hundred dollars that she can hit more common English pins, one inch long, stuck into a frame, to be set in motion to travel twelve feet in one and a quarter seconds, distance thirty feet (out of fifty shots) than any one else in the world using a rifle 22 calibre."[56]

Still no prominent takers. Levi wrote, somewhat desperately, to the editor of *Breeder and Sportsman:*

> In your paper of the date of November 24th, 1883, you
> remarked that at present there were in California two young
> ladies that were professional rifle shots—Miss Lillian F. Smith
> and Miss Hartman. I cannot ascertain of the whereabouts of
> young Miss Hartman, and now I will say if there is any such
> person or young lady we will give her a chance to make herself
> known, as I issue these challenges open to any one male or

female on the Pacific Coast or in the world, with the exception of the last one mentioned, using the Winchester Rifle, which is only open to ladies.[57]

He offered to back his daughter with a purse of one thousand to five thousand dollars. Yet there was still no word from Carver, Bogardus, Stubbs, or anyone else.

Despite the lack of attention from professional shooters, Levi pushed Lillian to refresh her act. On January 27, 1885, for example, the *San Francisco Chronicle* offered a small mention of the California Girl learning to skate, so that she might "give exhibitions of rifle shooting while whirling on wheels."[58] In August of the previous year, his daughter had turned thirteen, and he must have known that she could not be touted merely as a "child prodigy" much longer, especially since she had started to show some signs of pubescence.

On April 1, 1885, Crittenden Robinson (no relation to Rebecca), who was considered the wing shot champion at that time, attended one of Lillian's shows at Eintrecht Hall, in Stockton. Robinson observed that the fourteen-year-old girl showed no hesitation or nerves when she hoisted her seven-pound rifle. From a distance of thirty-three feet she targeted glass balls that were attached to a wooden figure of a deer that was suspended in midair. With unfailing aim, she fired from both the right and left shoulder, shooting with the rifle held upside down and backward over the shoulder, sighting with a hand mirror. Not once did she miss. Remaining backward and using the same mirror, she shot at ten glass balls that were sprung in quick succession from a trap—and hit them all before they fell to the floor.

Robinson was so assured of the girl's abilities displayed at this exhibition that he volunteered to hold up an ace of clubs, the middle of which she perforated without pause in firing. For her finale, the little lady performed her most noteworthy feat: using a Winchester, she shot one hundred glass balls in two minutes, thirty-five seconds, beating champ Carver's record of two minutes, thirty-six seconds.

Besides shooting from various shoulder angles and backwards with the mirror, she broke glass balls revolving on a wire in a horizontal circle, with a radius of about six feet—never missing. She also broke twenty balls attached to a swinging wooden deer, and shattered every single one inside of a minute, with no misses. "Two small balls no larger than a hazelnut shared the same fate," and for one of her finales, a five-cent piece was concealed behind a playing card, and pierced directly in the center from a distance unrecorded, but probably her usual twenty feet for precision shots.

Robinson, who had "acquired such confidence in the accuracy of the aim of the young lady," came on stage and proffered his playing card, which Lillian promptly cut in two with a bullet.[59] The *Chronicle* remarked that Lillian had justified Robinson's confidence. Very soon, Lillian would earn the interest and confidence of someone who would change her life drastically: William F. "Buffalo Bill" Cody.

Chapter Two

BUFFALO BILL, QUEEN VICTORIA, AND LITTLE SURE SHOT

> It is no exaggeration to say that [Lillian Smith] will
> cause the famous rifle shots of the country considerable
> trouble to retain their laurels.
>
> *Daily Alta California,* April 4, 1885

O n April 16, 1886, an exhausted but exhilarated William Cody
returned to western Nebraska, after disbanding his latest Wild
West theatrical troupe in Denver. He and close friend cowboy William
Levi "Buck" Taylor retreated with some other actors to Cody's new
Scout's Rest Ranch, some four thousand acres of prized farm and
grazing land near North Platte. Things were lively with the Wild West
proprietor home, with members of the troupe coming and going, and
lots of drinking and debauchery going on with Cody's straitlaced wife
nowhere near the place.

"Major" John Burke—Cody's loyal and tenacious publicist—
stopped off for a few days en route to St. Louis to help reorganize the
Wild West. All of Cody's entourage and many in North Platte were well
acquainted with the colorful Burke and looked forward to his visits.
But of considerable more interest to the townspeople was a newcomer,
fourteen-year-old Lillian Smith, "The California Girl."[1]

Lillian most likely met Cody in San Francisco, in March of 1886.
He had been staging his play *The Prairie Waif,* in which he played
a frontier detective fighting Pawnee Indians and "border ruffians."

Lillian had been making occasional appearances at agricultural fairs, but for the most part, she had been passing the time hunting with her brother in Tulare and Merced counties. On March 15, she took part in the annual San Francisco Schuetzen Club festival; Cody probably saw her shoot there.

It is not clear who approached whom, but either way, Cody had added Lillian to his troupe by the first week of April, and excitedly started having press materials made up for her. He sent photographs of her to his poster maker in Baltimore, remarking that Lillian was to be a member of the Wild West for the next two years, and "we want to advertise her all we can. She is a wonderful Shot."[2]

After *Waif* broke up in Colorado, Cody brought her on to North Platte, where, according to the *Lincoln County Tribune,* she was billed to give an exhibition of shooting at Cody's beloved Lloyd's Opera House on the evening of April 20.[3]

Cody knew he had snapped up a star. He spoke confidently of Lillian to an *Omaha Bee* reporter, "There is one new artist I have engaged who is simply a prodigy. She is a young girl, only 15 years of age, and her powers with the rifle, shotgun or revolver are perfectly marvelous. She can beat the world shooting. I don't bar anybody. Her name is Lillian Smith, and she comes from California."[4]

Similar to the way Broadway producers today test their shows in smaller venues, Cody took note of how North Platte audiences reacted to Lillian's performance and how she might be useful in a reformulation of a Wild West show. She made quite an impression. Ira Bare, editor of the *Tribune*, referred to Lillian Smith as "the best shot in the world." Her performance, he wrote, bordered on "marvelous," breaking 20 glass balls in 24 seconds with a Winchester rifle, and 20 balls with a single loading rifle in 54 seconds. "This is shooting as fast as an ordinary gunman can shoot his piece," he continued, "to say nothing of taking aim at a fast moving target." Another of Lillian's beautiful feats, he said, was breaking two balls with one shot as the balls swung past each other in the air.[5]

On the last day of April, Lillian and the other members of the show left for St. Louis, where the Wild West would open a few days later. Levi and Rebecca Smith accompanied them.

The St. Louis exhibition was a huge hit, too. The *Omaha Daily*

Herald proudly reported that Cody, its adopted Nebraskan, had wildly entertained more than 25,000 people on the Wild West's opening day. The *St. Louis Republican* reported that its citizens got to see "the grandest exhibit of the scenes of the extreme western plains and the most complete representations of Indians, buffaloes and cowboys ever presented here." During the show, after many crowd-thrilling exhibitions and chases, Cody would let the audience breathe for a moment while he rode up to the famous Civil War general, William Sherman, his old friend and acquaintance, and the two bowed to each other.

But one of the best features, the *Republican* noted, was the "exhibition and skillful handling of the rifle and revolver" by a California girl, Miss Lillian Smith. She seldom missed a ball that was thrown, and the shooting was "no less wonderful for accuracy than rapidity; no more pleasing for either than for the magic ease and grace with which it was done."[6]

There was, however, another young lady mentioned in this article as having done some "pretty shooting" as well: Miss Annie Oakley.

Annie Oakley was born Phoebe Ann Moses in Darke County, Ohio, on August 13, 1860.[7] When she was six years old, her father died from pneumonia. Phoebe's mother tried valiantly to provide for the family, but ultimately, she had to send her children to others to care for them. In 1870, Phoebe went to live at the Darke County Infirmary, about two and a half miles from Greenville. She was bound out to a family that abused her both physically and mentally, and she eventually ran away, back to the infirmary.

Eventually, Phoebe found caring in the superintendent's household, and here she learned how to sew dresses and quilts and also run the dairy. These times, notes biographer Shirl Kasper, left an indelible imprint on the girl and formed a "deep and abiding pride" that would mark her character for the rest of her life.[8]

Phoebe vowed never to want again, and made plans for her future. When the teen left Greenville, she stopped at a town grocer, whom she had known well because she ran errands there for the superintendent. She was going home, she told the owners, and planned to hunt and trap again up in the north county woods, as she had for a few years after her father died.[9] She struck an agreement with the grocers, whereby they

America's Best Female Sharpshooter

would purchase any small game she shipped to town. For the rest of her life, she would earn her living with a gun.

Like Lillian Smith, Phoebe Moses was a market hunter in her younger years, and was so productive she eventually earned enough to pay off her mother's mortgage.[10] Like Lillian, Phoebe started to gain a local reputation for precision with a gun by excelling in turkey shoots, a popular pastime in the late 1870s and early 1880s.

Just like the California Girl, Phoebe was eventually barred from participating in these shoots so as to encourage other contestants. Thus, when she received an invitation from Jack Frost, a hotel owner in Cincinnati, to shoot against a well-known marksman on Thanksgiving Day, 1875, she was only too happy to oblige out of boredom and intrigue.

Phoebe's opponent, Irishman Francis "Frank" Butler, was touring with several other marksmen in search of prize money, and felt comfortable that he would pocket an easy $100 put up by Frost—more so when he saw that a teenaged girl was his match. Much to his and everybody's surprise, Phoebe won, scoring all of twenty-five shots, while Butler missed one. Despite her besting him and an eight-year age difference (he was at least twenty-three, maybe as old as twenty-eight) to her fifteen years, Phoebe entranced Butler, and they married on August 23, 1876. About this time, Phoebe Moses changed her name to Annie Oakley.

For about five years, Butler performed his stage act with a male partner, while Oakley tagged along. This changed on May 1, 1882, in Springfield, Ohio, when the partner became very ill; Butler asked his wife to hold the targets instead. As the story goes, Butler kept missing that night, and someone in the audience shouted, "Let the girl shoot." She did, successfully, and from then on, Annie Oakley was the star attraction while Butler spent more time on management, finances, and show logistics.[11]

In spite of the audience's delight with Oakley, she was still struggling for recognition in the spring of 1884. To make sure they had steady income for the upcoming season, she and Butler took a job with a traveling show called the Arlington and Fields Combination. While in St. Paul, one of Oakley's greatest publicity coups came to pass, by way of a distinguished prisoner of war in Dakota Territory, Sitting Bull, who was touring St. Paul with agent Major James McLaughlin.

The Lakota chief, who was blamed for the murder of General George Armstrong Custer at Little Big Horn just eight years before, went to see the Arlington and Fields show on March 19, where he saw Oakley snuff a burning candle with a bullet from her rifle. According to Oakley, Sitting Bull's messengers begged her to meet with him, and eventually she relented, and after their meeting, Sitting Bull insisted on "adopting" her.

Oakley was charmed, while Butler saw the pecuniary value in the exchange. A couple of weeks after the alleged adoption, he put an advertisement in a trade publication called the *New York Clipper* that proclaimed, "The Premier Shots, Butler and Oakley, Captured by Sitting Bull."[12] From that day forward, the press and fans affectionately referred to Annie Oakley as "Little Sure Shot," the English translation of "Watanya Cicilla" in Lakota.

Ironically, it may have been Annie's popularity that convinced Cody and show manager Nate Salsbury that they should add three other women performers—which included Lillian Smith, Della Farrell, and Georgia Duffy. The latter two were cowgirls from Colorado and Wyoming who staged pony races.

It may have been that Lillian had no chance at camaraderie with the shotgun champ because Annie would have been insulted and made suspicious by the addition of any female shooter—understandably so, given that there were not yet very many celebrity women shooters. Of course, Cody had a tendency to acquire "shiny things" in the form of immensely talented people, without giving immediate thought to how to manage their expectations and how to praise each performer for his or her unique contribution.

It did not take long for Lillian Smith to get on Annie Oakley's nerves. Certainly, Cody's obvious fascination with Lillian did not sit well with Oakley, writes Wallis. Oakley already faced heated competition in the arena from teen cowboy Johnny Baker, and was well aware of the favorable reviews of Smith in the press. It must have stung Annie a bit to read articles in which gun enthusiasts were already hedging their bets as to who was more precise, even with regard to trapshooting—a shotgun event. "We saw Miss Oakley shoot a few days ago," wrote a *Breeder and Sportsman* correspondent in April 1887, "and could not help admiring her command of the handsome little weapon which she

America's Best Female Sharpshooter

uses. She is very quick, but not a snap shot." Furthermore, "A match between Miss Oakley and Miss Lillian Smith would be an interesting event. Loyalty to locality should incline us to believe Miss Lillian the better, but we cannot venture so far."[13]

Cody, notes Oakley biographer Glenda Riley, had obviously failed to think through the introduction of the "stout and vocal Lillian Smith" to the rest of the company, especially to her direct competitor.[14] He may not have cared—a rivalry could be good publicity. In her autobiography, Oakley reported Smith's boast to other Wild West performers that "'Annie Oakley was done for,' once they saw her own self shoot." There was no one to corroborate Lillian's remarks, although it sounded like her. The slander may have originated with Levi.[15]

Certainly Annie Oakley felt threatened professionally by Lillian Smith. Personally, she could not stand the sight of her. True to her Victorian mores, Oakley never attacked Lillian by name when she complained about her, at least not in writing. Her last thinly veiled snipe toward Lillian in her diary reads, "Well, they saw both her work and her ample figure" and, as a consequence, cut her salary in half.[16]

This is doubtful. Cody's rollercoaster financial situations made everybody's salary a moving target, and the showman was not above pitting acts against each other as a salary negotiating tactic. And Lillian gave Cody no reason to be displeased—she faithfully fulfilled her obligation, which was to hold the attention of the crowd while the big acts were being changed. The historian Glenn Shirley describes her usual performance at Erastina and a few months later, at Madison Square Garden. She would hit a plate thirty times in fifteen seconds, and then break ten glass balls hung from strings and swinging around a pole. When ball after ball had been shattered, she would destroy the strings without a miss. For the final part of her act, Lillian would toss a ball into the air, then fire at it three times and then purposely miss— bringing the crowd to its feet with suspense—but always shatter it on the fourth shot.[17]

Oakley was incredibly anxious about Lillian Smith joining the troupe. "Though she would never admit it," writes Shirl Kasper, "Annie dealt with the problem quickly and decisively: she simply lopped six years off her age." From then on, she would tell interviewers that she was born in 1866, not 1860. The lie was not hard to cover, continues

Kasper, because Annie was so petite, and because she did have a younger-looking face.

By the time Butler and Oakley parted ways with Cody a couple of years later (temporarily, it turns out), Lillian had obviously learned what a functional, husband-wife partnership could do for a woman performer. In 1904, Lillian mentioned the couple in a letter to her close friend Alf Rieckhoff, in which she seems to be lapping up Frank Butler's casual compliments, while putting Annie down as a "has been":

> Frank Buttler [*sic*] was out yesterday and after the show he came and told me that I had a fine act that it was catchy and pleased the people and that all we needed to do I thought that it was pretty good for him to say dont you think so? He looks old—Annie was down in New York state some where attending one of those lieble [*sic*] suits as they say that they are getting a lot of money out of it. She will need all she can get if she goes out with her show again and I hear that she is going.

Clearly, Lillian clung to Butler's compliments, maybe allowing herself to feel better about the stinging barbs he he had thrown years earlier. Lillian's next sentence is almost certainly her way of telling herself that she had managed to do as well as Oakley after all, noting they sat in "the privaledge car" section and that, even though they sometimes had to pay extra for their upgraded accommodations, it was no problem because they were getting paid so well for their acts.[18]

Again, Lillian was probably blithely unaware of Oakley's chagrin during her first couple of months of Wild West employment. She was consumed by her new practice schedule and her father's aggressive marketing of her name. While in St. Louis, Levi Smith challenged Doc Carver to shoot against her, and according to papers, all arrangements were made for a contest at Pope's Theater on May 13. Carver did not show, and thus, according to the press with some probable direction by Levi, Lillian had every right to say she had "frightened off the Evil Spirit of the Plains."[19]

Either Cody gave tacit or direct approval for Levi to try to pit Lillian against well-known male shooters, or Levi simply did not understand relationships within the show circuit. Or Cody did not care. Any way, this "non-event" with Carver only added fuel for those who labeled

Lillian as unsophisticated. On June 20, she wrote to the *San Francisco Chronicle,* reflecting upon her recent week performing in the District of Columbia: "While at Washington, I met Senator George Hearst of California. He witnessed my exhibition and said it was the universal opinion of the people of Washington that I was the champion rifle shot of the world." The *Chronicle* added its assessment of this: "One hardly knows which to admire the most, 'Uncle' George's adeptness in taffying a handsome young lady or the naivete with which Miss Smith gives the old man away."[20] Lillian's sharpshooting talents were light-years ahead of her worldliness. This unworldliness could have had potentially disastrous results in the weeks following, were it not for some happy accidents.

To remain profitable, Cody needed a forum where he could put down roots for a while, and not pay the enormous transportation and local publicity costs required of a traveling Wild West show. Fortunately, the Canadian Erastus Wiman had seen potential in Staten Island for securing a situation just like this. As a young man, Wiman came to New York as manager of the Dun Mercantile Agency, a commodities speculation firm. As his salary rose, he purchased large tracts of land in what was then the borough of Richmond, and lobbied hard to make Staten Island the entry point for the Baltimore and Ohio Railroad for New York.

Wiman failed at this, but he did manage to consolidate local railway and transit lines, and increase the number of ferry routes from other parts of New York and New Jersey. In order for people to have a reason to use these lines, Wiman created "Erastina," a huge exhibition space in what is now known as Mariners Harbor, in the northwestern part of the borough. He eventually opened casinos there, and hired stage shows like Forepaugh's Circus, but the earliest and by far the most popular draw was Buffalo Bill's Wild West show.

On June 25, 1886, about twenty thousand people jostled their way into the stands at Erastina, to see Cody's inaugural presentation. From that day until the show's close in August, seventeen steamboats daily brought full loads of passengers to the island to see Indians, cowboys, riding, shooting, and the re-creation of the Old West. The *New York Times* reported: "The warmest interest was manifested in every feature, from the moment that the Indians and cowboys, assembling at the head of the inclosure, rushed their horses in picturesque platoons to the front of the grand stand until the thrilling finish, when Indians, cowboys, horses and powder smoke were flying in confusion all over the field at the end of a sham battle." Noting a theme that would be heavily discussed by historians in the century to come, the *Times* observed, "The Indians had to suffer defeat every time, but they seemed to have become used to it and entered the contest with no less spirit on that account."[21] The paper also noted audiences would go especially crazy with the loud cracks of pistols, and the "scurrying" of Indians.

For the performers—about two hundred in total—the grounds were about as perfect as possible for a traveling show. The *New York Herald* described the environment from the point-of-view of a spectator, but the actors and workers must have appreciated the cool, dry weather, especially the breezes that tamped down the stink of horses and sweat. The scenery was a welcome sight after they traveled so far in crowded train cars: "On three sides [of the arena] were rolling hills clothed in fresh greenness and walled with dark woods. In front was the shimmer of the sea." There were fifty acres in the grounds devoted to the exhibition area and just as importantly, the camp. "Gleaming in a grove at one side are the white tents of the Indians, painted over with fantastic designs"—that was how the *New York Herald* described some of the grounds.[22]

Lillian's own tent is visible in one of the few extant photographs of her in a group setting from Erastina. She is perched at the edge of the opening, with two cowboys and a show executive standing, seemingly protective around her. One of these men is James "Jim Kid" Willoughby, a native of Clay, Missouri, who was fourteen years older than Lillian, although he looked younger. The sharpshooter was entranced, and the two started a secret affair of some sort.

A champion rider and roper, Willoughby was very handsome, about five feet, ten inches tall with green-blue eyes and a gentle manner, despite his rough-and-tumble profession. During his "down" time, he liked to write songs and poetry.

Given the age difference and their brief acquaintance before starting a romance, the pairing of Jim and Lillian might seem at first like a publicity ploy launched by John Burke, Levi Smith, or Cody himself. But Lillian needed no extra pitch at this time, nor did the Wild West in general—the stands were selling out daily and the show had been extended through August from July. Conversely, the acknowledgment of a romance between a teen and a man so much older could have a detrimental effect on Nate Salsbury's efforts to keep the Wild West wholesome for family patrons.

Lillian and Jim's marriage incensed Levi, especially since it happened right under his nose. If the couple was truly in love and wanted to start a family, that would be the end of Lillian's shooting career. If they were taking simple infatuation too far, then she was "damaged goods" in the eyes of more appropriate groom prospects in the future. Worst of all, another man was now legally and morally in charge of her future: if she managed to stay in show business, all earnings would ostensibly be managed by Willoughby.

Lillian's account of her nuptials is fair testimony to Levi's displeasure. She told a reporter for the *London Tropical Times:* "Well, now, I'll just take you into my confidence. My mother was determined I should not marry anyone, and my father seemed to have taken a decided aversion to 'my Jim.' They tried every thing to prevent my seeing him, and I used to worry myself to death about it." The teen's solution to this problem was similar to a ruse a teen might use today:

> I suddenly developed a mania for ice-creams, which were sold
> in camp, right below the line of tents, and I used to be always
> down there eating them. Jim's tent was down at that end,
> and when my mother and father thought I was filling up and
> making myself ill with creams, I used to drop them like a shot
> when they were not looking, and pop into Jim's tent and have a
> quiet flirtation. Jim had a boy scout always on watch, and when
> mother and father were coming down the walk he would give a
> whistle, and I would dive into the ice-cream shanty again.

This furtive behavior went on until the 27th of September, when the two of them decided they were tired of hiding their fondness for each other—the whole camp knew she was "dead in love with Jim, and he with me," but her parents would not listen to anything Jim had to say.[23]

That evening, Lillian got her friend to make some arrangements with Jim and a local judge. Buck Taylor, who was also a good friend of Willoughby, had moved his tent just opposite Lillian's, and appointed himself "master of ceremonies" for the next morning. "I shall never forget it," said Lillian to the *Topical Times* reporter. "As we were going to breakfast, my father caught me talking to Jim, which nearly sent him mad; and forbade me ever speaking to Jim again." Showing her youthful naïveté, Lillian remarked that she thought this was hilarious, considering she and the cowboy were just about to get married.[24]

If the bride was giddy, the groom was wary. They got married two days after the show officially ended, when everybody was packing up their tents and the blow to her parents might be softened by commotion. Even then, neither had the nerve to tell them. Levi and Rebecca supposedly found out on a train ride to Providence, where Lillian had an engagement. "I meant to let them find out for themselves," the teen recounted to a reporter, "and so they did, for the papers got a hold of it, and the first thing I saw my father reading the next day was 'A Marriage in Camp.'"[25]

Probably sensing that she had this reporter's rapt attention, Lillian quickly veered from a generally accepted version of her marriage story to one of high drama and intrigue, which underscored her reputation as a very clever young lady. "There was a scene, you bet," she told the newspaperman. "My mother said she would kill herself if it were true, and my father promptly whisked me two hundred miles away from New York and put me in solitary confinement." Lillian supposedly remained sequestered for weeks, until she got permission to go buy some ribbons. According to her, she "at once took this opportunity of jumping on the cars," in an attempt to reunite with her love, "After about forty miles of the journey was done, a policeman came looking into all the cars. My parents had telegraphed to stop me. Fortunately, a gentleman, who turned out to be a friend of Jim's—and strange to say, knew me, but I didn't know him—got hold of the policeman and told him he would point out Lillian Smith; and when he [the policeman] came to me he told the policeman I was not a bit like her, so he never even asked my name." Lillian was very happy to get back to New York, and went "straight away" to join her husband. "This was on the 22nd of November last and I was married on September 25. Quite a long time back, wasn't it?" she remarked. The shooter must have thought she sounded very worldly when she said, "You know there is an old saying, 'Marry in haste, repent at leisure.' Old sayings are not always true, and

America's Best Female Sharpshooter

I have proved this one to be so, for I would not part with my Jim for anything."[26]

Strangely, at least on the surface, a series of contradictory letters appeared the following week in New York and Massachusetts newspapers, some purportedly from Lillian, some from "The Kid." The young shooter denied she had ever married, and gave a detailed explanation as to how Willoughby could have misunderstood the situation; the cowboy shot back that he held the marriage certificate, signed by both, and that she must be under her father's thumb. "Mr. Smith is a good shot," the Kid stated to the papers, "Well, so is Lillian, and I'm a pretty smooth shot myself. She never signed that letter. I am her husband and am going to protect her."[27]

Lillian, or someone claiming to be her, replied yet again, threatening to sue if Willoughby did not retract his statements about them being married—betraying any notion that it might have been a misunderstanding.[28] However, in 1897, when Lillian married a saloonkeeper in Santa Cruz, she used "Willoughby" as her last name on the license.

At some point, Levi finally accepted the fact that a marriage of sorts took place. The Smith family stayed with relatives in New Bedford, Massachusetts, in October and November, after which the Champion Rifle Shot went back to New York, where rehearsals commenced for Cody's latest undertaking, a play called *A Drama of Civilization.* Buffalo Bill merged his crew with "the zoological treasures" of Adam Forepaugh, a well-known circus impresario.

Cody, Salsbury, and Forepaugh contracted with Madison Square Garden for a winter program, which would consist of scenes of "human nature," such as the arrival of immigrants, a prairie fire, an attack on a train, the capture of women on the train and stagecoaches and their subsequent rescue, visions of a "rude mining camp," and the sports of cowboys. The partners spent tens of thousands of dollars having scenery painted for the inside of the venue, and adapting it for the "live denizens of the forest," the animals, that Forepaugh provided.[29] Lillian entertained with sharpshooting between the four epochs into which the play was divided.

Exactly how much money Cody and his partners made from *Drama of Civilization* is not known, but by all accounts, this indoor version of Wild West was a huge success. On Thanksgiving Day alone, for example, two performances brought nearly twenty thousand attendees who paid from $0.25 to $1.50 each, depending on their seat preference, and a privileged class paid for box seats that cost up to $12.00 each. Thousands were routinely turned away every night.[30] At Erastina, Mark Twain had commented: "Down to its smallest details, the show is genuine . . . the effects it produced upon me by its spectacles were identical with those wrought upon me a long time ago by the same spectacles on the frontier."

Twain made another point: "It is often said on the other side of the water that none of the exhibitions which we send to England are purely and distinctive American. If you will take the Wild West show over there you can remove that reproach."[31] Twain was referring to Queen Victoria's Golden Jubilee, scheduled for the spring of 1887 in London. American promoters had organized "An Exhibition of the Arts, Industries, Manufactures, Products and Resources of the United States." They took note of Twain's suggestion—and Cody's outrageous successes in North Platte, St. Louis, and Erastina—and offered Cody and Salsbury an engagement that created a sensation around the world: the Wild West in Europe.

On the morning of March 31, 1887, the chartered steamship *State of Nebraska* left New York harbor, ferrying eighty-six white cowboys and "Mexican heroes," ninety "native specimens" in the form of Oglala Sioux, Pawnees, and Cheyennes, and twenty-three passengers, some of whom were British citizens returning home in a most entertaining way. Accounts vary, but Yost gives a good estimate of the animals on board as eighteen buffalo, ten mules, ten elk, five wild Texas steers, four donkeys, twenty deer, and one hundred and eighty horses and ponies. Bill Sweeney's thirty-six member cowboy band, wearing uniforms of grey shirts, slouch hats, and moccasins, played "The Girl I Left Behind Me" as the *Nebraska* weighed anchor before the cheering dockside crowds.[32]

Presumably, Lillian did not sit by or dine with Annie Oakley, who was seen "bubbled over with good spirits," nor was she noted by the *Times* as being among the cowgirls. Most likely, she spent the better part of the two-week voyage with Jim Kid and the cowboys, although she must have practiced her shots on deck with Cody and Oakley from time to time.

America's Best Female Sharpshooter

The *Nebraska* sailed up the Thames on April 14, and anchored at Gravesend. The actors and their crew were transferred to three trains and taken to Earl's Court, in West Brompton. The year before, Earl had been a triangle of empty land at the confluence of three railway lines until developer John Robinson Whitley came up with the idea of an "American Exhibition," and signed Buffalo Bill's when he saw a performance in Washington in 1886. Now, it was twenty-three acres of gardens, courts, and exhibition halls. It also had horse stables, a corral, and a huge grandstand that could seat twenty thousand people. Additionally, it had a "camp village" for the Wild West performers and executives that was similar to, but more elaborate than, the one at Erastina. It was set up amid a grove of newly planted trees; each tent had a wooden floor and a slow-combustion stove inside to ward off the damp English spring.[33]

Cody's press agent, John Burke, and his business manager, Nate Salsbury, had done their jobs very well. It is doubtful that Londoners would have had much interest in American industrial and commercial goods on their own. Londoners were tired of trade fairs, especially since the Colonial and Indian Exhibition had played there the year before. "The American Exhibition," writes Kasper, "in fact, probably would have fallen flat on its face if Buffalo Bill's Wild West had not been secured as a side attraction." Indeed, when the exhibition officially opened on May 9, 1887, ten thousand people who had come early stampeded past the main exhibition and headed to the Wild West camp.

Ticket payers filled the best seats in the grandstand more than an hour before the show was to begin.[34] The audience, which swelled to at least twenty thousand by the time the show started, was treated to "an exact reproduction of frontier life," comprised of "Indian life, 'cow-boy' life, Indian fighting and burning Indian villages, lassoing and breaking in wild horses, shooting, feats of strength, and Border athletic games and sports," which could mean any number of ball games played from the backs of galloping horses or sprinters who raced the horses.[35] There were no visible problems with horses getting stuck in the mud, despite a sudden downpour that morning.

A few days earlier, on May 5, Cody had given a special performance of Wild West for Albert Edward, Prince of Wales, and his royal party. This was a coup in itself, but it also spurred a publicity boost the Wild

West partners could only have dreamed about: the attendance of Her Royal Highness, Queen Victoria.

The monarch was impressed by the glowing accounts that filtered back to the palace by way of her son and daughters, so she decided to see for herself. On May 11, two days after the formal opening of the Wild West, the Queen came to Earl's Court for a command performance. She had planned to stay for only part of the show, but was so enthralled she stayed until the very end.[36]

Queen Victoria's interaction with Annie Oakley and Lillian Smith has been reported any number of ways since the second it happened. The queen sent for the "American Girls," Lillian and Annie. Annie made "the prettiest of curtsies," according to the *London Daily Telegraph*, and later remembered that Victoria turned to her and said, "You are a very clever little girl," which, if true, greatly boosted Annie's spirits. On the other hand, some historians say the queen specifically sent for "the California Girl," and the *Illustrated London News* ran a large, impressive drawing of Lillian being introduced to the queen.

The truth was, Victoria made very little, if any, distinction between the two. She said pleasantries to both, according to the *London Times*, which gave a detailed account of the royal pilgrimages to the show. Victoria's personal diary merely notes that she attended the performance, and "saw two girls shoot at glass balls."[37] By many accounts, the sovereign was most enchanted by the "papooses" of the Sioux.[38]

Whatever Queen Victoria's thoughts were of the female shooters, the London press made much of Lillian, both before and after the monarch's interaction with her. The *Illustrated London News* exclaimed, "The sensation of the day was created by 'The California Girl' whose forte is shooting at swinging targets. She complicates her feat by adding all kinds of difficulty to her aim, and her crowning achievements of smashing glass balls made to revolve horizontally at great speed, and clearing off ball after ball on the target just mentioned to the number of twenty were really marvelous."[39] The American *Rifle* magazine reported that during her tour, Lillian had changed Europe's perception that only British ladies could achieve a high level of sophistication with the gun. "We were recently privileged to see a public and private exhibition with the rifle and pistol of the skill of Miss Lillian F. Smith, a young American lady of 15 years of age, who has attained a marvellous degree of skill."[40]

In 1888, Cody recalled Lillian's interlude with Victoria: "Young California spoke up gracefully, and like a little lady. She showed the Queen the mechanism of the firearm, unloaded and stripped it in order that each part might be examined, then handed it to the gracious sovereign . . . all the time conversing with her Majesty as if she had been a member of the troupe."[41] Cody might have been willing to add something just as laudatory about Annie Oakley, but she and Butler left the Wild West before its last London performance that year, allegedly bitter about Lillian's seemingly brighter publicity. It was probably a combination of this and a dispute over pay.

Smartly, Oakley and her husband cultivated invitations to elite British gun clubs. These clubs, such as Hurlingham and one at Notting Hill, paid the couple to give exhibitions to Britain's upper class and also to show off new models by Lancaster Arms.[42] Lillian simply did not have the maturity or finesse to attempt sponsorships like this.

Still, Lillian was growing up a bit, and although she may not have been schooled in proper English etiquette, she knew that London society and aristocracy favored Oakley's presence. Mrs. Butler routinely received flowers at her tent; she and Frank were often invited to tea with dignitaries—Miss Smith and Willoughby were not. Lillian started to realize that no matter how talented she was, Annie Oakley would always be England's favorite shooter.

This weighed heavily on Lillian, as evidenced by a long letter to *Breeder and Sportsman* signed anonymously by "California." The newsletter printed it in its original form, spelling and grammatical errors untouched. In it, the Wild West show was lauded as an extreme success, thanks in very large part to the teen prodigy: "Miss Lillian F. Smith the 'California Girl' is knocking the English shooters all crazy. She performed before all the Royal Family, and was presented to the Queen Victoria. The Queen complimented her very highly on her shooting and took her Gun in her hands and examined it and I have learned since it was the only Gun she ever held in her hand."

The rest of the column is an embarrassing reflection upon Lillian, whether she wrote the letter or not: "There was considerable Jealusy as Miss Smith and Buffalo Bill was the only whites presented to her Royal Magesty. Miss Oakley being left out in the cold. The English people can not understand rifle shooting such as the California Girl does. . . . But shot gun shooting is quite common in London as most every one does wing shooting." The writer finally got to the point:

> Some of the Papers had it that Miss Oakley was presented
> to the Queen but she was not I happened to be present one
> this occasion being an American and having been born in
> California I was anxious to see the results of the day and
> Frank Botler never lets a chance go, he is Miss Oakleys
> Husband but it is not known here. He is passed as her brother
> he manages Miss Oakley and has nothing else to do, while
> Miss Lillian Smith's manager is a Cowboy and takes part in
> every act in the Wild West Performances and has no desire to
> put stuff in the news papers Reporters heads that is not so,
> while this man Botler is an old Showman and will do anything
> for notoriety and publicity but is no use for them to struggle
> for California is bound to win . . . for she can well boast of the
> Champion Rifle Shot of the World.[43]

Butler responded firmly to California's letter. He did not use Willough-by's name, but he might as well have. He charged that the document had originated from the Wild West camp, and that the writer's "bad English was as good as his signature." Nate Salsbury enclosed a letter with Butler's, chiding *Breeder and Sportsman* for publishing any gossip about the camp.

On September 3, *Breeder* printed a letter merely signed "Cowboy," which acknowledged that Smith was indeed "marvelous," but which also defended Oakley's and Butler's character:

> I have had the pleasure of meeting Mr. Butler . . . and I must
> say that I have found him a very honorable and straightforward
> gentleman, and he has never to me tried to pass as anything
> but Miss Oakley's husband, and I, as correspondent to sporting
> papers, have never yet had him try to fill me up with news
> unless I asked him for information. . . . Now, Mr. Editor, when
> I write this in no way reflecting on Miss Smith, but when 'A

California' asserts that Miss Oakley is left out in the cold, I wish to say that he is much mistaken.[44]

It was not enough: Butler wrote a rebuke on August 16, after Annie Oakley had "bested" Lillian Smith at Wimbledon—indeed, he included a report of her doings there. Lillian's remarks about shotgun shooting being commonplace in England touched a nerve with the Butlers. Frank Butler assured *Breeder*'s readers that this was no big thing: "As regards Miss Oakley shooting a shotgun, nearly every shooter east of the Rocky Mountains knows that for the first three years before the public Miss Oakley did nothing but rifle or pistol shooting, and gave it up because she could not get a living salary for doing it." Moreover, Butler said defensively, Oakley specifically turned away from rifle or pistol shooting because in the early 1880s, it was not unique: "This was owing to the fact that gallery or fancy rifle shooting was very early learned, and at that time there were about twenty girls and women giving exhibition in that line." And certainly, it was no big deal in England, where Smith was plying her craft: "And I find by actual count there were no less than sixteen here, some of them at present playing in music halls here, while Miss Oakley is the only lady trap shooter seen here yet."

Oakley had proven that she had not forgotten her rifle expertise, Butler wrote, as evidenced by her performance on July 20, 1887, at England's shooting mecca, Wimbledon, though he did not present a score.[45] It is not even clear whether British sportsmen thought Oakley could shoot any better than some among them, but rather, they thought she possessed the composure needed to be a novelty in a man's world. One of these sportsmen was gun maker Charles Lancaster, who saw a marketing opportunity after watching Oakley shoot at one of the early summer Wild West shows. A source named "Purple Heather" wrote to *American Field* magazine with some revealing comments about Oakley and her new coach: "I met Miss Annie Oakley the first day she shot at his private grounds, and I was also present when she first came to our club ground (the Gun Club). At this period Miss Oakley could kill about one blue rock [pigeon] out of five. After Mr. Lancaster had finished his course of instruction she killed forty-one rocks out of fifty, and for these performances she selected her Lancaster 20-bores—a pair of beautiful guns built for exhibition—in preference to her Lancaster 12's."[46] Thus, the British press followed the evolution of Oakley's improved marksmanship during the Buffalo Bill Wild West show, crediting this improvement to British advice and British guns—a source of national pride.

Lillian Smith had no such endorsements, no matter how well she could shoot. Even when Oakley had a particularly bad day at a gentleman's shooting club, where she hit only five out of twenty clay pigeons, the manager softened his criticism by telling her she was much less of a shot than he expected, but much more of lady.[47] In reality, her rifle was probably too heavy and the shot too light for the windy weather, much like the problems Lillian had at Wimbledon. But because of her proper countenance, reputation, and involvement with Lancaster Arms, England's elite was favorably predisposed toward Oakley's performance at Wimbledon, no matter what her score was.

Sadly, even the *Sacramento Daily Record-Union,* the biggest newspaper from Lillian's hometown region, once her biggest booster, took a swipe at its homegrown shooter. The paper noted that her "highly polished language" in a published interview would astonish people who knew her in nearby Woodland. "In Woodland, she usually said: 'Swab off the target, Pap, and let me bang de eye,' or else, 'Swing de apple dere, young fellers, an' let me bust his skin.' How great are the changes."[48]

Indeed, the grounds of the National Rifle Association, formally known as Wimbledon Commons, were really where the simmering rivalry between the two women congealed. The London Gun Club invited the famous shooters from the Wild West to participate in its annual championships there, although Cody did not attend. Annie Oakley's and Lillian Smith's actual scores are not recorded, but by most accounts, Oakley performed better.

Lillian appeared at England's hallowed shooting grounds on Tuesday, July 19, 1887, accompanied by "a number of cowboys and other celebrities," including a small Indian boy, "most resplendently arrayed in a blue silk shirt, and a pair of red silk trousers," according to the *Weekly Dispatch.* Lillian herself wore a flouncy white summer dress, "incongruously accompanied by a yellow silk Mexican sash and plug hat."[49] The Queen's Prize winner of 1884, one Mr. Gallant, escorted Lillian and her entourage around the grounds.

America's Best Female Sharpshooter

Gallant must have been disappointed when Lillian picked up a rifle at the "shooting deer" target and made some pitiful shots. The first two bullets missed the target entirely. Worse, the next few hit the haunch of the iron animal—this was considered especially poor shooting, because in real life, the deer would have escaped, only to suffer. But Lillian's most heinous crime was to leave without paying a customary fine for this misfiring.

Annie Oakley fared better, though it is not clear how much. The *Evening News* wrote that Oakley had been "more successful at Wimbledon" than her "comrade in arms" had been the previous day, making a "fairly good record" at the running deer.[50] The Prince of Wales had invited Oakley to be on the grounds this day, and shook hands with her, testifying to her charm for Victorians. Sure Shot's prim clothing got no mention in the papers because it was most certainly less flashy than Lillian's.

Thirty years later, in an interview with the *Pinehurst Outlook,* Oakley revealed that she had had some coaching on the running deer target prior to her shoot—coaching that Lillian Smith was not privy to. "They took a fancy to the idea of a country girl from the West outshooting their professionals," Oakley said coyly. "I don't believe however that it was there that the Grand Duke got the idea of tackling me himself." She related that just a little while later, "the Prince asked me down to Wimbledon where they had the ranges and the military camp, and we took a crack at the running deer. . . . Earl [de Grey], who was probably the best shot in the Europe at the time, gave me some confidential and careful advice before I took the stand, and I succeeded in hitting the bull's-eye on the four-quarter five times running." Also in this recollection, Oakley took pains to describe the disgrace of someone hitting the metal animal in the hindquarters, a clear swipe again at Lillian Smith.[51]

On the whole, Smith's and Oakley's appearances at Wimbledon were not as significant to Brits as they were to the American shooters. There was a novelty in having "Yankee" Wild West actors appear on the grounds, but more ink was spilled about royal participation, the Queen's Prize, and whether or not the National Rifle Association would continue to contract with the venue. There was a bit of speculation as to why Buffalo Bill Cody did not come at all.

Even the most seemingly scathing report of Lillian's performance is quite tepid when put into context. For example, the *St. James Evening Review and Gazette* admitted that Lillian's "non-success" might have been due to the weight of her rifle, and that even "the best of shots is hopelessly at sea when shooting at a novel target."[52] The *London Evening News* concluded that Lillian's poor performance was due to her unfamiliarity with the rifle handed to her and its recoil, and that she would one day come back with an appropriate rifle.[53]

Still, the blandly positive reports of Annie Oakley's performance at Wimbledon must have stung Lillian, especially since she already resented Annie's popularity among the upper crust, as evidenced by what was likely Willoughby's letter to *Breeder and Sportsman*. It did not help matters that the Butlers posted this letter in their tent and made fun of it any time someone stopped by for a visit. Furthermore, the rifle was supposed to be Lillian's bailiwick, not Annie's.

The Wild West played London from May 9 until October 31, 1887. The Victorian comedian Marshall Wilder declared it "the greatest, most unapproachable, thoroughly howling success" that America ever sent to England, and called Cody "the hero of the season."[54] Unfortunately, it further soured relationships between its most talked-about stars: Cody, Smith, and Oakley.

Cody did nothing to settle hard feelings between his female sharpshooters, though to be fair, there may have been no upside for him to get involved. The Butlers never publicly discussed their reasons for leaving the show, but leave they did, after the last performance on October 31. After spending some time with new friends in Europe, the Butlers sailed back to the United States around Christmastime.

Lillian Smith most likely breathed a sigh of relief with Oakley gone, but she may have also wondered if the Butlers had gotten the better deal: enjoying the privacy afforded couples traveling on their own, and being able to keep every dime they earned, even if the star did not know where she would be appearing from one week to the next. Buffalo Bill's Wild West performed in Birmingham and Manchester through the spring of 1888, when finally, the troupe boarded the *Persian Monarch* on May 4 and sailed back to New York.

Summer in Staten Island was a virtual repeat of the prior year, except that the Wild West garnered even more throngs of people because of its publicized blessing by "sophisticated" Europeans, particularly Queen Victoria. There were some new acts, like the "bucking horses," which was a feature the cowboys had perfected in England. Cody augmented his "tribes" of Arapahoes, Sioux, and Cheyennes, who were "bare-limbed and paint-bedaubed," to "yell and dance and fight," just as they were supposed to do on the real frontier.[55]

Before returning to the States, Lillian had been promoted to a bigger act, consisting of trick-shooting off the backs of horses, along with Cody and "the Cowboy Kid," Johnny Baker. In spite of this, her time with Buffalo Bill's Wild West was coming to a close, and so was her first marriage.

Chapter Three
A TOUGH TRANSITION

Had the woman who shot [railway executive] Chas. T.
Johnson been as skilled with her gun as Lillian Smith,
the champion rifle shot of the world, Johnson would
never have lived to tell who shot him.
                    Santa Cruz Sentinel, June 20, 1897

I n late October 1888, the Wild West show shut down for the winter
at Richmond, Virginia. Before heading back to North Platte for a
long-deserved rest, Cody took his "red men" to visit the White House
and see Congress in action. He smoked a peace pipe with show asso-
ciates Nate Salsbury, John Burke, Red Shirt, Rocky Bear, and others
at the Bureau of Indian Affairs. The Great Father himself, President
Grover Cleveland, received the Indians in the East Room and by all
accounts was impressed with their "majestic bearing" as they filed by.

There was no such fanfare for Lillian after the Wild West disbanded.
Before they had even left England, Cody signed contracts to open his
extravaganza in Paris during the exposition of May 1889, which was
going to celebrate the centennial of the French Revolution. Annie
Oakley was invited to renew her contract with the pageant; Lillian
Smith was not. The terms of the Butlers' rapprochement with Cody
were never revealed, but most historians agree that one condition was
probably that Lillian had to leave the show. Neither Smith nor Oakley,
nor Cody for that matter, ever publicly discussed details of Smith being
dropped from the Paris excursion.

Like Oakley, Smith never expressed anger toward Cody in public—and she had every right to be angry. After arriving in England back in May 1887, she had excitedly written to *Breeder and Sportsman* about her new surroundings, noting that she expected to go to France with the Wild West in October. Although a Parisian tour did not come to pass until the exposition in 1889, she was surely disappointed at being left behind as the show visited the rest of the continent.

Thus, the California Girl spent Christmas of 1888 on the East Coast without Jim, who had returned to Europe with the Wild West. On January 20, she wrote to *Breeder and Sportsman* to let her fans know her latest activities: "I am at home with my parents this winter, resting from my European tour, which was a great success." She described a 12-gauge shotgun she received as a Christmas present from one Westley Richards, of London, and said that she looked forward to a rifle shooting exhibition in a few days, when she would attempt to "beat all records of rapidity shooting," notably by breaking five hundred balls in fifteen minutes.[1] Smith wrote that she would return home to California for the summer of 1889; presumably, her parents had been staying in the East with relatives during her Wild West sojourn.

Whatever exhibition it was, it warranted no report in the papers. Reporters watched Annie Oakley instead, wondering what her next move would be after her brief acting foray came to a disastrous end. The Butlers' play, *Deadwood Dick: or, the Sunbeam of the Sierra's,* was panned by critics, and suffered the loss of its leading man the night before its debut, incurring major last-minute script changes. The theater company fell apart in Chambersburg, Pennsylvania, in late January when the assistant manager absconded with the show's receipts.[2]

Annie Oakley had wasted no time getting back into the exhibition circuit, especially because the Butlers had no source of income until Wild West resumed in May. On February 23, in Long Branch, New Jersey, she won a $500 purse in a pigeon shoot against Philip Daly, Jr., stockholder of a new athletic club there and a rather notorious gambler. (Not surprisingly, Levi Smith opened a shooting gallery nearby.)

This was one of many wins or near-wins at trapshooting Oakley had garnered just before and after her brief dramatic foray. She demurred when papers called her "The Championship Rifle Shot of the

World," in spite of the fact that she had used the shotgun in the majority of her *Deadwood* performances and most of her matches. Oakley again refused a shooting challenge from Lillian, proffered through the magazine *American Field:* "I will say that for reasons which it is not necessary to mention here, it is impossible for me to enter in any competition with Miss Smith. . . . The word 'champion' I have never used myself. . . . If the title benefits her any . . . I hope she will make better use of it than she did when she visited Wimbledon."[3]

Lillian could not have known it then, but Oakley did her a favor by distancing herself. Her refusal to match with Lillian, coupled with her pending absence from the country, would force Lillian to find an identity for herself that was not yoked to other sharpshooters. While the *Persian Monarch* sailed away with Buffalo Bill and his cast of hundreds on April 28, 1889, the eighteen-year-old Lillian was somewhere between the East Coast and California, hurtling toward home by way of the Union Pacific Railroad.

She most certainly knew she was headed back to the clutches of Levi, but was probably very homesick, too. After all, she had not seen her brother for the better part of three years. And California had always been very proud of its home-grown prodigy. Platitudes such as this one from the Sacramento newspaper appeared often during the summer of her return: "The young lady whose remarkable skill with shotgun and rifle—particularly the latter—has surprised the people of the New and Old world. . . . while abroad Miss Smith gave exhibitions before the British royal family and other foreign notables, and was the recipient of many costly presents."[4] Lillian was feted by the owners of the newly-refurbished Bartlett Springs resort, in Lakeport, in the lower end of the Mendocino National Forest. Here, she spent part of the summer "rusticating," resting with wealthy merchants from the state, and going on the deer hunts that took place three times a week.[5]

Lillian shook off the last residue of Buffalo Bill's Wild West show by breaking up with Willoughby, either directly or by proxy. A cowboy with the show, C. L. Daily, wrote his parents from France that his tent mate, Jim Kid, had received a letter that Lillian had "gone off with another cowboy, 'Bill Cook,' by name, half white and half Indian."[6] Kid, according to Daily, "almost went crazy" when he received the news: "He [Bill Cook] was with the show last year and was a great friend of

Kid's. He [Kid] has been drinking hard ever since. He will probably go back to America and hunt Cook up and kill him. I pity the poor fellow. He thinks an awful sight of Smith. Some nights he doesn't come into the tent at all but walks around all night. He doesn't think she is at all to blame but blames Cook."[7] Kid's different perception of his marriage was apparent when the *Cheyenne Leader* printed his letter on July 30, 1889, praising his wife: "All of us have learned a little French, and I'll sling the lingo at the boys when I get back. We are treated like Princes by the people. A member of the company can keep drunk all the time if he wants to, and some of them come pretty near doing it. My health isn't as good as it use to be, and I take good care of myself. Besides, I'm married now and must keep straight. My wife is the champion rifle-shot, and has made a great hit here."[8]

Evidently, Kid was missing Lillian and trying not to take to the battle. Plenty of the showmen—Cody included—boozed fairly heavily to relieve boredom and homesickness between shows. And it is likely that Kid was taking another opportunity to remind people that his wife was a bigger star than Annie Oakley, and that he had not abandoned her. Lillian never publicly stated why she separated from Jim. Clearly, she had been too young when they married and had simply fallen out of love.

Instead, Willoughby's estranged wife was setting her sights closer to home again. The western states and territories presented some alluring opportunities for rare talents like Lillian Smith at the dawn of the 1890s. More so than New York, New Jersey, Pennsylvania, and other eastern seaboard states, which were very similar to Europe by this time, with strict social codes, high buy-ins, and the support of Annie Oakley, who would not deign to a match with Lillian. On the other hand, Washington, Idaho, Nevada, Arizona, and California were still much more wide open in terms of settling land with firearms and providing entertainment for large numbers of unattached young men still flooding into those regions.

One form of entertainment was shooting ranges. The Smiths set these up in coarser California towns such as Marysville, Oroville, Chico, and Hanford. They were marginally profitable, and the family acquired or built them off and on over the next five years or so, whenever other obligations permitted. Levi constructed the framing and counters, painted lime-white on the targets, and oiled the machinery of the clockwork attachments that caused figures to play in lively fashion on a drum or hand-organ when a bull's-eye was made.[9] Lillian's mother Rebecca and sister Nellie, or a hired boy, could busy themselves by removing the spatters of lead from misplaced shots and painting out cracks and rust spots.

These ranges could make some money if a famous shooter sponsored them. As a proprietor in San Francisco told the *Chronicle* in May 1889, there was good cash to be made not from the nickels of twelve-year-old boys or dimes of dry-good clerks but rather from "sailors, cowboys and young sports that come in about half full and get up a wager." There was no shortage of these types in the rough-and-tumble San Joaquin and Central Valley regions of California at this time; Lillian made no distinction between drunk and sober egos when picking wagers.

While the Smiths could easily have cleared a hundred dollars a week or more with Lillian's celebrity, at least half of that was needed for rent, capital, and taxes on the locations, not to mention hotel pay, which might explain why the ranges were temporary and far-flung. Often, townships were happy to have the entertainment that the Smiths brought, if only to soak up the extraneous drinking men during the rowdy evening hours of seven o'clock to midnight. But hamlets also wanted a piece of the range's profits, especially if it was popular. In 1899, for example, Nellie Smith haughtily told a Fresno license collector that, although she was co-owner of a gallery there with her sister and father, she was in charge, at which point he hauled her to court to pay a five-dollar fee, plus interest. These financial considerations might account for the rapidity in which the Smiths' galleries opened and shut, but the family still opened at least a dozen in California and Oregon.

At this time, elite sportsmen were starting to take aim at subsistence and market hunters, labeling them "game butchers," "fish pirates," and "pothunters," in contrast to the "gentleman" who practiced a British-style sportsmanship. By the time *Field and Stream* and *Outdoor Life* debuted in the 1890s, magazines had already begun the work of creating and popularizing an image of reformed hunting associated with recreation and respectability.[10] Arguably, this trend offered diminished wage opportunities for subsistence hunters like

Levi Smith, but in the western states and Pacific Northwest, he could still find ways for his family to use guns to make a wage, and not just with galleries.

One way was to teach housewives how to shoot. Popular magazines and social clubs increasingly encouraged women to "share men's outdoor pursuits as a way of upholding, rather than undermining, Victorian notions of respectable, family-centered recreation."[11] During this decade, Lillian was highly sought after as a draw for women and children to come to shooting ranges and learn to fire.

In the spring of 1890, Levi started reading about the heavy speculation of metals taking place in Oregon, Washington and Idaho. The Seven Devils mining district titillated the minds of thousands of men who missed out on the California Gold Rush a generation before, and Levi was no exception. "There is quite an influx of miners and prospectors to this point on their way to the Seven Devils mining district. . . . No other mining camp is talked of among prospectors, and it is confidently expected that at least five thousand men will rush to the Seven Devils district this summer." This *San Francisco Bulletin* reporter wrote of the exceptional copper and silvery-blue "peacock ores" (bornite, a copper ore mineral) found plentifully there.[12]

Seven Devils, spanning a swath of land in eastern Oregon and Washington and a piece of western Idaho and containing about 125 mines, turned out to be richer in copper than anything else. It was not the precious metal that interested Levi, but rather the question of how prospectors were going to get to its most prosperous sites, like Lick Creek, Salubria, and Weiser. Senator John Hipple Mitchell of Oregon appropriated tens of thousands of dollars to improve the Snake River at certain junctions, making navigation between the mines and shipping outlets easier throughout the entire year. One Mr. Albert Kleinschmidt, a wealthy Helena entrepreneur, commissioned work on the steamship *Norma* to carry the ore by way of the Snake; possibly, Levi got work on the vessel.

Meanwhile, Lillian got work showcasing her talents in bigger cities like Portland, Salem and Astoria, especially during the colder months of the Pacific Northwest: "The California Girl is attracting great crowds in her shooting room in [Portland's] Bank Block where she gives marvelous exhibitions of her skill with the Rifle. Miss Smith will give instructions to Ladies and children in the use of fire arms, as it will many times prevent accidents."[13] The Smiths spent Christmas of 1890 in a boardinghouse, in Astoria, Oregon.

Hunting and surveying were in full swing by 1891, with transportation systems opening up and scores of people flooding into the district for mining and also the clearing of rich fruit-growing land. The *Idaho Statesman* wrote about the large parties traipsing throughout Seven Devils territory: "Some load a boat on a wagon and haul it up the Weiser twelve or fifteen miles and float down the next day, generally securing plenty of game. Others lay in the brush near the slough on bright nights and crack away at the ducks, geese, etc., flying over. In the morning the slough is generally pretty well littered up with game, which is gathered up, taken home and socked into the frying pan."[14]

Hunting and surveying in these western states provided yet another opportunity for Lillian. Prospectors C. A. Williams and E. James hired her to hunt and provide protection from wild animals, but the party could not leave until the snow melted completely in mid-May. Never ones to waste time or money, the Smiths continued to give exhibitions in and around Tacoma, until there was favorable weather for going into the wilds. It may or may not have been a true emergency that required Lillian's services when President Benjamin Harrison made a stopover in the city on May 6: "The big banner on the grain arch erected in honor of the presidential visit threatened to demolish the structure. . . . Producing a small rifle, she shot away at the halyards, though they were swaying at a lively rate in the strong breeze. The feat was watched by a large number of people and heartily applauded."[15] After she completed her Seven Devils hunting expedition, Lillian gave exhibitions at gun shows in cities like Spokane, Anaconda, and Helena. Her career might have petered out here, in the sparsely populated Northwest, had she not come up with an ingenious publicity stunt.

A couple of months prior, during the first week of April, some outrageous proclamations began to appear in Oregon and Washington papers, ostensibly written by Lillian in New York, but more likely written by Levi in Salem: "Lillian F. Smith . . . is going to return to Oregon to hunt, then have a boat built and go down the Columbia river to the Pacific ocean and then to San Francisco. She will then take the boat to the world's fair and put it on exhibition." And the usual wager: "At the same time she will be ready to arrange a match to shoot against any one in the world with the rifle.[16]

The Smiths had been back in California for at least six months when a revised version of this grand plan emerged in the press.[17] "Miss Lillian Smith of Fresno," reported the *San Francisco Call,* is building a boat in which she proposes to journey down the San Joaquin River to San Francisco." Moreover, she planned to make the trip alone.[18]

True to her word, Smith embarked in her "little tule boat" on Saturday, June 11, 1892 in Herndon, a river-entry outside of Fresno. Crowds of reporters and friends she had made at her shooting gallery on J Street came out to cheer her, or maybe catch a last glimpse of her. Lillian christened the bark "The California Girl." The vessel, which the papers declared she had made herself, was only six-and-a-half feet long and three-and-a-half feet at its widest—twenty-five pounds in total weight, before she added provisions and her body load.

A *Chicago Daily Inter Ocean* correspondent asked how long she had been contemplating this trip. She replied with a half-truth, which might have been slightly refined by the editor: "Only about ten or twelve days. The thought struck me what a fine opportunity such a trip would afford me to enjoy myself in using my rifle and to see the beautiful country through which I should pass." She explained that this was a "pleasure trip," and she was in no hurry to get to San Francisco, intending to stop many times along the way, including once at [Henry] Millers' Home Ranch. The correspondent pressed Lillian: would she be afraid to sleep all by herself at points along the river? "Afraid!" Smith exclaimed, "Why, there are no alligators in the river, and if anything else comes along I'll make it think that a whole regiment of riflemen has broken loose." What about waves, and weather, asked the reporter. "When I encounter the big waves of the bay," she responded, "it will be the nicest part of my trip to see my boat scoot through them like an arrow: now up, now down, like a swing, you know." As for the rain, she did not think enough would splash into the "California Girl" to bother her.[19]

There is no account of any stops Lillian made on the way, or of any features except for passing references to choppy waves at Antioch and the Carquinez Straits.[20] Then, like today, the river was approximately four hundred miles long, starting in the High Sierras, near Yosemite and not far from Lillian's place of birth. By entering the San Joaquin in Fresno, she cut roughly 140 miles from its total length, but it would have been fairly suicidal to begin at the river's headlands, where today the thundering rush of water over the mountains is strong enough to churn the turbines of about twenty hydroelectric dams. Still, rowing and sailing the San Joaquin through its Central Valley course for the remaining 250 or so miles to San Francisco required Lillian to use all of her brute strength and hardiness, fending off mosquitoes and pulling her little boat to safe harbor in order to sleep at night. But she did arrive in San Francisco safely with her boat in hand, exhausted and badly sunburned, on July 5. One of her childhood neighbors later recalled that Lillian was the first person to make such a trip. "Afterwards Frank Latta went down the river in a boat," the neighbor said of a Bakersfield high school teacher who replicated Lillian's journey, although he did so nearly forty years later, and with a small crew and an outboard motor.[21]

The family met her and took rooms at a hotel on Mission Street, where she rested for a few days. Then, the navigator lugged her little boat to what is now Golden Gate Park to show curiosity seekers, and also to do some "fancy and practical" shooting.

The crowds especially loved Lillian's trademark for this year: shooting fifty glass balls in one minute or less (at that point, she held the world's record for doing it in forty-two seconds). The wind in the Park could be pretty fierce, so she had a little trouble with another new act, which was to hit glass balls the size of cherries while they spun rapidly in concentric circles from a rack thirty-five feet away. Using two-and-a-half inch glass ones, she was able to "slaughter" from the same distance, but shooting from the right shoulder as well as the left, sometimes using a covered sight. Smith fired with unerring aim at three-quarter-inch balls thrown in the air, and from a trap.

These exhibitions were a family affair, noted the *San Francisco Call,* with a transparent nod toward Levi's exploitation: "The young woman possesses remarkable skill with the rifle, some of her feats almost surpassing belief. She was ably assisted in the performance by the entire Smith family, who have found life worth living since Lillian learned to shoot. Mamma Smith takes tickets at the gate, Papa Smith tosses glass balls into the air, and Lillian's younger sister

America's Best Female Sharpshooter

opens boxes of cartridges and swabs out the guns while her gifted relative is entertaining the audience."[22] Lillian wore a Buffalo Bill hat and a dark dress trimmed with bright yellow stars and medals tacked on here and there—a childlike costume for a plump, twenty-year-old woman.

The Smith family had planned to be in Chicago during the fall of 1892 for commencement of the World's Fair, but the exposition was postponed by almost a year, and was not open to visitors until May 1893. Moreover, Lillian was not invited to participate. This was more than likely due to the fact that exposition developers felt Buffalo Bill and his ilk were too "low brow" to be considered proper entertainment for the extravaganza, and surely Lillian Smith was considered much less cosmopolitan than Annie Oakley, who performed for Cody's "Congress of Rough Riders" just a few hundred yards away from the exposition's confines.

Instead, Lillian signed as the star attraction of San Francisco's Arizona Historical Wild West show in late July, which featured her exhibition shooting, along with Pima Indians playing football, rough riders, vaqueros, cowboys, and horseback versions of the Virginia reel. However, this would be Lillian's last ensemble employment for many years. Levi may have felt she was exposed to undesirable elements, not the least of which were young men, many of them not local and maybe not even white. His daughter's liaisons with Jim Kid and possibly the "half-breed" Bill Cook were embarrassing, but more importantly, they were reminders that he was unable to control her time and pay.

Keeping Lillian local for the time being was also a way for Levi to advertise his own new business, which centered on the development of a new watercraft that he hoped to patent. The "father of Lillian Smith, a famous rifle shot" was building a boat in Stockton that when completed, he announced, would "speed away from anything in the line of steam craft now in the channels." Levi's aim was to design a vessel that was extremely light and portable, appropriate for navigating the artificial waterways opening up around the San Joaquin River, and yet one that was strong enough to carry eighty or so yards of canvas aloft and attain speeds up to twenty miles an hour.[23]

Unfortunately, the craft failed. On August 22, 1904, Levi sailed out of Stockton, in an attempt to reach Tiburon in northern San

Francisco Bay by Friday, August 24, where he would participate in a regatta. He never arrived, and on the following Tuesday, the *San Francisco Call* told readers that friends and family were apprehensive about his fate, fearing that "the father of Lillian, the famous rifle shot" had capsized and drowned. He did not perish, but he did not make it to Tiburon in his boat, and now at age sixty, he made no more attempts at furthering a career of his own.[24] Instead, Levi signed up his daughter for grueling rounds of vaudeville appearances. She would perform at San Francisco's "Free Chutes Theater," on a section of the future "Playland," a ten-acre amusement park next to Ocean Beach, and at the Orpheum Theater on O'Farrell Street, between Stockton and Powell.

Vaudeville and Orpheum theaters across the United States were usually opulent buildings with interiors often modeled after the architecture and décor of various countries and time periods, including Viennese palaces and medieval English castles, Gothic cathedrals and Spanish-Moorish mosques. The structures were the ultimate escape for the masses—a place to go for those with a little spare cash and weekly leisure time. They could get affordable entertainment on a regular basis, and not worry about content that was too dirty for their wives or children, as variety shows sometimes were. Vaudeville was popular in an America where phonographs, film, radio, and television did not yet exist, and something new was needed to fill the gap. Even in the hardest of times, vaudeville shows sold out on a regular basis.

In 1895, Lillian booked several months at the Orpheum on South Main Street in Los Angeles. According to the *Los Angeles Times,* her performances there were bright spots, among such acts as a labored impersonation of Presidents Cleveland and Harrison, aided by a pig, and a turn by "darkey comedians."[25] As chance would have it, Doc Carver was engaged for his rifle shooting at nearby Westlake Park, today known as Griffith Park. While Lillian was shooting glass balls and wooden targets inside a theater, Carver was shooting oranges, apples, and baseballs, pieces of which flew into the faces of crowds sitting in the lower rings of the arena.

Smith again challenged Carver. There is no question she did this to bring publicity to wherever she might happen to be performing for any length of time, but Carver was genuinely an obsession for her. With a friend, John Travelsted, acting as agent, the shooter challenged Carver in the *Los Angeles Times:*

> Dr. W. F. Carver: Dear Sir—as you have failed to answer the challenge written by me on this . . . and refused to see me at your rooms in regard to the matter, I will here publicly challenge you to shoot a bona fide rifle match with Lillian F. Smith for the sum of two hundred dollars ($200) a side, or as much more as you may wish to make it, and gate receipts. Also, I put up forfeit of twenty-five dollars ($25) in good faith in the office of The Times. If said challenge is not accepted in one week the forfeit will be withdrawn.[26]

And withdrawn it was, for a week later the *Times* reported that Carver "has paid no attention" to Lillian's test of marksmanship. "It is not known why Dr. Carver declines to take up the challenge to compete with a woman for the championship honors, but it is supposed that it is owing to his gallantry."[27] Maybe. But even if Carver considered it, he may have scratched his head at responding to Travelsted, a transient ranch hand who, less than a year before, had been arrested for trying to steal a wagon in San Joaquin, and received a leg full of buck shot for his trouble. No doubt Travelsted was looking to make a buck off Lillian's talent, and the two of them cooked up this plan without Levi's knowledge. For Lillian, it was worth it to try, even if she would have to share money with her erstwhile friend.

It took resourcefulness and energy for a freelance performer to piece together a career. The new mobility belped. As gun historian R. L. Wilson notes, advances in mass transportation played a key part in letting female shooters like Lillian Smith and Annie Oakley earn their reputations, and this was absolutely true of Lillian in the mid-1890s. The Southern Pacific Railroad had, in 1876, completed its north-south line between San Francisco and Los Angeles, instigating the building of dozens of local connections, too. Lillian could take any number of shorter lines criss-crossing east-west between valley cities and those on the coast. For example, in April 1896, she likely took the California Southern from San Diego to Riverside to open a shooting gallery, and then on to San Bernardino to perform at Rabel Hot Springs.

Back in northern California during the holiday season of 1897, Lillian did "excellent business" with her sister Nellie and her father in San Francisco at the Chutes, an amusement park on Haight Street that featured a precursor to the modern rollercoaster. The following year, Nellie assisted her older sister at the Alhambra, a popular theater at the corner of Eddy and Jones streets.[28] When Lillian was not booked for any substantial amount of time, the family would head inland and open a shooting gallery in rural, tough places like Jamestown, or Tuolumne, or the city of Merced, or Point Richmond just east of the San Francisco Bay.

Traveling could get lonely, and often Lillian was without someone near in age to pass the time with. She set her sights on Theodore Powell, a football player for Santa Cruz's two-year-old team, whom she had met at a saloon. On July 8, 1897, the two married at the Calvary Episcopal Church in the center Santa Cruz, with a stranger as a witness. The *Fresno Republican* noted the marriage while it good-naturedly praised the town's rival team and also alluded to Lillian's large personality (and possibly her large figure): "The report that Lillian F. Smith, the champion rifle shot, has married a Santa Cruz ball player justifies the impression that some of those Beachcombers are not afraid to tackle anything in their line."[29] Exactly how long the marriage lasted is not known, but within a few years Powell had remarried and become a barkeeper in San Francisco. Lillian may not have been in love with Powell, but having someone to shoot with and drink with helped relieve the crushing boredom of giving yet another gun-holding lesson for housewives in places like Crockett and Gilroy.

Chapter Four

WENONA AND FRANK

"What," said he, "has you interested in shooting?" "What
has interested me?" she said. "Everything. I was on an
outing with my husband; they gave me a gun to shoot;
I fired it, and, although it almost deafened me, I fired it
again, and again, until my shoulder was black and blue.
I learned to hit a stationary mark, and then, when I
killed a bird, it was the proudest moment of my life."

William Bruce Leffingwell,
The Art of Wing Shooting, 1895

Charles Franklin Hafley threw up all the way back to San Francisco. It was several days after Christmas in 1899. And until he
had embarked on the SS *Australia* and started toward Hawaii a month
before, the former sheriff had only traversed such water as the swamps
in upper Fresno River while chasing outlaws like "Indian Dick." Like
Lillian, he was born in 1872, albeit in Tennessee. His father, Samuel
Houston Hafley, moved his family to Stockton around 1880, and—like
Levi—followed jobs around the Central Valley.

Lillian may have met Hafley through her brother—they lived near
each other in Visalia, a farm town in Tulare County. When not running
down horse thieves and worse criminals, Hafley competed there in
shooting matches with fellow National Guardsmen. No doubt Lillian
was aware of his prowess with the rifle and with catching ne'er-do-
wells. Hafley was not a conventionally handsome or tall man—he

stood at five foot, seven inches, with a mop of dark hair, and already leathered skin—but he was witty, very intelligent, and his twinkly brown eyes attracted women and inspired confidence in men.

Hafley mustered into the U.S. Army as a corporal on April 29, 1898, as a sharpshooter for the Sixth California Volunteers, three days after the Spanish-American conflict broke out. But after about a month of service, he left to deal with severe abdominal pain. Eventually, Hafley was diagnosed with a hernia, and had surgery at Lane Hospital (now Stanford) in the fall. He was honorably discharged in December, his service noted as "honest and faithful," and his character "excellent."[1]

Nonetheless, when he returned to the Central Valley, Frank found that his job as sheriff of Tulare County had been given away. The only thing left for him to do was to appear as a minor hero in the occasional town parade and give shooting lessons. Similarly, Lillian found herself sharing the spotlight with her father, mother, and sister Nellie as part of the "Smith family of rifle shots" in San Francisco's vaudeville circuit. Both Lillian and Frank needed a way to reinvent themselves, and they found it in each other.

It is not clear if Frank and Lillian ever bothered to make their union legal. Hafley's grandson, Tom Shelton, remembered that they seemed "light years ahead of their time" in terms of cultural norms, and that they simply lived and traveled together until about 1908, when Hafley fell in love with trick rider star Mamie Francis.[2] Even then, they continued to work and travel together, if not sleep in the same tent.

It might seem strange that the duo never had children, given the relative stability of their relationship, and the length of it. It is impossible to know whether a physical issue or personal choice kept Lillian from motherhood. Shirl Kasper theorizes that Annie Oakley's childlessness was probably because of the constraints of a career that could be physically and mentally exhausting—and Lillian may have had to face the same practicalities. They were both working women preoccupied with making a living and dedicated to their craft. This, coupled with the fact that they traveled nearly every day of the year, did not lend itself to settling down and raising a family. Perhaps Lillian could have gotten away with carrying a child under her Indian tunic without too much public focus on her belly, but it would have been risky to both her and an embryo to do the rigorous equestrian tricks she performed regularly.[3]

America's Best Female Sharpshooter

Lillian, according to Michael Wallis and other sources, never got over her split-up with Hafley, the "dashing Frank Smith" (he had taken her surname professionally), and it would be hard to believe she felt nothing, given their decade-long partnership. But whatever Lillian's feelings, she showed only kindness and loyalty to Hafley and Mamie Francis, and the two women even formed an unlikely friendship. Tom Shelton recalled that Lillian was always very kind to him as a child, and that his mother and grandmother were always cordial to her in return.

Smith and Hafley could not have been unaware that Oakley and Butler were pulling back from the public a bit, and they may have sensed an opportunity to grab some of the spotlight from the duo. The year 1901 was a tiring one for Little Sure Shot and her husband. Cody's Wild West experienced some bad fires and accidents on the set, due to equipment malfunctions. There were several train accidents, one of which included the Butlers' car in the early morning hours of October 29, on the way to Danville, Virginia.

While Annie would later falsely claim it was this train wreck that turned her hair prematurely white, it was true that the carnage of dead animals and the financial loss probably encouraged her and Butler to start thinking about a less hectic schedule. On January 17, 1902, the *New York Sun* printed an announcement from Annie that she would "never go into the Wild West business again," and within days, her husband wrote Bill McClure, Cody's aide-de-camp, that he had been offered a job with the Union Metallic Cartridge Company, of Bridgeport, Connecticut. Frank Butler was now going to take on the job as wage-earner for the couple.[4] To be sure, Annie Oakley went on to enjoy a satisfactory acting career and shooting exhibitions of her choosing for the next two decades, but the attention they garnered as a couple was mostly due to their battling defamation cases in court.

Lillian and Frank Hafley's first big excursion together was a mixed blessing. According to descendants, they were hired by Queen Liliuo-kalani of Hawaii to teach marines stationed in Oahu how to fire Smith & Wesson firearms—possibly one reason Frank adopted Lillian's surname.[5] They then had to flee when local unrest unfolded at the announcement of Hawaii's annexation as a territory by the United States. Since the island had become a territory a year and a half before, this account probably owes something to the power of Frank's storytelling as shaped by memory.

What is absolutely certain is that on December 12, the first recorded victim of bubonic plague died in Honolulu's Chinatown, and although officials quickly quarantined the area, the government started restricting inter- and extra-island travel. On December 26, the *Honolulu Evening Bulletin* reported Frank and Lillian's departure for Hilo underneath a plea for citizens to "keep cool" in light of the black plague.

The couple caught a schooner back to San Francisco at the end of the month, perhaps because theater gatherings were being cancelled, but most certainly due to fear that all ways back home might soon be cut off. And while Frank retched over the side of the boat, Lillian savored her newly found ability to work outside the sphere of her father, and resolved to never again share billing with oddities like Aimee the Human Fly.

The year 1900 was a good one for Lillian—a fresh start in every sense of the phrase. She moved to Chicago with Frank, where they had been engaged to perform at the Masonic Temple Theater while they perfected their act. Shooting within the confines of indoor stages obviously required some adjustments from performances done in an outdoor arena. They did not need to make many changes to the firearms themselves, although Lillian—like Cody and so many other Wild West performers—probably used a smoothbore-chambered rifle instead of her usual grooved barreled one, using shot instead of rifle bullets to increase her chances of hitting more animated targets, and more importantly, to reduce the risk of hitting and hurting an audience member.

In October of 1900, Smith reminded a vaudeville friend that if Frank came to call on them at the Tremont House hotel, to please refer to him as Lillian's "brother," likely because her separation from Powell was not finalized.[6] To be traveling with a man who was not technically one's husband would have been a public relations disaster. She may have been taking a page from Annie Oakley's book. The Butlers had taken great pains to promote their true marriage date as June 20, 1882, as opposed to August 1876 because Frank may not have divorced his first wife when he started courting Annie.[7]

Importantly for Lillian, her father was out of the picture for good. Her decision to partner with Hafley was one that gave her the financial and social freedom she deserved, and one she wished for her younger sister, too. In late 1899—coinciding with Lillian's exodus to Hawaii with Hafley—Levi had taken Nellie to Arizona, where she performed in territorial fairs and where he tried valiantly to capitalize on the Smith name: "Mr. Smith and daughter Miss Lilly [Nellie] Smith, are in Nogales. Mr. Smith has conducted shooting galleries throughout the United States for the last thirty years, and has come to Nogales for the purpose of opening a gallery here. He is the father of Miss Lillian Smith, the celebrated lady rifle shot, who has for several years held the championship of the world."[8] Before leaving the mainland, Lillian made an effort to get Nellie enough public notice to strike out on her own. The *Tombstone Prospector* and the *Phoenix Republican,* for example, noted that Lillian was with her father and sister for a few days, watching Nellie perform.[9]

A few years later, Smith lamented to a friend that her younger sister was seemingly unable to pull herself from Levi's sphere of influence, as she had: "Thanks for the clipping about Nellie, I'm glad you met her—it was a nice thing for her to have her picture in the paper—she wrote me from Indianapolis—I guess she is going West again—I was in hopes that she would stay East, I wished she could do so much better here. Now as she says the old man is a draw back for her as he was with me for almost 17 years."

This letter is the only surviving one that gives a first-hand account of Smith's relationship with her younger sibling. Clearly, Lillian thought of her as a blood sister, though she very well may have not been. Vital records for Nellie have yet to be discovered, and Rebecca Robinson's 1900 census entry clearly states she had given birth to only three children, with two still living at that time. Allowing for the death of baby George, this left only Lillian and Charles, who were the only two children mentioned in her 1901 obituary. Perhaps she was a relative from Rebecca's side, named after her father Cornelius Robinson. In the one extant photograph of Nellie, she bears a family resemblance.

There is a more sinister possibility concerning Nellie's shadowy birth. While it is true that Annie Oakley did not want Lillian Smith to come back to Buffalo Bill's Wild West when they returned to Europe in 1889, it may be that Lillian was simply unable to. After a fantastic showing in Newark in January, where she set a new record, breaking five hundred glass balls in twenty-three minutes using two rifles, Lillian and her family suddenly packed up and left their Newark gallery. After this, Lillian disappeared for seven months or so, emerging at Bartlett Springs resort, where she stayed about a month, ostensibly to recuperate from her eastern and European tour, although those had long ended. It is entirely possible that Lillian became pregnant by Kid during the last month or two of Buffalo Bill's Wild West, and the family hid her at the resort in California until she gave birth, emerging a bit slimmer. It is noteworthy that the family took pains to announce her divorce from Willoughby in August 1889, about the time she would have given birth. As noted above, Kid was surprised to learn of his own marital split. This public embarrassment effectively kept him from seeking Lillian out after his Buffalo Bill tour—and from possibly stumbling over a tot that looked like him. This scenario also means that Nellie would only have been ten and three-quarters years old at her 1900 appearance in Arizona as a sharpshooter, but such a young age was certainly not a barrier-to-entry for this family. In her 1904 photo, Nellie looks to be anywhere from fifteen to twenty-five years of age.

Whatever the case, taking on a newborn child to mold as another Lillian fit right into Levi's desire to be an integral part of a shooting franchise. In her letter to her friend, Lillian wrote, "The best thing she [Nellie] could do would be to marry or go with some man who was smart enough to manage her—else she will never win with this old man around her neck." In a statement that could be reflective of jealousy on the part of either sister, or perhaps just a straightforward assessment, Lillian confided that neither Nellie nor her father liked Frank because the latter had "made a success." Smith asked her friend hopefully if he had seen Nellie show some interest in a man named "Ross," with whom she had been performing—probably sharpshooter Fred C. Ross from Brooklyn, who was making a name for himself in rifle circuits.[10]

And Frank *was* successful, or rather, "Frank and Lillian Smith" were. They were booked solidly throughout the midwestern and northeastern United States in the Orpheum route, which was a chain of vaudeville theaters owned by impresario Gustav Walter. In 1899, Frank sent out press kits entitled "The Only Real Novelty of the Century," consisting of a dapper profile photograph of himself dressed in a tuxedo, and Lillian with a Victorian caped dress and a fancy feathered hat.

The language in the release was embroidered, but not by much. It

America's Best Female Sharpshooter

noted that Lillian had been presented to 170 members of royalty thus far, and owned the only rifle ever held in the hand of Queen Victoria.[11] "Enthusiastic crowds," wrote Michael Wallis, "marveled at Lillian's ability to snuff out a candle flame with her rifle, shoot the ashes off the cigar in her partner's mouth, and break small balls suspended from Frank's hat." In some private exhibitions, she even shot a dime from Frank's fingers, or ashes from his cigar, without leaving a scratch.[12]

The Smiths sent clever promotional cards to venue managers in advance, usually a stack of ace cards with a bullet hole in the middle of the club, reading, "Shot by Lillian F. Smith, 'The California Girl,' Champion Rifle Shot of the World, While Held in the Hand of Frank C. Smith." And perhaps most important to many club owners, the Smiths could perform "the Most Daring Novelty Shooting Act in Existence" while taking only three minutes to set the stage, leaving no damage, and no smoke.[13]

If Lillian ever tired of criss-crossing the country, performing in dirty outdoor arenas and smoky saloons, she never said as much. It was an exhausting life of noisy train rides, seedy hotels, and one-night stands. Their shooting act might be sandwiched in between the turns of a bawdy songstress and a scantily clad acrobat.[14]

Because mail and telegrams sometimes did not reach itinerant performers, Lillian probably did not hear that her mother had passed away on March 6, 1901, until a month or so after the fact. She may have been dismayed to learn that Rebecca had been living without her husband in the Orleans Lodging House in San Francisco's Mission district, perhaps working as a housekeeper or laundress.

Before their second year together was over, Frank and Lillian decided that second or equal billing with others was not appropriate for performers of their talent. Thus, when Frederick Cummins' Indian Congress approached them to join it, they jumped at the chance. Cummins had a contract with the upcoming exposition—a World's Fair— which would run from May through November 1901, in Buffalo, New York. Lillian proudly wrote to a friend, using letterhead that carried images of the Congress and Wild West stock certificate: "The picture at the head of this letter shows the winter quarters of the big show that we go out with next summer it opens on the 1st of May[.] Frank is the assistant manager and we have stock in the company, it will be larger then Buffalo Bills and will be a real indian and cowboy show. . . . this is going to be a big money maker."[15]

Unfortunately, this particular World's Fair is now most famously noted in history as the event at which an anarchist assassinated President William McKinley. Its objective was to present in microcosm all of the trends, developments, and innovations of these years immediately following America's victory in the Spanish-American War. The great and colorful buildings along the Grand Canal, built in ersatz Spanish colonial style, symbolized American suzerainty over the hemisphere. The amazing Electric Tower announced to the world the nation's technical superiority. Buffalo was chosen as the fair's location because of its size (at the time it was the eighth largest city in the United States with a population of approximately 350,000) and also because of its well-suited railway connections. The grounds spread across 342 acres between Delaware Park Lake to the south, the New York Central railroad track to the north, Delaware Avenue to the east, and Elmwood Avenue to the west.

Sometime during their stint in Buffalo, Frank Hafley and Lillian Smith slipped away and gave an interview at the New York City offices of the gossipy *National Police Gazette.* "I have a brand new one-thousand-dollar bill in my inside pocket," Hafley said, "which says that Wenona is the champion pistol shot of the world—in fact, the 'Police Gazette' champion." He was even willing to up the stakes if someone who was quite good presented himself or herself, and he had no qualms about meeting all comers. "I ought to know what she can do for she has been shooting at me for years." To say she created a sensation at the World's Fair, wrote the *Gazette,* was putting things mildly. People who came to challenge her, it continued, quietly went away after seeing her do her act, apparently forgetting what they came for. "On the Midway, the question of the day was: 'Have you seen Wenona shoot?'"[16]

Little is known about Frederick T. Cummins. According to his 1901 biography, he had been an Indian trader, prospector, cowboy, Indian Service agent, "gallant soldier of fortune," and bronco breaker in Deadwood and Helena.[17] At some point, he designated himself with the military title "Colonel," as many showman did. It was a coup for Cummins to get Lillian-Wenona—he desperately needed a celebrity sharpshooter to compete with Buffalo Bill's Wild West, which had Annie Oakley this season. Lillian fit seamlessly into Cummins's ethnological narrative, not just because of her enormous shooting talent but also because she was an "extra special" Native American.

Cummins's show was the most popular attraction on the Midway. It featured sham battles, Indian heroes, military scouts, and "long-haired painted savages in all their barbaric splendor"—a description a young spectator, Will Rogers, wrote to his father. The Colonel gave the Smiths several hundred shares of stock in the show, though it is possible he did so in lieu of paying them entirely in cash.

Lillian and Frank must have thought long and hard about the sharpshooter's debut with the Indian Congress. To make absolutely sure they stood out from the crowd of performers with Cummins, "Lillian and Frank" became "Wenona and Frank." A drawing of a svelte, delicate-looking "maiden" started to appear in advertisements of the couple's programs at Keith's Orpheum. The image could be interpreted to be that of an Indian woman, or that of an Anglo pioneer teen—the dress and shoes in the sketch suggested a prairie girl, but the braided hair could belong to a young lady of native ancestry.[18] If one wanted to believe she was at least half Sioux, she could just as easily be that, wearing pseudo-Indian clothes.

The name "Wenonah" was that of a beautiful young Native American in Henry Wadsworth Longfellow's epic 1855 poem, *The Song of Hiawatha,* still a bestseller at the turn of the twentieth century and featured in any number of songs and plays at that time. Lillian-as-Wenona headlined newspaper reports of Cummins' Indian Congress, her name placed between the names of Geronimo, the embattled Apache chief, and Calamity Jane (Martha Jane Canary), the famous frontierswoman. Wenona's sudden appearance on the national scene as a lost-and-found Sioux princess was infinitely more believable than the eighty-eight-year-old Geronimo's ferocity, or the critically alcoholic Canary's plan to marry at the Congress, as circulated by many exhibition publicity flyers.[19]

Changing from "Lillian" to "Wenona" certainly created a new era of publicity for Lillian Smith, and may have also had a more secondary, practical advantage. It was difficult, if not impossible, to do certain shots with fancy Victorian capes and velvet dresses bedecked with feathers and ribbons, as Lillian had heretofore been doing. More importantly, a scaled-down costume had much less of a chance of catching fire from an errant spark from a gun or, worse, the gas lighting used inside the theaters.

Truthfully, Lillian's "prairie wear" also smoothed out her large bosom and behind, though extra weight was not something that Smith ever seemed to care much about. The little that historians have written about her almost always contain Oakley's derisive comment about her weight, but that never bothered Smith as much as questions about her shooting ability. Still, she must have noticed (or someone pointed out to her) that she looked nearly twice Frank's size in press photos, such as one that appeared in the *New York Police Gazette*.[20] It was one thing to show how one could delightfully shoot the ash off her spouse's cigar—quite another to look like one was hunting him.

Lillian's foray into Native Americanness was well-received at Cummins' Indian Congress. In 1926, an unnamed contributor to *101 Magazine* reminisced about meeting "Winona" there:

> Mr. Moore escorted me through the village one day, and through him I met many of the famous chieftains as well as the beautiful Winona [*sic*]. "Winona, shoot!" he exclaimed in a burst of warm admiration for the lovely young Indian girl's prowess. 'Winona shoot! Why, I wouldn't be afraid to let Winona shoot the ashes from my cigar at twenty paces.'
>
> 'Suppose you let me try,' said the little champion. To our amazement the young secretary took from his pocket a cigar[,] lit it and drew a few puffs until he had about a half inch of ash. Winona called for her rifle. We gathered around Mr. Moore to bid him an eternal farewell.

Workers who had seen Wenona shoot many times murmured tongue-in-cheek "goodbyes" to the young press assistant, scaring the writer even more. 'Ready!' called Wenona. Mr. Moore measured off the twenty paces, and held up his head with the cigar between his teeth. Winona raised her rifle, aimed, and fired. "And the next thing we knew," said the writer, "the smiling countenance of Moore leaned toward us, displaying the weed with the fiery end smoothed off clean and clear."[21]

The play princess charmed the throngs of dignitaries who visited the Congress show each week by adding personal touches to her tricks. One of them honored "Dry Dollar" Timothy Sullivan, a Tammany politician who, as a youngster, peeled a revenue stamp from a beer keg and put it aside to dry, thinking it was a dollar, Wenona took a silver dollar from her pocket. She held it up high for the crowds to see, and then dramatically dipped it in a bucket of water someone brought her. She made a big show out of wiping it dry on her tunic, and then threw it up in the air, took aim, and shot and wedged a bullet directly in the center of it. Sullivan accepted the dollar from her gleefully, and the audience roared with laughter.[22] For Mayor Maybury, of Detroit, Wenona shot from one hundred yards the shape of a horsehoe into a band of metal, which she then presented to him, eliciting wild applause from the stands and lots of bonnet-and-hat tossing.[23] For others, she shot their names or favorite slogans into large pieces of thin wood, which she gave to them as souvenirs.

Wenona and Geronimo dutifully submitted their palms to be read shortly after the Congress arrived for rehearsal at the Midway. No doubt the spiritualist gave the newspaper a more full account of her findings than she did the participants. "He is not so hostile toward whites as he was in the past," she reported, "but as he is of a very obstinate disposition, he cannot see where he was in the wrong." As for the former "California Girl," the soothsayer was not far off the mark in some respects, telling her she was prone to be "impulsive," but more in speech than in action. She accurately reported that Wenona had a lot of vitality and strength, but would be so much more content if another woman would challenge her in short- and long-distance shooting.[24]

Of course, this palm reader's proclamations were a ploy by show promoters to spur Annie Oakley to challenge Wenona this summer of 1901. Little Sure Shot and her husband arrived in Buffalo with Cody's Wild West on or about August 25, for a two-week run just outside the Pan-American fairgrounds, similar to the way Cody set up at the 1893 World's Fair. Eight thousand people went to see Cody and his Rough Riders of the World in the spacious enclosure just outside the East Amherst entrance, and in addition to all the horsemen and their tricks, the audience applauded Oakley, who gave a fine, if not extravagant, display of her marksmanship.[25]

It seemed as though Cummins' Congress was an opportunity for Wenona to avenge her shut-out of the Chicago World's Fair eight years before, when Oakley performed with Cody outside the Midway

Plaisance and the California Girl was stuck in her home state. Wenona may have gloated when Tom Marshall, a trapshooter from Illinois who had recently won his second open-field championship, gave an interview in which he not only downplayed British trapshooters but also lauded Wenona: "Mr. Marshall says that the Glasgow exposition is a very small affair, and not up to date. When asked about Wenona, the Sioux Indian girl at the Indian Congress, who does rifle shooting, he replied: 'She is beyond doubt a marvel. She uses bullets, while those who claim to be in her class use shot. In a contest, it is my opinion, that she will make anyone who tries to wrest the championship from her look like eight cents.'"[26] Wenona privately cherished the compliment, but did not try to engage Oakley in a match at this time.

The press, on the other hand, took matters into their own hands. On August 23, the day before Oakley was scheduled to arrive, someone planted a story in local papers that was obviously meant to spur some kind of match, or perhaps a heated encounter, between Oakley and Wenona. The *Buffalo Sun Times* claimed that someone placed a target alongside one of the New York Central Railroad tracks, near the mill town of Echota. Hafley placed a silver dollar in the center of this target; Wenona went to Niagara Falls, continued the story, and took a New York Central train for Buffalo. Handlers told her where the target was, which was just to the right of a road north of Echota. The *Sun Times* and other area newspapers relayed the breathless account: "Wenona kept a strict lookout, and as the train passed the target she raised her 44-caliber Winchester, and pulled the trigger. The Winchester belched forth its load of lead. California Frank, who was standing near the target, went to it and found the bullet wedged in the silver dollar."[27] Naturally, there is no firsthand account of this escapade from anyone else who might have been on the train or on the side of the tracks. Whenever he was asked about this amazing feat, Frank would pull out a silver dollar with a bullet in it and say something like "You shoulda been there!"

Other New York papers dutifully printed the unlikely account, and so did *American Rifleman,* which called it "absurd" and added that "everything seems to go" in Buffalo during this exhibition year.[28] Not absurd was the likelihood that Wenona could hit a target in this manner—she had precisely hit targets going faster on the bouncing back of a horse—but it was unlikely that Frank and Wenona would take a

America's Best Female Sharpshooter

Friday off to prove that while paying customers awaited at the Midway.

Despite the dramatic nature of this story, it was not Wenona's marksmanship that the public was meant to consume—it was her quote at the end of the *Sun Times* article, intended to stir up jealousy between two women sharpshooters. Referring to her day of shooting on the rails, Wenona allegedly responded to a question about her nerve with, "I have only one fear, and this is: Those who know that I hold the championship title might in a fit of jealous rage have me arrested for mutilating [a] federal coin."[29]

Whether or not Wenona actually said such things publicly is irrelevant—the quip was an indirect response to a blistering manifesto written by Mr. Annie Oakley in *American Rifleman* in the middle of the summer. Butler's manifesto was in response to a thousand-dollar wager Wenona had proffered to Oakley in May through the papers, inviting a match at the exposition. He wrote: "During Annie Oakley's shooting career I think she has received more so-called challenges than anyone in the same line, with the possible exception of Dr. Carver. . . . I send a few samples of these challenges, and the kind of people who write them." He cited the time he accepted a match for Annie with a Mrs. Jesse James imposter, and on another occasion narrowly avoided one with a homicidal housewife. But there could be no misunderstanding about whom he meant when he wrote the following, pointing out that Wenona was formerly Lillian Smith: "During one of my visits to London there was a woman shooting in one of the music halls under the name of Winona [*sic*]. She never missed ringing the bell, and was making quite a reputation, and, as a matter of course, issued the usual challenge. A few days later she called on Annie Oakley in her dressing tent. During her visit I took pains to show her some American rifles in which she seemed to take little, if any, interest." If this was disingenuous, what Butler wrote next was patently false: "I think she must have had a brandy and soda more than was good for her, for she grew quite confidential and more than surprised me by saying, 'Pon my word, Miss Oakley. I don't know a thing about rifles. My cartridges are all blank, and my husband rings the bell by pulling a string.' This may seem strange, but I have see many of the shooting acts on the English stage worked on the same principle, and not only the audience but the managers as well swallowed [them] bait, hook, and all."

In the next paragraph, Butler meandered off about a shady theater manager, and then circled back to denigrating Wenona: "One woman, who often challenged Annie Oakley, has three living husbands, or said to be such, and I have clippings from western papers which, if half true, would keep any respectable man or woman from entering into any contest or controversy with her." To hammer his point home, Butler ended his letter by saying that Oakley would never enter into a contest with a woman with "a shady past or doubtful reputation" while he was managing her, and that because she "values her private reputation far more than her shooting one," she would never use the word "champion," and begged their "friends" omit it in connection with her name.[30] It was probably because of Oakley's own license with her birthdate that Butler neglected to point out the obvious, which was that press materials had shorn twelve years off Lillian-Wenona's birthdate, and were touting her as an Indian maiden only eighteen years of age.

Wenona's soothsayer at the exhibition also noted that she very fond of nature and animals—not a difficult conclusion, given the sharpshooter's obvious history of living and working outdoors. However, the Pan-American was an event that forced her to make some personal sacrifices for her profession, with regard to living creatures. To be sure, Wenona had killed thousands of birds in her lifetime—as had Annie Oakley and many other marksmen. Pigeons were considered pests of the highest order, and shooting game fowl was necessary to survive. But because of Wenona's professed Indian heritage, she had to participate in a practice that must have turned her stomach at least a little.

In order to fulfill Cummins's mandate that everything about the Congress be authentic, at least as audiences thought at the time, managers arranged for at least four "dog feasts." Pat Ryan, a superintendent from the Bureau of Indian Affairs, ordered hundreds of dogs from northeastern animal shelters and citizens in August 1901. "Wanted! 700 Fat dogs, fat dogs!" read an advertisement in the *Courier* and other Buffalo papers. "No number too large. Indians are going to have a dog feast."[31] On September 27, the *Buffalo Commercial* reported that a number of Buffalo, Tonawanda, and Lockport dogs had disappeared and "700 Indians thoroughly gratified their hunger." The poodles, rat terriers, hounds, water spaniels, and other breeds were allegedly killed in the presence of 12,000 spectators.

According to area papers, Geronimo and Wenona were responsible for dispatching the dogs. "Geronimo handled the bow and arrow and Winona [*sic*] the rifle. They took their turn killing the dogs. Geronimo put the arrow through the heart every time and Winona was just as successful with the powder and lead."[32] The "bravest bucks" got to dress the dogs for cooking, according to another local paper, and the mutts were fried, broiled, or baked. Geronimo supposedly ate two dogs at this particular feast, and said they tasted like "fried froglegs."[33]

This version of events is hard to believe, even for the kind of ethnological extravaganza Cummins presented. It is true that some Sioux, Apache, Cheyenne, Kiowa, and Arapaho bands historically had dog feasts, although the Blackfoot, Nez Perce, and Crow tribes—among others represented at the Congress—did not. But such a wholesale slaughter of domesticated animals would have certainly aroused the displeasure of at least some of the 10,000 spectators who came on September 26, the day one feast was planned. As it happened, the Buffalo Humane Society called upon managers of the Congress to see why they thought they could do such a thing. Supervisor Ryan supposedly showed them government records that permitted Native Americans to hold public dog feasts.[34]

What most likely occurred is that while in the arena, Wenona put down perhaps a few dozen sick or old dogs with her rifle, while Geronimo snapped arrows as best as he could. The animals were carted away, and the show went on. Dignitaries paid up to seventy dollars extra for the privilege of dining with Geronimo and other Native American celebrities after the shoot; Generals Joseph Wheeler and Captain Richmond Hobson late of the Spanish-American conflict did so, and may have actually nibbled on a piece of cur. All of these actions were a sort of "sleight of hand"—the general public assumed more dogs were slaughtered later, for special guests only.

Wenona certainly cringed at performing this ritual. She shot wild animals for food and safety reasons, and smaller, nonedible animals that were pests—not domesticated creatures. And while she may have been doing a kindness to some of the dogs proffered up at Cummins's exposition, it is noteworthy that when she retired to the 101 Ranch in the late 1920s, she made it a point to gather up as many sick and old dogs as she could and let them have the run of her land until they died of natural causes. And, perhaps attempting to soften her image or her soul a bit, Wenona spent extra hours training "Teddy," a horse named after Vice President Roosevelt that Cummins loaned her for the Congress, for an act she performed for several weeks following the dog hunt:

> She has taught Teddy to go to the center of the arena and there drop as if dead. . . . While posing on the supposed dead horse she does fancy shooting and through it all Teddy never moves. Her trained doves are let loose. They fly all about the horse and peck him. Teddy plays his part and remains motionless. The doves fly to the barrel of Wenona's rifle and perch upon it side by side. She shoots and shoots but neither doves nor horse move. Finally the Indian band strikes up "White Wings." The doves fly away, Teddy rises to all fours and darts off across the arena apparently proud of his performance.

The most amazing part of this feature is that Wenona did it standing upright on Teddy for almost the entire time.[35]

Hafley was dynamite as an assistant. He was Wenona's usual mark for holding or swinging glass or plastic balls, and had his fair share of adventure, too. His was more of a practical nature, such as rescuing a native boy who had fallen from his saddle during a pony race from getting stomped. Naturally, Hafley became a more integral part of Wenona's biography, as the "old scout" who brought her before the public after she got bored with life among white military folk, at Fort Bennett, South Dakota. In this 1901 version of Wenona's biography, her father was Chief Crazy Horse, of the Sioux.

Wenona and Frank were resting after the afternoon performance on September 6, 1901. Inside the Temple of Music on the grounds of the Exposition, Leon Czolgosz reached with one hand to greet President William McKinley, and shot him with the other. Eight days later, McKinley died from his wounds, casting a pall over the exhibition. On Sunday morning, September 15, 1901, President McKinley's casket was closed and the honor guard placed the casket into a hearse. Following close behind was now-President Theodore Roosevelt with Secretary Elihu Root and other members of the Cabinet. The procession moved through a vast throng to the Buffalo City Hall, where more than 150,000 people viewed the body, lying in state.

Toward the end of the afternoon, Indians from the exposition filed by, followed by their women. The Indians had liked President McKinley, the Great White Father. A few hours before, they had sent a wreath of purple asters accompanied by the inscription, "Farewell of Geronimo, Blue Horse, Flat Iron and Red Shirt and the seven hundred braves of the Cummins Indian Congress and Wild West Show. Like President Lincoln and Garfield, President McKinley never abused authority except on the side of mercy. The martyred Great White Chief will stand in memory next to the Savior of mankind. We loved him living, we love him still." As the Indians passed, each of them dropped a white carnation upon the president's coffin.[36]

The exposition officially closed November 2, 1901. It lost more than three million dollars—a financial disaster, but one that gave millions of visitors to the "Rainbow City" and its environs the memories of a lifetime. Cummins' Indian Congress, writes James McLaird in his biography of Martha "Calamity Jane" Canary, attracted audiences because of open-air performances in its "monster arena" that could seat 25,000 people, and because of its expert shooters, animals, and sham Indian battles complete with 700 real Native Americans. Probably its romantic image of the West attracted visitors, the most appealing of representatives embodied in "Geronimo, the human tiger, Winona, the wonderful Sioux rifle shot, and Calamity Jane, famous in song and story of frontier days."[37] McLaird's point is underscored by the man who wrote his local paper to say he was very disappointed to discover Wenona was, in fact, a white woman when he chanced to see her and Frank at an art gallery in town—probably the gallery of Wenona's future paramour, Emil Lenders.[38]

Canary joined Cummins's show on or about July 30 that summer of 1901. Either the Montana reporter Josephine Winifred Brake—who was Canary's benefactor and companion at that time—or Frederick Cummins himself threw the frontierswoman a reception at the Iroquois Hotel in Buffalo. In the days following, Canary gamely made parade appearances that featured her, Wenona, and Geronimo. The triad stirred the crowds to fever pitch. But within a few short weeks, Calamity Jane was gone. Tired of Brake's restrictions on her movements, salary, and alcohol intake, Canary waylaid William Cody when he arrived in Buffalo with his own show on or about August 26, asking for money and a railroad ticket home, which he gave to her.

It is tempting to think of what conversations might have transpired between Wenona and Canary during the few days they paraded together. Probably, Wenona as a child had read about Canary's exploits as a pioneer scout and her involvement in shenanigans surrounding the town of Deadwood in the Black Hills of South Dakota. She certainly would have read at least some excerpts of Canary's 1896 autobiography—a heavily embellished work that newspapers plucked from constantly in the years leading up to the 1901 World's Fair. But if Wenona and Canary had words, there is no record of them. As many historians note, Canary was mostly a curiosity at this point in her life, as opposed to being a full-fledged performer. Wenona and Canary's time together was likely limited to the few minutes for a few days that they were on horseback near each other. As for Annie Oakley and any interaction of the two with Annie Oakley, Canary was on her way back west shortly after Oakley's arrival, and Wenona and Oakley only met in the imaginations of newspaper reporters.

Cummins' Indian Congress recreated Custer's Last Stand for the last time, followed by endless rounds of fireworks in the arena. Although we do not know if the Colonel's financial affairs dovetailed with those of the exhibition, we can assume Frank and Wenona were paid what they expected, because of Wenona's appraisal of him as a "good enough fellow" in future correspondence.

With the exposition over, the Smiths turned to vaudeville. The duo obtained nonbinding agreements with three different exhibitors who had established venues across the country: Keith and Proctors, Kohl and Castle, and Orpheum Theatres. "Wenona and Frank" circulated around theater hubs like Indianapolis, New Orleans, New York, Boston, and St. Louis, fulfilling engagements in those cities. Chicago remained their "home base" for much of that time; it was here that the Smiths found a rather lucrative opportunity.

Casimir Zeglen, pastor of a North Side Catholic church, had recently received a patent for his bulletproof vest invention. The shield consisted of intricately woven silk fibers—a family secret he had brought with him from Poland several years prior and perfected in the States. Later press accounts gave the impression that Wenona and Frank were the first people to test this vest, but plenty of local law enforcement officials had already allowed themselves to be shot at in order to test the product's reliability. What Zeglen needed was publicity, so that more cities would purchase it for their forces. Zeglen got his publicity in the form of Wenona and Frank, who incorporated the vest into their Orpheum act.

For this more modern version of the shield, Frank would advertise a week before their appearance that he would pay anyone in the audience to wear the vest and let him take a shot. He was deluged with applications all week, but would-be targets usually lost their nerve by show time. Frank would feign disappointment, and ceremoniously come up on stage and don the shield himself. Crowds would gasp as he passed Wenona his revolver and let her take aim at his heart.[39]

According to one reporter, after the "Crack!" of the pistol, it seemed like a full minute instead of a split second between the hiss of the bullet leaving the chamber and the "plink" of the piece of metal hitting the floor after the vest turned it away. "How does it feel to face a 38-caliber revolver, at five paces, and be shot at?" this employee of the *Denver Post* asked Frank, during one stop on the couple's "vest tour," in December 1903. "It is hard now to describe the full sensation which comes over me when I am shot at," answered Frank, "but even with that vest on I experience a strange thrill when I face the pistol." The sensation, he recalled, was only slightly different than the "rush" he got when he engaged in gunfights with criminals, in his job as sheriff—he had the protection of a vest now, but the adrenaline surge was similar: "As near as I can remember the first time I knew a man was shooting at me to kill it felt as if all the blood in my heart was rushing to my head. For a moment, I was blind. I could feel the hot blood burning my face and my arms and limbs seemed paralyzed. Then I heard the bullet whiz past my head. That aroused me, and I mechanically shot back. With the crack of my gun I was fully alive to the situation."[40] Frank Hafley, of course, had long learned how to subdue the impulse to fire back.

The couple did not have a lot of leisure time because there was always work that needed to be done between programs: publicity assignments, dreaming up and practicing new acts, acquiring new animals and equipment if need be, and of course, cleaning and replacing gun parts. But with what little time she had, the champion was fond of collecting picture frames, and cooking chicken dinners for herself and Frank—probably a chicken whose neck she had wrung with her own hands.

Lillian and Frank's favorite thing to do when time permitted was to hunt, although they were aware that shooting game was becoming less socially acceptable. On November 28, 1902, Lillian responded to a letter from her faithful friend Alf Rieckhoff, telling him she was "glad to know you can handle the papers" and that (the newspapers) "are so afraid in this country that they will put something in that will help the shooting cause along."[41]

Smith was referring to a bill that New Jersey and New York lawmakers were considering, which would outlaw live bird shooting from a trap. Shooting pigeons, argued proponents of the law, was not in itself bad—the birds were bred to be killed—but the fact that they were often not killed immediately. Even when expert marksmen fired their best, according to the New Jersey humane societies, five to twenty percent of the birds escaped the boundary, and were found in surrounding neighborhoods still alive but with their legs blown off or disemboweled. The agitation and notoriety attached to trapshooting were so great at this point that back in April of this year, 1902, the Grand American Handicap, the blue-ribbon of the shooting season, had decided to transfer its annual competition from New York to Kansas City, and it was the last time the tournament used live pigeons.

It was also the last time Lillian and Annie Oakley were within shouting distance of each other. Out of 493 shooters, only three were women: Smith, Oakley, and one Mrs. S. S. Johnson of Minneapolis. Smith did slightly better than Oakley in the qualifying rounds on April 1, missing one bird out of twelve to Oakley's two, but all three women did well enough to advance to the main competition the next day. Then, Mrs. Johnston was the only woman to have hit all of her birds, while Oakley had missed two, and Smith three—not a large discrepancy. Ultimately, none of the three women did well enough to advance to a trophy-taking position, or even a cash prize. If either Oakley or Smith had any thoughts about the competition or each other here, they did not get aired in the press.

Meanwhile, Lillian and Frank felt that audiences were tiring of exhibition shooting, no matter how intricate. To remedy this, they added some comedy to their routine, such as a dog and monkey act, whereby the animals would dance with each other to a tune created by Frank and Wenona by shooting at different-toned metal strings. It

America's Best Female Sharpshooter

worked. "Now I don't suppose that I can talk any thing but shop," she wrote Rieckhoff of their refreshments, "but anyway I want to tell you that the act is the hit of the bill (I know that they say that) and the bill is such a good one that the manager says that the Orpheum Road Show that comes next week will have a hard time to make good."

No matter how good their shooting act was, though, the Smiths had to fend off imitators and competitors. Wenona enjoyed proving them insufficient: "Frank goes up in the gallery just after I do my ten with the little gun and shoots 5 balls stationary, and 5 swinging and it makes a hit, we put this trick in because [sharpshooter John] DeLoris was here not long a go and some of the people thought that it was such a great thing to do that long shooting, and they were not so sure that we could do it, so I went up one night and showed them, and then we figured it out that I could hold the stage better." Lillian could not even resist putting her friend Alf in his place, claiming that she had not forgotten to write him, but "you know how it goes with these show people that have so much to do, and really have nothing to do, now if we were as busy as you are, I don't know when we would get anything done."[42]

The Butlers were out of Lillian's mind as a competing husband-wife act, but the shooter was keeping an eye on some other potential rivals for her vaudeville money. Frank and Myrtle Chamberlin were receiving some good if short-lived press, billed as adept at novel rope juggling and lasso handling, and also at "Queer Tricks with Ropes and Whips," and "Shooting by Aid of a Mirror." An August 12, 1902, news article stated that the Chamberlins had appeared in all of the best vaudeville theaters in the United States as well as Europe, and another on September 24 noted that "the Chamberlins are likewise famous rifle shots and will give exhibitions at the range, shooting accurately from thirty different positions."[43] The couple happened to cross paths with Wenona and Frank's show in Rhode Island the last week of November, 1902, though they did not receive top billing, which was reserved for the Smiths. Still, Wenona was keenly aware of their presence, and wrote her assessment of them to Rieckhoff: "The Chamblins are on the bill with us this week. . . . his wife works in the act now and she is a sight, and you cant tell them any thing to help their act out. I think that he intends to put shooting in the act and will take of our stuff and work it in they watch every show we give, they are in the theatre all the time."[44]

Another shooting couple was making news as well, as Winchester Arms missionaries. Adolph Toepperwein married Elizabeth Servaty within weeks of meeting her in 1903, at the gun maker's Connecticut factory. Adolph, who was already a well-regarded rifle marksman, taught his wife how to shoot. Apparently a natural shot, Elizabeth took to it immediately, and allegedly within three weeks of her first lesson, she was shooting chalk from between his fingers with a .22 rifle.[45] After their debut as a couple at the St. Louis World's Fair in 1904, the press dubbed Elizabeth as "Plinky," for her ability to hit so many metallic targets in a row and elicit the "plinking" sound.[46] Wenona made Frank go watch their act when he could get a spare day.

She need not have worried about any other shooting couple. Even allowing for the usual hype of reviews and vaudeville advertising, newspapers always gave Wenona and Frank glowing reports, and Keith's Theater managers—notoriously stingy with both praise and paycheck—were glad to have the two on their roster, making such notations in their log books as: "Unquestionably the best in the business. . . . the woman is exceptionally fine and they go strong here"—"They are wonders in their line"—"This is the best shooting act in vaudeville." Wenona must have worked on her plump appearance so evident in her *Police Gazette* photo from 1901—a year and some months later in New York, the Keith's manager noted that "The appearance of the woman has improved wonderfully since their last time here.[47]

Performing in the vaudeville circuit was not for the faint of heart. Many theaters were poorly heated in winter and became oversized ovens in summer. Dressing rooms were small and filthy, with little if any ventilation. Musical accompaniment could be anything from a full orchestra to a lone pianist, and the quality of those musicians varied—most performers could make do with a poor one, but Frank and Wenona depended on certain tempos and crescendos to keep the rhythm and timing of their shots.

Frank and Lillian had no agent—Frank acted as agent and manager—so there is no record of how much they earned in a typical week of vaudeville work. Booking agent Martin Beck, in 1900, managed to get fledgling magician Harry Houdini $60 a week for his show, which was upped to $150 a week within a year; the Orpheum reluctantly paid tramp juggler and comedian W. C. Fields $150 a week, in 1900. Agent

William Morris got sultry singer Eva Tanguay $35 a day from the Orpheum chain around this time, before her rise to stardom a couple of years later, and actor and singer J. C. Nugent earned a robust $150 a week performing only twice a day for twenty minutes.[48] The *Chicago Tribune,* in 1903, pegged vaudeville salaries in large cities as $35 for the most basic, unknown act, working sometimes eight times a day, six days a week, to $300 a day for the biggest moneymakers.[49] Given these clues, Lillian and Frank—as mid-to-high-tier acts—probably earned about $100 a week together, at the height of their stage popularity in late 1902 and early 1903.

This was a healthy salary—the equivalent of more than $2,700 per week in today's value—and the Smiths had to perform only twice a day for twelve minutes, four or five days a week. Their act consistently drew full houses and good press, but because of the inherent limitations of indoor theater, it was not one that could not be revised more than a few ways and draw repeat customers. Therefore, when Gordon Lillie, otherwise known as Pawnee Bill, offered them both a job on his new Wild West show going out in spring of 1904, they readily agreed.

By the summer of 1904, at least in private, Frank and Wenona-Lillian's business and personal relationship had started to mature. They were both thirty-two years old, and while this was still young even by standards of that time, the physical demands of their profession were not easy on the bones. While they were happy to work with their beloved equine companions again, shoot outdoors, and have a steady paycheck, they had somewhat forgotten the rigors of practice. The start of a typical day, according to Lillian, was to get up early, get Frank's horse from the cars, and take it back to the grounds, which could be anywhere from one mile to six miles away from the train. They would work the crowd until "saddle up call," then go back into the show for two hours.[50]

Lillian urged Frank to "break an Indian into the act soon" so he could have some help and stay off the leg that was recently crushed by a stallion. They visited Frank's parents in Tennessee from time to time, and clearly Frank must have spent time with Lillian's family: his brother Oliver was living with and maybe caring for Rebecca Smith in San Francisco when she passed away. But by the beginning of 1906, Lillian's letters started to indicate that her partner was looking for a place to settle down in the future, but not necessarily with her: "Frank is still away in Oklahoma. . . . we have been wanting to buy a home or some land I should say Frank has been looking around to see what he could get to suit him[;] he was up in the Osage country but he don't like it much so I don't know where he will buy." Lillian was complaining about the time he spent away from her, but not necessarily because she missed his affections: "I think that he will come home before long. I hope so he has been gone two weeks and ever and I am getting tired doing all the work. Mrs. Liesys hand is not well yet so it keeps me busy doing all the work at the barn and in the house, we have a cow and some chickens and a horse to look after." She quickly recovered from her disposition, and put on a sunnier one, in spite of her faithful housekeeper's temporary disability. Lillian noted that, after all, the cow milking was probably helping her strengthen the hand she had injured in a fall in Kansas the previous September.[51]

Lillian's irritation with Frank might have been casual and passing, or it might have indicated fissures within their relationship. Whatever the case, "Wenona & Frank" were determined to present a united front when it came to show business. This became obvious during their first year with Pawnee Bill's, when some strange events happened in the traveling pageant.

According to some newspapers, two performers left the show in Massachusetts, and the Major sent agents to scour Boston and Taunton to find them. One of these missing performers was a "dashing, handsome knight of the lariat," twenty-five years old and the owner of a ranch in Oklahoma. Night after night, it was noticed, he walked around with his beautiful companion, shyly exchanging smiles and greetings. No one was particularly worried about the cowboy mistreating his love, because "a better fellow never lived," and both would be welcomed back to the show with a celebration of their elopement. The young lady was a noted as being a full-blooded Indian, the daughter of a chief, and one of the prettiest maidens that ever left the territory. The groom's name was "withheld by authorities," but the bride's was printed for all to see. She was We-no-aye-te—Princess Wenona.[52]

Possibly the earliest surviving photo of Lillian, taken in the spring of 1886 while in St. Louis with Buffalo Bill's Wild West. She was fourteen years old. *Buffalo Bill Center of the West, Cody, Wyoming, P.69.1532.*

Undated photo, probably taken in winter or spring of 1886, when Lillian first joined Buffalo Bill's Wild West. This was likely the first time Lillian had worn such a fancy dress. *Western History Collections, University of Oklahoma Libraries, Rose 786.*

Lillian, age fifteen, still with Buffalo Bill's Wild West. By the time the show reached New York, where this photo was taken, she was clearly more comfortable with publicity photos.
Buffalo Bill Center of the West, Cody, Wyoming, P.69.1785.

One of many Buffalo Bill's Wild West publicity photos, probably taken in winter of 1887.
Buffalo Bill Center of the West, Cody, Wyoming, P.6.0022.

Lillian in characteristic pose. Possibly taken for Buffalo Bill's
Wild West Madison Square Garden run, in late 1886.
*Western History Collections, University of Oklahoma
Libraries, Ferguson Collection 463.*

Undated, but most certainly taken during her 1886–1887 Buffalo Bill's Wild West season. *Buffalo Bill Center of the West, Cody, Wyoming, P.69.1786.*

Lillian with her trademark hat and a rope-detailed corduroy dress, which her mother likely made. This photo was probably taken just before she left for Britain in April 1887. *Buffalo Bill Center of the West, Cody, Wyoming, P.69.1588.*

Lillian at her tent in Erastina, New York. Immediately left of her is Jim "Kid" Willoughby.
Buffalo Bill Center of the West, Cody, Wyoming, P.69.1133.

Portion of a photograph of the cast of Buffalo Bill's Wild West, ca. 1887. Annie Oakley stands six persons to the right of Lillian.
Buffalo Bill Center of the West, Cody, Wyoming, P.6.0067.

A London newspaper printed this sketch of Lillian showing her rifle to Queen Victoria shortly after the shootist's performance with Buffalo Bill's Wild West in England, May 11, 1887.
Illustrated London News, Mary Evans Picture Library.

Portrait taken sometime in the 1890s. The shoulderless tartan-wrap is an interesting choice. It may have been a nod to the fashion Queen Victoria had started, thus reminding the public of Smith's performance for the monarch, or it may have been simply a homemade costume.
Courtesy Grigsby Family Collection.

Nellie Smith posing on the grounds of the St. Louis World's Fair in the summer of 1904. Nellie performed with the famous cowgirl Lucille Mulhall, but despite her talent for rifle shooting, apparently did not continue in her sister's footsteps.
Black-and-white reproduction of glass negative, DN-002043. Chicago Daily News, 1904. Courtesy Chicago History Museum.

This photo was used with a *Police Gazette* interview with Frank Hafley and Lillian Smith during their performance run at the Pan-American Exhibition in Buffalo, New York, in 1901. The duo was experimenting with identities and costumes this particular summer.
Courtesy Grigsby Family Collection.

The Departure of Minnehaha

In 1905, Pawnee Bill (Gordon Lillie) took a slew of publicity photos that featured Smith (as Wenona) in reenactments of stories featuring Native Americans—not always true, and not always Sioux. Here, she is Minnehaha from Longfellow's poem. *Library of Congress.*

This photo of Lillian as Princess Wenona was probably taken
when she joined Pawnee Bill's Wild West in 1904. Except for a
brief return to other dress in 1908 and 1909, she continued to
wear this sort of costume for the rest of her career.
Library of Congress.

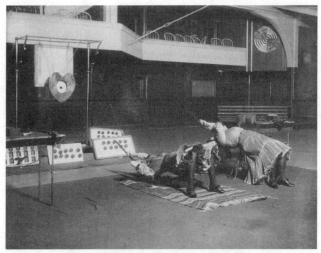

Wenona and Mamie Francis rehearsing their vaudeville act, ca. 1908. Here, the women practice hitting targets while upside down.
Hafley-Shelton Wildwest-Rodeo Collection.

Wenona practices shooting tiny glass balls off Mamie's hat. The man standing in the background is likely Sam Cross, who was a prop master for Wenona and the Hafleys and went on to a long vaudeville career of his own.
Hafley-Shelton Wildwest-Rodeo Collection.

This photo was taken in Nashville at an unidentified vaudeville theater. The pair is holding .44 magnum lever action rifles. Despite the fact that Mamie Francis married Lillian's longtime love, the two formed a friendship that lasted at least two decades. *Hafley-Shelton Wildwest-Rodeo Collection.*

Lillian practicing with a fellow 101 Ranch performer, ca. 1915.
*Western History Collections, University of Oklahoma
Libraries, Nesbitt-Lenders 2306.*

Besides being a remarkable shootist, Lillian was an accomplished equestrienne.
Western History Collections, University of Oklahoma Libraries, Nesbitt-Lenders 658.

Lillian with her horse.
Western History Collections, University of Oklahoma Libraries, Nesbitt-Lenders 601.

Chapter Five

SIOUX LEGACY, THE 101, AND EASIER LIVING

There is no rule that I know of that will teach a man how to be a great shot. . . . A man may have the finest gun that ever was made and the best of ammunition and practice for years and then not be a first-class shot. You see, the brain, the eye and the trigger must all work with the same impulse. When everything is just right if it's within range you feel the object you shoot at rather than aim at it.

William Cody, 1887

No matter how many years she spent traveling the vaudeville circuit, Lillian never got used to the frostier cities, and she hated the long, dark days of winter. The warm-blooded performer kept boredom and depression at bay by furiously sewing moccasins, scarves, and hats and decorating them with Native American–inspired beadwork. She made these items for the children of trusted friends, but mostly to sell as curios at their performances. The chill merely depressed Lillian, but it gave Frank physical discomfort in the form of aching bones and joints from injuries he had received over the years. Still, as long as the weather allowed them to avoid frostbite and have some visibility, the couple would go outside and shoot, warming up their limbs and improving their mood.

The Smiths vigorously promoted Lillian as a real Native American princess, though it was not hard for audiences to overlook the fact that her skin might have been darkened with a little greasepaint. Pawnee Bill and vaudeville audiences were more than willing to receive her as a member of a "noble race," albeit one doomed by the progress of "civilization."

Native Americans were icons of American identity, and citizens wanted to feel a natural affinity with the continent—it was Indians who could teach them such aboriginal closeness.[1] Another fantastic version of Lillian's life before she signed on with Pawnee Bill was printed in a magazine article that came out about the same time that "We-no-aye-te" was taken away by her groom. The author describes how Wenona came to be with Frank Hafley: "One day when the autumn sun lay hazy over the prairie, when the little summer folks whined and buzzed through the binding grasses, a cowboy with wide sombrero and flying leather trappings galloped along the trail past the spot where sat Wenona, the Indian princess, dreaming of the days she had left behind her at Carlisle." In this story, the cowboy did not notice the maiden, who stared at the dust of his horse trailing off into the horizon for hours, until he returned the next day and saw her smile, "This time he looked and stopped and came back, for Wenona's smile was irresistible. Day after day he came and tarried, until one day he came and carried her away as his wife. This cowboy was Frank Smith—known as 'Fighting Frank' [Hafley]—at one time Sheriff of the famous Larimer County, Col., where his chases after outlaws made him known throughout the West."

After reading several columns of Wenona's romantic biography, which included a short stint at the Indian Industrial School in Carlisle, Pennsylvania, one might have been surprised at her boldness in speaking to a reporter with "little or no trace of an aboriginal accent" about firearms, most definitely with Annie Oakley on her mind: "You know, of course, that because a person is an expert in the use of a shotgun it does not follow that the same person is a good shot with the rifle; but did you ever stop to think that the reverse is also true? One may be very accurate with the rifle and yet be only ordinarily successful with the shotgun." Wenona expanded: "I can take my rifle and hit anything I see within the range of my gun, but were I to go into a shoot at live birds or clay pigeons, where the hard ammunition was a handful of shot instead of one ball, I should make only an ordinary score."

But just so it was clear that the "princess" was absolutely more than proficient at every kind of shooting, she clarified further: "Of course, I do not mean that I cannot kill live birds or break targets with a shotgun; but there are plenty of amateur sportsmen who could beat me at that game. The reason of it is that we who use the rifle 'hold too close' to the object. We are in the habit of having only one bullet to do the work, and we cannot make allowance for the scattering of the shot. Nothing so interferes with accuracy in rifle shooting as does the occasional use of the shotgun."

And again, Wenona, or Lillian, could not help but "take aim" at someone who would not shoot with her: "This has been abundantly proved in the case of Dr. Carver, at one time probably the leading rifle shot of the world. He began giving exhibitions in circuses and using the shotgun. It was easy work for him after he fell into the habit, and he grew careless. A few months of that sort of thing will undo what has required months to accomplished [*sic*] in the way of securing absolute accuracy." She closed the interview with an entirely practical reason why she did not claim to be an expert with the two-barreled weapon. "The recoil of the shotgun must to greater or less extent, bruise the shoulder," she said. "Sometimes this is not noticed by the shooter, but the constant jarring has its effect just the same. In the kind of work which I do with the rifle, there is nothing more important than that the shoulders should be in perfect condition." She emphasized that when cutting the ashes of a cigar held in someone's mouth, or putting a bullet through a card held in someone's fingers, the slightest involuntary twitch of the muscles of a sore or lame shoulder could cause serious injury to that person.[2]

In the spring of 1904, Wenona and Frank joined up with Pawnee Bill. A one-time employee of Cody's, Pawnee Bill, or "Colonel" Gordon Lillie, had created his own Wild West show in 1888. While a translator for the Pawnees in the Buffalo Bill Wild West show's debut season in 1883, Lillie grew to idolize Cody. Despite the competition that his show gave Cody's, the two remained friends and talked often. Both knew that the Wild West format was beginning to show some wear with the public. As historian L. G. Moses explains, many of the Show-Indian personalities who had once been objects of curiosity in the various Wild West shows were either dead or, frequently, too old to travel.

America's Best Female Sharpshooter

Survivors of the late Plains Wars no longer starred in columns of newsprint. Therefore, Buffalo Bill and his competitors were always changing features to remain current or to increase the novelty of their performances. Lillie's solution, continues Moses, was to restyle his show as Pawnee Bill's Historic Wild West and Great Far East.

Lillie made Wenona one of his main features, often having her ride in with him at the opening parade, with her on his left and his wife, May, on his right. The *Harrisburg Independent* called Wenona the champion wing shot, heading "a band of Western girls, noted for their true shooting," and remarked upon her astonishing ability to shoot twenty glass balls in twelve seconds, while riding a "fierce broncho."[3] In June, First Lady Edith Roosevelt took her children to see Wenona and the rest of the program when it was in Washington, D.C.[4] Pawnee Bill's Far East also included Hindu magicians, Singhalese dancers, Madagascar oxen cavalry, Australian Aborigines with boomerangs, Boers, Zulus, Chinese and Japanese Cavalry, Arabian horsemen and many other "exotic" actors.

By all accounts, Wenona and Frank liked working for Lillie, and got along well with the other actors. Lillie even gave Wenona a piebald pony, after a horse she had been using for years in the arena broke its leg. The Colonel told her to take her pick from his herd, and she picked "Rabbit" because he was "picturesque in appearance" and also, "an Indian always likes a spotted or calico pony." But most likely, she picked him because he was completely malleable in terms of the training her acts required. Nonetheless, she fell completely in love with Rabbit, and he dutifully traveled with his mistress all over the United States from then on.[5]

"Dusky Winona" shot at pennies and other objects, both while stationary and from the back of a galloping horse. An Ottawa, Kansas, reporter exclaimed that she was equal with shotgun and rifle, and that "both afield and upon horse she displays equal aptitude and skill and she claims especial distinction as the only one of her sex performing shooting 'stunts' from the back of a galloping horse."[6] This may very well have been true. The only male performers who could do this were Cody, Buckskin Bill (W. C. Cahoon), and possibly Cody disciple Johnny Baker.

On September 21, 1905, while performing in Burlington, Kansas,

Wenona's horse spooked and bucked her clear off. When she tried to rise, the still-stomping horse kicked her in the head, knocking her unconscious and slicing part of her scalp. The accident must have looked horrific to the audience, because a porter for the Santa Fe Railroad who left shortly thereafter to work his route told the newspaper at his next stop that Wenona had to be dead, given the way her horse fell on her.

The sharpshooter was taken to the hospital, where her wounds were deemed non-life-threatening, although she most certainly checked herself out before any possible brain or neck injury could be observed. In these days, long before disability pay and safer working conditions, time was money. If word got out that Wenona was not well, Pawnee Bill's Wild West stood to lose advance bookings—which meant Frank and Wenona would lose pay. As it was, the show received bad press the following day for not having any headliners, and for its performers seemingly just "going through the motions." This knowledge, along with her sheer physical strength and mental fortitude, spurred the markswoman to return to work in a couple of weeks, without showing any limp or grimace to the audience, though she was in a lot of pain.[7]

Gordon Lillie's working conditions were thought to be some of the best among traveling shows, and the performers always got the Sabbath off. Management was not chintzy when it came to hiring hands to keep the animals clean and maintained—something that was very important to the couple. This extra support helped Wenona recover, and on December 16, 1905, the couple posted a letter in the *Clipper* to their fans: "The season of the Pawnee Bill show closed November 4 in Malden, Mo, and we have since been out in the swamps of Southern Missouri, resting and busting. There are plenty of deer and wild turkey here, and we have no trouble getting all we want to eat with our rifles. Wenona has entirely recovered from the injury she received from her horse falling."[8]

Pawnee Bill's Wild West also allowed Wenona and Frank enough time to pursue a side business—making and selling curios to supplement their income. Frank's leg was still hurt from a fall the year before, and sometimes this kept him from performing. Thus, he created another job for himself within the show, which was head of its "Indian Curio and Ethnological Department." The couple hired a salesman from Hyde and Benham's Trading Company, an outfit that sold Navajo textiles and other Native American creations to customers all over the United States. Wenona and Frank designed the sale items—mostly tomahawks—with input from show Indians. The couple also hired Robert Hartley, a metals worker and inventor in Pittsburgh who often helped replate their guns, to mold the axes. Wenona bluntly ordered Hartley not to worry about expediency over craftsmanship, and to "fix it so that no one else can get Tomahawks from our model and [to get them] out as soon as possible."[9] They sold these, along with Wenona's various beaded handiworks, at their performances.[10]

According to some of her few letters, Wenona enjoyed the work with Pawnee Bill's Wild West and the outdoor life it afforded her. Therefore, it was probably just the prospect of a better salary that spurred Frank to open negotiations with the Miller brothers of Bliss, Oklahoma. On March 16, 1907, the *New York Clipper* announced that Wenona and Frank would not go out with Pawnee Bill again, but instead would join the 101 Ranch for the Jamestown Exhibition, America's tercentennial celebration of the first permanent English settlement, to be held in Norfolk, Virginia, from April 26 to December 1, 1907.

The Millers were Joseph, George Jr., and Zack, sons of Colonel George Washington Miller. George, or "G.W." as he was often called, became a cattle merchant after serving in the Civil War. Miller sought to expand his cattle and agricultural interest following the opening of the Cherokee Strip by land run. He and his sons began buying additional property along with lease agreements with the Ponca Indian tribe.

The 101 Ranch expanded to some 75,000 acres of pasture and farmland. With skillful management, the ranch grew to an estimated 110,000 acres (a little larger than the city of St. Louis at that time), and its boundaries eventually expanded to the northern Oklahoma counties of Noble, Pawnee, Osage, and Kay. The communities of Marland (originally Bliss), Red Rock and White Eagle were within the bounds of the giant farm and ranch operation.

When Colonel Miller died in 1903, Joe, George, and Zack continued expansive operation of the ranch. The brothers hired experts to develop agricultural applications that became enormously successful, while they built a herd of 25,000 longhorns. The brothers also developed large herds of Holstein and Shorthorn dairy cattle along with Duroc-Jersey hogs.[11] Starting in 1904, the 101 Ranch made headlines almost weekly, for its bumper crops of wheat and breeding experiments with animals like Abyssinian zebras.

The 101 Ranch, writes historian Al Ritter, earned the title of a "Fabulous Empire." It had its own packing plant, ice plants and cold-storage lockers, and such innovations as a tannery, a cider mill, an alfalfa mill, an electric power plant, a dairy and a cannery, along with a telephone system and mail service. *Show World* described this empire as entirely beneficial to the thousand or so Ponca and Oto Indians living on reservations within the 101's confines, to whom the Millers paid roughly $30,000 a year in rent: "Many of these Indians live in the natural state in wigwams, but there are hundreds more civilized, and some of them have homes worth $5,000, showing evidence of thrift. Miller Brothers have always done everything in their power to help the Indians and their efforts in behalf of the red-skinned race entitle them to much credit. They have built churches for them and have in many other ways assisted the government in educating the aborigine."[12] Later when oil was found on ranch land, the Miller brothers built their own refinery producing gasoline, kerosene and fuel oil.

The Smiths met the Miller brothers while wintering in Malden, at the end of 1905. Some of the Pawnee Bill performers, including Frank and Wenona, stayed there to make some extra money breaking out some colts for farmers. At ten dollars per head for each horse "broken," Wenona could easily make several hundred dollars. And she loved to tame even the most unruly young ones. She took exceptional pride in breaking one "real freak" of a colt she named Spider, because it was "all legs" and seemed to jump straight up into the air and then sideways.

Earlier in 1905, the Millers entered the entertainment field. Joe Miller got an endorsement from the National Editorial Association of St. Louis to hold its annual newspaper editors convention in Guthrie, Oklahoma Territory. The brothers spared no expense or imagination to produce an extravaganza they promoted as a "Round Up"—really, a Wild West show. The men hired at least two hundred local cowboys, ranch hands and Indians, and even arranged to have the imprisoned frontier warrior Geronimo brought to the ranch under military guard from Fort Sill.

America's Best Female Sharpshooter

Among other larger-than-life promotions, the Millers placed a tongue-in-cheek advertisement in area newspapers that they would offer a thousand-dollar prize to anyone who would submit to being scalped by Geronimo. It was a huge success, as described by Ritter:

> More than 65,000 people attended the long afternoon of events of June 11, 1905 and overflow crowds easily filled a huge grandstand built for the event. Performing ranch honed skills, cowboys and cowgirls paraded that huge grandstand on the south side of the Salt Fork River along with vividly costumed Ponca, Kaw, Otoe, Missouri, Tonkawa, Pawnee and Osage Indians, marching bands, soldiers and Geronimo. Along with Geronimo's mock 'buffalo hunt,' trick riding, bucking horses and a performance by the bulldogging 'Dusky Demon' from Texas, Bill Pickett, the evening ended with an unannounced frontier style wagon train attack by Indian performers.

The Millers treated the editors to a "buffalo barbecue," featuring meat Geronimo allegedly procured on his last hunt.[13]

Frank Hafley (Smith) approached the Millers about joining the 101 as a partner, not just a performer. He had tried to make similar arrangements with Pawnee Bill—after all, Hafley was a dynamic arena manager and location scout—but Lillie was consumed with joining forces with Cody, and could not see his way to work out a partnership with Frank. So in March 1907, Hafley announced that he and Wenona would be going to a special exhibition in Virginia with the 101 Ranch, not back to Pawnee Bill.[14]

President Theodore Roosevelt invited the Miller brothers to bring their Wild West program to Jamestown. Almost every day at 2:30 and 8:30 P.M., the 101 Ranch show performed mightily on the Lee Parade Ground, in a vast amphitheatre. The performance consisted of about five hundred cowboys, cowgirls, Mexicans, and members of several tribes of Native Americans. There were hundreds of "the finest horses and ponies," long-horned steers from Texas, and herds of buffaloes. "The Millers," reported the *Atlanta Constitution*, "had such tremendous resources to draw from that it is no wonder that they put together a Wild West show that has created a sensation. . . . To miss this show is to miss the treat of a lifetime."[15]

The *New York Times*, in previewing a re-creation of the original Jamestown settlement, made passing reference to "an Indian village close at hand."[16] This had nothing to do with Wenona, but referred to a historical exhibition by the Powhatan Indians, who hoped that by participating in the exhibition, they would remind fellow Americans of their existence and raise awareness of their low standard of living in the state. But they were overshadowed by the 101 Ranch Wild West show's Plains Indians, whose whooping, flashy presence was more recognizable and attractive to paying customers.[17] The Powhatans were not permitted to contribute to any official attractions of the tercentennial exhibition but were relegated to the "amusement" area. There, they were compelled to stage Pocahontas's rescue of Captain John Smith from execution ordered by her father, chief of the Powhatans. Wenona had occasionally performed in a similar recreation for Pawnee Bill's show, in effect giving visitors the impression that the Indians were "savages" in feathers.

A number of scholars have considered why Native Americans chose to take part in Wild West shows. Philip Deloria suggests that some motives are simply unknowable; he pointed to a number of possibilities: "escape; adventure; economic need; cultural celebrations; educational outreach." Early testimony from Indian performers, writes Alison Fields, reported poor conditions on western reservations, including hunger, disease, and boredom. In contrast, Wild West shows, particularly large ones like Buffalo Bill's, Pawnee Bill's, and the Millers', provided attractive opportunities for Native people to travel, earn a living, and engage with a broad variety of people. Furthermore, for some performers who were involved in the earlier Indian Wars, participating in a Wild West show actually shielded them from government persecution or imprisonment.[18]

Although all of these shows shared similar formats, the Miller Brothers' Real Wild West show set out to compete against and distinguish itself from Buffalo Bill's. The show placed more emphasis on everyday aspects of ranch life, as well as popular cowboy pastimes such as "trick riding, broncho busting, wild steer riding, and fancy rope spinning."[19] In addition to the featured cowboys and cowgirls, the Miller Brothers hired more than 150 Indian performers from South Dakota and Oklahoma for their early shows. These performers included Oglalas and

Sicangus (Brulés) from the Pine Ridge and Rosebud reservations and Cheyennes, Poncas, Sac and Foxes, Comanches, and Kiowas from the former Indian Territory. Wenona and press agent Grant Richardson had no problem gleaning details about the Carlisle Indian School, as many true graduates of this institution and others like it found jobs in the 101 show as translators and showmen.[20]

The Millers gave Wenona and Frank top billing at the beginning of the exhibition, but it soon became clear that *Princess* Wenona was the star. Zach Miller had her outfitted in a buckskin costume and billed her as "The Champion Indian Girl Rifle Shot of the 101 Ranch."[21] This did not bother Frank; the couple had no professional jealousies between them.

The ex-sheriff had started using his real name again—Hafley—because he had set up a fledgling management business, nurturing new talent for the emerging rodeo format. He signed Ada Somerville, a talented and beautiful western performer possibly from Frank's hometown of Tulare, California. She was also one of the most respected horse trainers of her time, and had perfected the art of teaching horses tricks, like dancing on their knees, without a whip.

Women with horses were becoming very popular, and after the Jamestown run ended in October, Frank searched for more acts while wintering on the vaudeville circuit with Wenona. His goal was to bring fresh and thrilling performances to Dreamland, Coney Island, where he had been hired as arena manager for the 1908 season. *Billboard* magazine conveyed some mild disappointment at the fact that, contrary to what Hafley previously announced, Wenona would not be at Dreamland that season, but had not been booked elsewhere.[22]

However, Frank did engage "one of the biggest sensations ever seen in this country," a young woman who could dive sixty feet through the air into a pool of water on the back of her horse, Lurline. Her name was Mamie Francis, soon to be Mrs. Frank Hafley.

Chapter Six
NEW FRIENDS, OLD FRIENDS

Her eyesight is as clear as the best field glass, her nerve
is as true of steel and she performs shooting "stunts"
daily in the arena of the "Wild West" which put to blush
feats in markmanship offered by masculine exponents.
Council Bluffs (Iowa) Daily NonPareil,
August 19, 1905

Dreamland was the last of the "big three" amusement parks in
Coney Island built during the Progressive Era. It opened in
1904, and was designed to be a grander, more sophisticated version
of its neighboring venue, Luna Park. Some of its many attractions
included a "midget city," Frank Bostock's wild animal show, scenic
railways, a ballroom, a Japanese tea pavilion, and the Hell Gate boat
ride. Perhaps most famously, it featured Dr. Martin Couney's Infant
Incubators, an attraction showing how premature babies' lives were
saved.[1]

California Frank's Wild West show at Dreamland was somewhat
of a misnomer. To be sure, Hafley's program contained many of the
spectacles, cowboy and Indian chases, and re-creations of historic
events that other exhibitions did, but it really was more of a precursor
to rodeo than an evolution of Wild West. While Hafley's endeavor was
not quite the rodeo we know today, with clowns and cowboys competing to win a pool of money, it did incorporate a lot of sport and animal
tricks and scaled-down pageantry.

At first, Wenona decided not to participate in Frank's Dreamland venture, maybe because she was jealous of Frank focusing his attention on Mamie. But she managed to put her feelings aside and rejoined Hafley for the summer, and was no less dazzling than usual: "Princess Wenona, the world's champion rifle shot . . . rides around the Hippodrome track on the back of a running horse breaking balls with a rifle as fast as they can be thrown into the air by her assistant, who also rides a horse in front of her. She breaks five balls thrown into the air at one time, also shooting pennies thrown into the air."[2] Wenona's act was usually sandwiched in between Mamie's and Ada Somerville's. Frank was so busy with finances that he hired someone new to take over as arena director, a rugged twenty-five-year-old cowboy from Kentucky named Wayne Beasley.

By the opening of Frank's Wild West in May of 1908, Hafley and Francis had developed strong feelings for each other. Regardless of this, Wenona's demotion on the bill was not a symbolic gesture of "second best" but, rather, a good business decision. Mamie's act with Lurline was something few people had ever seen, and moreover, the rapid and loud shots from Wenona's act might spook Lurline were she to go first. And though Mamie and her white horse kept people sitting on their seats with anxiety and anticipation, Wenona was still America's favorite. A visitor to Hafley's act in Omaha later that year recounted his experience: "In this Wild West direct from Coney Island he applauds above all else the remarkable marksmanship of Princess Wenona who pierces glass balls thrown in the air in sets of three and four. Even more skillfull than this is her feat of breaking twenty glass balls on a swinging frame in just twenty shots, no more and no less. Princess Wenona was one of the features of the carnival and her recognition was well deserved."[3] Wenona represented the bygone era of conquering the frontier, as well as the emergence of the modern-day circus.

On April 25, 1908, while Wenona was prepping for the opening of the Dreamland show, Levi Smith passed away. He was seventy-two, and had suffered from cancer of the bowel. The old man died alone at a hospital in Stockton; a housekeeper from the rooming house where he had been staying signed the certificate. He was buried without fanfare or tombstone in Stockton's Rural Cemetery. Virtually every part of

Princess Wenona's "Lillian Smith" life was now gone. Even Nellie was in the wind, traveling with lesser-known shows like Texas Bill's Wild West.

The last vestige of Wenona's life as Lillian Smith was shed when Charles Frank Hafley and Mamie (Elba Mae) Skepper Francis quietly married on November 19, 1909, in DeKalb County, Georgia. There was no announcement in any of the usual vaudeville circulars, nor did the Hafleys ever speak of it outside of family and close friends. Wenona-Lillian purportedly "never got over her split-up with the dashing Frank Smith," but there is no evidence of this.[4] In fact, the three of them—Hafley, Francis, and Smith—began an aggressive tour of the eastern and southern states, headlining huge fairs in cities such as Pittsburgh, Philadelphia, Augusta (Georgia), and Greensboro (North Carolina). The two women occasionally handled the show quite ably without Frank as "Wenona, Francis & Co." when he needed to dash off to secure other talent. On another occasion in March 1909, he went to Henryetta, Oklahoma, to help Zack Miller quell an uprising led by the Sioux chief Crazy Snake.

The 1910 season was a pivotal one, with Wild Wests, circuses, and vaudeville shows jockeying for audiences and financial solvency, by combining, splitting up, or poaching talent or managers from others. The "Two Bills Show," Cody's and Lillie's merger, had been relatively successful, but this was mostly due to the fact that Cody announced that he would retire this year.

Meanwhile, circus executive Edward Arlington left Pawnee Bill's show when the latter combined with Cody, and formed a partnership with the Miller brothers, taking total responsibility for all business affairs of the Millers' Wild West show. This freed the brothers to take care of their flourishing ranch and farm concerns.[5] The competing Ringling Brothers had three shows under their control, including the Forepaugh-Sells and Barnum circuses.

All of these traveling shows, along with Sells-Floto, Tammen and Bonfils, and Wallace-Hagenbeck, frequently butted up against each other in cities where appropriate venues were limited, and where consumers no longer wanted to pay to see essentially the same thing more than once a year. Hafley was smart to keep his show simple and nimble: he could dart in and out of small towns before the bigger Wild

Wests or circuses lumbered in, and not lose as much money if weather prevented a showing. Additionally, Hafley had Wenona, who in turn had built-in name recognition, and could shoot indoors or out, small arena or large: "Of Princess Wenona, the world's greatest rifle shot, it is difficult to speak. A pen picture gives an inadequate idea of her skill. She is admitted by such authorities as Buffalo Bill, Pawnee Bill and Colonel F. T. Cummins . . . to be the greatest Wild West attraction before the public today."[6]

As for Mamie, all she needed was her diving platform—set up by a few of the Sioux who accompanied the show with their "chief," Eagle Eye—and a trench of water, often dug by local baseball teams eager to make a few dollars. Frank would crank up the waltz *Sobre las Olas* on his portable steam calliope machine to attract crowds, and continue to do so while Mamie's horse Serpentine was coaxed to the top of the twenty-five-foot platform (Lurline had passed away the year before). Serpentine was a riderless filly of "Babe" and always went first, because she was not distracted by the music or the hustle of the crowd. After the applause for Serpentine's dive subsided, Frank stopped playing his music, and demanded complete silence from the crowd. Mare Babe climbed and dove flawlessly, as long as there was no noise.

Mamie Francis was a very proficient rifle shot by this time, and she could even hit the occasional stationary target from a galloping horse. In the 1920s, the press sometimes referred to her as the Champion Lady Rifle Shot. But during the first decade of the twentieth century, there was simply no one except Annie Oakley who could come close to Wenona's skill, and Frank trusted no one besides Wenona to perform the dangerous tricks audiences craved: "Another thriller is when California Frank takes in his teeth a quill of about three inches in length, at the end of which is a glass ball about the size of a marble, and this she splinters, repeating the act six times. It can well be imagined that California Frank has no doubt as to her accuracy, as a deflection of a hair's breadth in her sight would mean death." As usual, noted a Southern paper, she performed these death-defying acts actions modestly and gracefully, even while galloping at speeds up to forty miles per hour.[7]

Putting a positive spin on his streamlined organization, Frank maintained that his show might be shorter than most, but that "people would rather witness one hour of high-class exhibition" than two hours' ordinary fill-in show.[8] Still, Hafley maintained a close friendship with Arlington and the Miller brothers; they were, after all, the richest showmen in the country, and actually owned a large chunk of the "real" West.

Anyone taking a group picture of California Frank's Wild West in the spring of 1910 would have captured Wenona at one of the most content periods of her life. In May, just before beginning a long campaign in Georgia and Tennessee, her troupe mates consisted of performers who would remain lifelong friends, both to her and to each other.

First and foremost, of course, there were Frank and Mamie, married and in the throes of legal paperwork for Frank to adopt Mamie's daughter. Mamie sometimes assisted Wenona with her shooting act, throwing up glass balls from a galloping horse beside or in front of Wenona's horse. In turn, Wenona would take care of Mamie's horses when she was busy with daughter Reine (who would later become a famous rodeo star in her own right), or, as was sometimes the case, when she was recuperating from injury sustained from her diving act. If Lurline or Serpentine spooked at the top of the platform for any reason, Mamie would suffer a broken nose or bruised ribs or both. Ironically, she could not swim, and members of "California Frank" always stood at the ready if horse or rider took too long to get out of the pool.

There was Bee Ho Gray, whose real name was Emberry Cannon Gray. He was a treasured show mate of Wenona's. Gray was a "wonder with a rope," able to catch the horse running past him by any foot that was asked for. One of his trademark lasso tricks was to throw two ropes at one time, catching the rider with one and the horse with the other.

Gray and wife Ada Sommerville met in 1904 at the St. Louis World's Fair, while both were performing in Colonel Cummins' Wild West Indian Congress and Rough Riders of the World, along with Nellie Smith. The Fair was Bee Ho's first Wild West show; Ada was already a veteran performer and thirteen years older.

Unlike Wenona, Bee Ho was part Native American, if only one-eighth, through his mother. He was renamed by Chief Quanah Parker, last chief of the Comanches, whose children he played with as a youngster at the nexus of Apache, Kiowa, and Comanche lands in present-day Oklahoma.

America's Best Female Sharpshooter

Bee Ho developed his western skills on the plains of Indian Territory, but had never seen a real trick roper until about 1900. He and his younger brother, Weaver, heard about the amazing tricks that were being performed by ropers in Wild West shows. Together, they rode sixty miles on one horse to the town of Chickasha to see the Pawnee Bill Wild West exhibition, making the trip in two days. They were very impressed with the trick ropers and began teaching themselves rope tricks, using clothesline and anything else they could spin. Within a few years, both were performing with Wild West shows. Both Gray brothers would enjoy amazing fifty-year careers in western performance.

Besides being incredibly talented with a lasso—one of his acts was to "catch" four cowgirls dashing on horseback at full speed about the ring—Bee Ho Gray had a great sense of humor. Ada taught their horse Onion how to do dances that were borderline offensive at that time. Gray would ask suggestively, "What sort of Oriental dance do you like to do, Onion?" and the horse would stand on his hind legs and gyrate suggestively. In his forties and fifties, Gray appeared on stage and radio with such luminaries as Bing Crosby, Will Rogers, and Tom Mix.

Wenona found Gray's qualities endearing, and she considered him to be one of her best friends.[9] Despite his sharply-honed silliness, Gray was extremely empathetic to Americans of all ethnicities and social standing, and was especially kind to animals and children. Many of Gray's friends and family remarked after his death in August 1951 that they thought of him as a humorous and accepting father figure.

Like Wenona, Adaline Hulen Sommerville Gray often felt most at ease around cowboys and horses, even though she had once been a Broadway actress. She was a talented and beautiful western performer and horse trainer who was one of the most respected equestriennes of her time. She coached several horses that belonged to famous people in the world of the Wild West shows, including, eventually, Ben Hur, the horse of Zack Miller of the 101 Ranch.

Offering support was nurse Fanny Liesy. Wenona had released Fanny to the nomadic household of the Hafleys, but she remained in service to Wenona whenever domestic or medical assistance was needed. She was truly the anchor for the California Frank Wild West show. Fanny's husband, William, died in 1886 when he was just thirty-two years old, and her two young daughters died in the early

1890s. Her brother-in-law was a sheriff in San Joaquin County and knew Hafley well. Frank remembered when, just before William died, Fanny gave birth to a stillborn baby. She kept plunging the tiny body in buckets of ice cold and then warm water, hoping to revive it.

Despite or because of these tragedies in her life, Fanny Liesy enrolled in the first class of a nursing program offered by Stanford Hospital. She graduated in 1897, and took such good care of Frank when he underwent his emergency hernia operation there that Frank and Wenona hired her. This stalwart woman was only too happy to leave California and its heartaches and take to the road with them. The daughter of a prosperous farmer, she even loaned the Hafleys and Wenona money from time to time. Fanny outlived almost everybody in the troupe.

This company was brought closer together by the tragedy that befell them in March 1910. The California Frank Wild West was preparing to showcase a phenomenally well-trained white horse named "Columbus," ridden by Ada and trained by both her and Wenona, and which had belonged briefly to William Cody. A fire broke out in the stable, and spread rapidly because of the colorful bunting decorations tacked on throughout the inside of the structure. Fanny Liesy tried desperately to unlatch Columbus's stall gate, but the animal had kicked the gate so many times that the latch was bent, making it impossible for her to open it without getting swallowed by flames herself. The gang cried for days over the loss of Columbus, and also the little Angora billy goat Ada had gotten to keep him company.[10]

Others in the congenial group included Johnny Hughes, whose main function was to keep Wenona's, Frank's and Mamie's rifles clean and oiled, and reload expended cartridges between shows. Billy "Clown" Lorette provided comic relief between sets with his trained donkeys. Chief Eagle Eye—really an erstwhile actor named George D. Fuerst—announced each act. There was Thomas "Tommy" Kirnan, a fourteen-year-old trick rider and fancy roper, who was also Reine Hafley's first equine tutor, and Julia Allen, a young singer, horse trainer, and bugler par excellence. And then there was Wayne Beasley.

Wenona and Frank met Wayne Anderson Beasley during their Pawnee Bill days. Born in 1883 to poor farmers in Fulton, Kentucky, he moved to Noble, Oklahoma, in his youth and got work as a ranch hand. Beasley was not conventionally handsome—he was only about five feet, eight inches tall and had a round, non-descript face—but he was incredibly strong and masculine, his body all tightly compacted muscle.

Beasley was fearless. All of Pawnee Bill's employees remembered how, in 1906, the cowhand saved Lillie's prized menagerie during a sudden and dangerous rainstorm that blew all the tents down and separated hundreds of family members. The show's veterinarian managed to get the elephants upright by administering doses of cocaine under their tongues, but the buffalo and camels were headed for Newark Bay. Beasley led thirty-three other cowboys after them. "They were lassoed just in time," reported the *New York Sun*, "A big camel was stepping into the water when Head Cowboy Wayne Beasley roped him and yanked him back with such force that he will have a pain in his neck for a long time." By midnight, Beasley had managed to round up all the horses, too.[11]

In turn, Wenona seems to have lassoed Beasley this season of 1910, at least for a spell. The *Los Angeles Times* noted a year later that it was a "romance of many years' duration," and it is possible Wenona may have turned her attention to him when Hafley turned his to Mamie. Still, there is no evidence that this was anything but a short-term physical attraction coupled with a healthy respect for each other's show-biz sophistication. If it was at all awkward for Wenona, Hafley, Mamie, and Beasley to travel together, they never said anything. After all, they had all worked together for many years at this point, and none of them ever placed their romantic attachments above their professionalism.

Once again, this was a romance that served Wenona-Lillian well. Beasley gave the shooter the confidence to move away from Hafley's sphere. The latter was making plans to enlarge his vaudeville–Wild West hybrid into a full-fledged circus, to capitalize on what he correctly perceived as the eventual demise of the Two Bills Show. Though Cody's and Lillie's combined program would last another three seasons, their dwindling profits were already the worst-kept secret in show business.

Frank thought a portable circus with well-known names and wholesome acts that hinted at the frontier escapades of yesteryear without requiring acres of land could make good money in both urban and rural locales. For performers like Wenona and Beasley, though, the loss of this "room to move" was tantamount to being locked in a cage.

In December 1910, Wenona wrote to Joe Miller, part-owner of the only "real" Wild West for the foreseeable future, apparently in response to an overture he had made to her:

> Your nice letter to hand having been delayed in the mail—I hear you are coming East so will send two letters one to Bliss and one to N.J. Now in regard [to] business—I think that the act is worth $50.00 a week—I will furnish—and pay a man to look after the act—that is make balls and care for the guns— and take care of my horses—you to furnish the makings for the balls and ammunition—And in regards [to] Wayne—you will find him a first class man—sober—and the best all around worker you ever had—a man that you can put in any part of your show—from the front door to the back and he will make good—he is a trick rider (got $50.00) a week here in vaudeville for his work—a Poney Express rider—practical roper—bucking horse rider in fact any kind of cowboy work.

Wenona added flirtatiously that if Joe did not find Wayne Beasley as good as any of his best cowboys, she would make him a "handsome present," and vouched for Beasley as a good showman.[12]

Miller hired them immediately for the following summer, albeit not at the pay Wenona had hoped, but rather, $250 per month. According to a 101 Ranch historian, this was the highest salary paid to any employee at that time, although that might be a reach since it is not known whether that included monies for Wayne, and if so, how much.[13]

Hafley attempted to incorporate his Wild West show with the Miller 101 as well. He sent Edward Arlington, manager of the 101's entertainment concerns, ideas for combining their shows in the 1911 summer and fall season. Just a few days after Wenona received her acceptance, Arlington received a less enthusiastic response from Joe Miller regarding Frank Hafley: "My candid opinion is that, under the most favorable conditions, the deal [with California Frank] would be a loser, although it might figure out good on paper, and I would prefer spending the money against the opposition than going into this deal." Miller appreciated the fact that Hafley would not ask the brothers to put up any money, but knowing the showman better than anybody, he predicted that a "show-down would come" and Hafley would not have the money to put up the draft stock, harness, canvas, lights, and "a world of other things" that would be necessary to frame up his show. Most importantly, Miller did not want his Wild West to simply be a repository for broken-up acts that were not strong enough on their own. He reminded Arlington that "California Frank . . . has lost Wenona, as well as Ada Somerville and Bee Gray," and thus had no strong features with his outfit.[14]

Wenona and Beasley wintered in Passaic, New Jersey, along with the other 101 stars, including cowboy clown Dan Dix, young fancy roper Chester Byers, and Goldie Wooden, otherwise known as Goldie St. Clair. The "Sioux princess" was just as horrified as the rest of the troupe when Wooden was gravely injured at an exhibition given for President Theodore Roosevelt in Philadelphia, a stop on their trek out West. St. Clair was known as the "Female Champion Bronc Buster," and besides doing tricks on "killer horses," she could rope, throw, and tie a steer in less than a minute. This time, she was thrown from Roan Devil, and the bronc stomped on her head and kicked her as she was down, causing a blood clot and some broken bones. She appeared so close to death that Philadelphia papers erroneously reported that she had died—she survived but was not able to continue with the show that season.[15]

After appearing at sixteen stands across Pennsylvania in June, the 101 Ranch troupe spent the rest of the summer in Michigan, Wisconsin, and Illinois. The musicians in the show quickly learned to duck when Wenona came out—at her first performance with the 101, the cornetist got a load of birdshot. Everywhere the show traveled, notes Wallis, it faced fierce competition from traveling circuses such as Ringling Brothers, Forepaugh-Sells, Barnum & Bailey, and the Al G. Barnes Wild Animal Show.

Finally, the show train headed west. The troupe anticipated its season finale scheduled for October 21 at El Reno, Oklahoma, but instead of calling it quits for the year, the Millers decided to extend the season and spend the winter in Los Angeles. After El Reno, they continued with stops throughout Texas, New Mexico, and Arizona until they reached the Pacific Slope.[16]

Wenona was no doubt thrilled to return to California in the autumn of 1911, as was everybody else connected to the 101. Los Angeles had changed a lot since Wenona had last seen it, possibly in 1901 or 1902. It was no longer a sleepy town. In the first decade of the twentieth century, the population had soared from slightly more than 100,000 to nearly 320,000.[17] After their months on the road, "Los Angeles looked like heaven on earth to the exhausted bronc riders, trick ropers, Indian entertainers, and sharpshooters. Joe Miller's performers were delighted for the chance to bask in the sunshine, feel the caress of warm salt breezes beneath stately palms and eucalyptus trees, and feast on luscious grapes, citrus, and abalone, fresh from the sea."[18] Some of the performers stayed at the St. Marks Hotel in Venice, just south of Santa Monica on the beach, while others rented oceanfront cottages.

The boarders at Venice included Don "Vern" and Edith Tantlinger, a husband-wife team. The duo joined the 101 show in 1908, and performed in it for nine consecutive seasons. Vern acted as arena director, the show's Indian agent, and eventually as "Chief of the Cowboys." He specialized in hunt-and-battle feats using the boomerang—his assistant was Zu-Rah, billed as an Australian aborigine, who always caught the flying weapon bare-handed as it whirled through the air.[19]

Edith, on the other hand, preferred trick-shooting with a pistol and trapshooting with a shotgun. She had been on the show circuit since the late 1890s. Given their early marriage, the Tantlingers probably met while students at Iowa State University and what is now Minnesota State University, Mankato, respectively. Vern was a professional baseball player for a while, and Edith was a schoolteacher before they turned to more specialized pursuits.

The Tantlingers' biographies are rather unclear, even though Edith left several diaries she had kept while touring with the 101 and with Wenona. They are filled mostly with minutiae about the weather, show schedules, tidbits about the towns they visited, and an occasional remark about co-workers. The only extant reference to Wenona is on April 17, 1909 in which she notes that Wenona's "horse fell with her, hurting her quite severely—unable to work."[20] This may have been the case, for the markswoman did not appear in headlines again for two more months.

Edith and Wenona do not appear to have been overly friendly, but this was probably due to their grinding work schedules more than anything else. Joe Miller paid Wenona almost as much singly as he did the Tantlingers together, or at least he did initially; Wenona was aware of this and perhaps the couple were. Edith was an exceptional cowgirl—there was no other as good with a lariat—and incredibly adept with both rifle and shotgun, but she was nowhere close to being the crack shot that Wenona was. And she never claimed to be, although on occasion, press biographies referred to her as an "Oklahoma Indian Girl" in a mild attempt to create another Wenona.[21] Edith was and always remained the quintessential cowgirl, a card-carrying "mistress of the plains" and leader of the rest of them on the 101.

Other performers who stayed seaside that winter included clown Dan Dix, the high-riding Parry twin sisters, and lady bronc rider and cowgirl fashion plate Lulu Parr, who may have filled in for the injured Goldie St. Clair; Parr was with the Two Bills Show for the regular season but quit to meet the 101 out West.

One other notable winter mate in Los Angeles was Jim Kid Willoughby. There was no rancor between him and Wenona after twenty-three years since their last meeting. Jim was a deeply sentimental man, and they likely reminisced about their heady years with Buffalo Bill. He posed no threat to Wayne Beasley, who was twenty-six years his junior, and who looked up to Kid as a legendary "cowpunch"—someone who had subdued even "man-eating French stallions" and suffered many broken bones and torn spinal cords for his trouble.

Both Wenona and Beasley were probably just as surprised as everyone else in the show to see Kid—many had assumed he was dead. The Miller brothers had paid a considerable amount of money to trackers to canvass western South Dakota and eastern Wyoming and find him—exactly why remains unclear, but it did not take much to persuade Kid to join the troupe. And even with his fifty-five-year-old, painful bones, Kid was determined to keep up with the others. In one anecdote divulged by the *Santa Monica Outlook*, Kid Willougby ran two miles alongside Beasley and cowboy William Saunders to lasso "Vicious Nic," a buffalo that had broken away from his corral and was goring passing autos.[22]

Wintering in Venice really was a welcome respite for Wenona and the 101 performers. The animals were well taken care of by some of the five hundred support staffers the Millers provided, and housed far enough away on the grounds of the Los Angeles Gun Club at Athletic Park so performers could have a break from the smell. The troupe loved the magnificent weather and the clean scent of the ocean, and like Kid and Wenona, many renewed friendships with co-workers and with actors from Barnes's Circus, which was also wintering in the resort area.

The developer Abbot Kinney had years before envisioned Venice as being the "Coney Island of the Pacific," and was happy to make a profit off sideshow freaks, amusement rides, and honky-tonk attractions: "The Midway-Plaisance, or simply 'Midway,' along the swimming lagoon featured rows of amusements and exhibits such as head-hunting Igorots from the Philippines, dancing girls, snake charmers, a bearded lady, camel rides, and a moving-picture theater. Some of the most popular attractions included Chiquita, a thirty-two-pound woman who stood twenty-eight inches tall, and 'Bosco Eats Them Alive,' a man who dined on wiggling reptiles."[23] Barkers wielding huge microphones enticed tourists into tent shows, and to the "Indian Village," a cluster of teepees and souvenir shops erected on the pier by 101 general agent Fred Beckman that was attracting almost four thousand ticket payers each Saturday and Sunday.

It was at this Indian village that Wenona earned some press for a "real life" exploit. One day, about a week before Christmas 1911, a young man from New York was leaning against a railing and lost his balance. He did not know how to swim, and as the shouts of those who saw him fall reached the "princess," she jumped into the surf, buckskin and all. She held his head above the waves until people threw some ropes and she was able to pull him to safety. True to form, she did not think this was worthy of any fuss, and barely tolerated his profuse thanks before heading back to sell her beadwork.[24]

Despite the announcement of their engagement in the *Los Angeles Times* and the *Santa Monica Daily Outlook,* Wenona and Wayne Beasley did not marry during their winter hiatus.[25] This was most likely a publicity ploy by the 101, and perhaps a way to explain some public displays of affection on the part of the couple. A show roster from the 101 publicity department had Wenona printed up as "Princess Winona [*sic*] Beasley," suggesting that a marriage had already taken place. Any disappointment about not having a wedding in their town did not stop Angelenos from swarming the 101 Wild West in the spring.

Even given Los Angeles's access to theatrical and athletic events, few of its dwellers had ever experienced anything like the Miller 101 Wild West. Most audiences had no idea of how many people and moving parts had to come together to make the Wild West such a wondrous break from reality. The show depended on the intricate choreography of scores of people: a legal team; supervisors for cars for sideshow events and performers; supervisors for cars for white working men and women and for "colored" people and Indians; musicians; clowns; ammunition shorties; clean-up teams; doctors and veterinarians; and more.

Arena director Tantlinger and his assistant, head cowboy Beasley, started rehearsing in early February, refining acts such as the horseback quadrille, trick riding, trick roping, horse roping, fights over the waterhole, the Wells Fargo stagecoach holdup, and so on. Tantlinger also made sure the Indians and their interpreter from the Pine Ridge Reservation arrived within a month of the show opening, for rehearsals. He also may have supervised the transportation and certainly the rehearsals for a band of Navajos contracted from New Mexico.

The Miller brothers' show formally opened in Santa Monica on March 23, 1912. For two hectic weeks the 101 Ranch outfit played bookings in nearly a dozen southern California cities—Long Beach, Pomona, San Bernardino, Pasadena, Anaheim, San Diego, Los Angeles, Escondido, Santa Ana, Corona, and Redlands. The three-day stand at Praeger Park in Los Angeles—deftly covered by the *Los Angeles Times*—included a contest of Olympic track and field stars designed to raise funds to send the athletes to the forthcoming games at Stockholm, Sweden. No strangers to public relations, Joe Miller and Edward Arlington saw to it that the Olympic Games Committee received a sizeable percentage of the advance ticket sales.[26]

The Millers spared no expense presenting this Wild West "as it was and as it is," and not as "fictionalists" and "eastern showmen" would imagine it, most certainly a reference to the Two Bills Show. This was the only show, management contended, that featured real western cowpunchers, and not eastern actors, being "organized in the West instead of the East, on fact instead of theory."[27] The 101 Ranch *Real*

Wild West, reported the *Santa Monica Outlook,* was most definitely not a circus, nor a mere vaudeville show, but rather a "Simon pure" Wild West show that came direct from the ranch at Bliss, Oklahoma. The *Los Angeles Times* described it in depth: "[It] is made up of as splendid specimens of cowboys and cowgirls as ever rode unbroken equines before a Los Angeles audience. Indians of both sexes, living in natural environment and performing the feats for which the race was noted, is another feature of the great show. . . . The numerous marksmen and equestrians of the aggregation are heralded as having no peers in the country"[28] There were no rings, observed the *Times,* and no tent. The acts were performed in "one great arena," and Miller asserted that his show had "that freedom of action and grace of motion" that could not be obtained in the confined rings of a circus.

This California extravaganza included the roping and riding of long-horned steers, an exhibition of Australian boomerang throwing, and displays of the punishing of horse thieves on ranches and cattle ranges. It featured the Cheyenne Champions, a "barbarous Mexico bull-ring sensation," football on horseback, a stampede, a round-up, and "sixty real Injuns." One of these Native Americans was "Princess Winona" who gave her usual remarkable exhibition with the rifle.

Of course, this "real" Wild West, although it was funded and sup-plied by a true working ranch, was a re-imagining of the frontier, just like Cody's, Lillie's, and to a lesser extent, Hafley's, Texas Bill's, and Texas Jack's. Audiences already had the suspension of belief required to watch reenactments of Pony Express adventures, Mexican rough riders prepare to cross the Rio Grande, and bloodless stampedes. Added to this were elements of a Wild West imported by Cody two decades earlier, such as Georgian Cossacks and parades, and the humorous aspects of vaudeville, such as clowns, trained donkeys, and cowboys who stood on their heads while on horseback. Despite its assurances that it was no circus in structure, the 101 certainly had circus elements, with sideshows and "freaks" such as bearded ladies and living human skeletons.

The 101 Ranch show and its prized shooter were as well received in San Francisco and the cities in between as they were in south-ern California. "Indian Princess Wenona the Favorite of Girls from Orphan Homes," blared the *San Francisco Chronicle,* which wrote that although the waifs screamed in delight at the cowgirls, cowboys, clowns, and animals, it was the Sioux Princess who shot glass balls from the back of a galloping horse who was their "pet."[29] By the end of the 1912 season, the retinue had toured 22 states and 3 Canadian provinces, staging 421 shows. The Wild West's exact profit is not recorded, but by August of that year, *Variety* noted that compared to most other circuses, the 101 was "cleaning up" and doing at least as well as the Two Bills.[30]

Wenona's former love, Frank Hafley, was not doing as well with his show. After she and Wayne left, California Frank's Wild West folded into the Mulhall Wild West, comprised of Colonel Zack, his son Charlie, and daughters Georgie, Mildrid, and Lucille—all trick riders, with the women destined to become famous equestriennes in the years to come—most famously, Lucille. Despite the addition of this talent, California Frank's show had problems breaking even. Although Miller had declined to have Frank Hafley's troupe along for his West Coast venture, Arlington was invested in it personally, and convinced Miller to let him brand it as "a smaller portion" of the 101 Ranch show.[31]

It was just not enough. "If Eddie Arlington was not a loser on the '101' venture," wrote *Variety*, "he did drop a roll with the California Frank attraction."[32] This was not the fault of either man. Wild West shows were extremely expensive to move around, and Hafley's show was plagued by costly rail car accidents. And while Bee Ho and Ada drifted back into Frank's fold in mid-1912, and Mamie had learned to shoot fairly well, the crowds wanted Wenona, and she was not there. Arlington, and the 101 by association, severed ties with California Frank's show sometime in the spring of 1912.

Lesser-known entrepreneurs like Con. T. Kennedy and Herbert A. Kline were happy to pick up Frank's show here and there throughout 1912 and 1913, but they were not connoisseurs of "true" Wild West. Kennedy and Kline were in the carnival business, and Hafley's troupe had to share billing with Rounds' Imperial Ladies Band Orchestra, Turpin and Schwartz's daredevil rides on their Motor Drome, Trixy the Six-Hundred-Pound Damsel, and John Ruhl's Flea Circus.

Ironically, the 101 Ranch's Wild West success in southern California also planted the seeds for its eventual demise, and that of Wild West extravaganzas in general. Its success led to a marriage between the Millers and entrepreneurs in the fledgling film industry, and though it would take another fifteen years or so, "moving pictures" and the western genre in particular, would permanently siphon away potential audiences from live shows. But for the time being, explains Michael Wallis, the Millers and their entertainers and animals provided ready-made content for the Bison Company production studio, founded by producer and director Thomas Harper Ince.

In 1911, when a Bison partner learned that the Miller Brothers' 101 Ranch Wild West show was in winter quarters at Venice, just a few miles from Edendale (a wide swath of land northwest of downtown Los Angeles), he paid Joe Miller a $1,000 deposit in exchange for film use of seventy-five cowboys, twenty-five cowgirls, and about thirty-five Indians and their wives. Additionally, the Bison people enlisted Jim Brooks, manager of the 101, who was a powerful ex-cowpuncher, able to rustle everybody up at sunrise and parade them up the coast to what would later be dubbed the Bison 101 Company.

The film outfit also gained use of twenty-four oxen, some bison, and a lot of horses, complete with trappings, as well as prairie schooners and stagecoaches.[33] It became a studio-ranch that specialized in westerns—the Millers started calling it "Inceville." Film titan Carl Laemmle eventually moved production units there too and produced his own westerns, which carried the 101 Bison brand name.[34] During the 1911–12 winter camp season, the Millers earned a cool $2,500 a week for the use of their cowboys and Indians and livestock.

Exhibitions like the 101 Ranch Wild West and the movies, wrote the *Fort Worth Star Telegram,* "have broken down the Indian's prejudice against being photographed." The Indians' natural dislike of being captured on film was a matter of curiosity and comment among transcontinental travelers, many of whom had their cameras snatched and broken by "irate Indian women." Among the Navajos and Pueblos, continued the *Telegram,* it was believed that the "devil machines" put a blight on children.

The 101 Bison filmmakers, on the other hand, never had any difficulty in securing the consent of an Indian to be photographed. In fact, according to the *Telegram,* Indian ranch performers competed to get their picture taken.[35] An "action" picture was preferred, and the Indian

America's Best Female Sharpshooter

"braves," as well as the girls, were constantly trying to excel each other in exciting and dangerous feats of horsemanship in order to attract the attention of director Miller.

Contrary to headlines, the "Indian" Wenona did not appear in Thomas Ince's thrilling recreations of Native American and pioneer conflict and reconciliation. Ince preferred actress Ann Little, whose real name was Mary Brooks, as his de facto Indian maiden—undoubtedly because of her stock theater experience, beauty, and youth (she was twenty-one in 1912). Her exotic, dark-eyed beauty was often in striking contrast to Grace Cunard's blonde-haired, blue-eyed "pioneer woman" character. Lillian Christy played some other Native American woman parts.

Wenona's age and less-than-lithesome figure may have prevented her from becoming a feature in 101 Bison films, but it is not likely she had much interest in participating. She loved to hear audiences scream with delight, not wait in the hot sun for hours at a time, readying to film one quick, artificial scene that would play to consumers she would never see or hear. Her friends Alf and Mae Rieckhoff thought she would reconsider and wrote Wenona a postcard with a picture of Bison star Tom Mix's house in Beverly Hills: "Wonderfull homes these movie show folks have, see this one of Tom Mix, cow puncher, he lived in a tent next to mine on the Cheyene [sic] Bill Wild West Show at Seattle. Who ever got such jack on a W. W. Show as Tom Mix gets in the movies[?] You should have gotten into this branch of the biz."[36]

Wenona would also most certainly have had mixed feelings about the way Native Americans were portrayed in film. This principle might seem improbable, given that she had completely hijacked a native American genealogy, but by 1915 she had spent the better part of her life living and working with Oglala Sioux. One of Wenona's friends was Luther Standing Bear, an advisor to Thomas Ince, who was adamant that Bison films were not depicting Indian life as it really was.

Wenona must have known of her co-workers' sensitivities to white actors playing Indians. "As I look back to my early-day experiences in making pictures," Standing Bear later reflected of his time with Ince, "I cannot help noting how we real Indians were held back, while white 'imitators' were pushed to the front." He complained to the director that not only were the actors and stories unnatural, but that most of the time, the costumes were not even correct. Although the Miller brothers and many performers in the 101 Ranch Real Wild West prided themselves on a program that was authentic, Ince blithely responded that the public would not know if it was not.[37]

To put an even finer point on things, there was a difference between actors who actually *lived* as Native Americans and those who simply put on garb and paint and spoke the stern, monosyllabic English that audiences had come to expect of Indians speaking English—a difference between those who adopted true tribal customs and language and those who used bastardized versions to appeal to non-Native consumers. Wenona's friend and coworker George "Eagle Eye" Fuerst appeared in many of Ince's films, and he had not one drop of Native American blood—he was one hundred percent German. But American Horse, a Sioux Nation chief, had truly adopted Fuerst when he was orphaned at fourteen years old. He was either fluent in or proficient with at least five different Native American dialects. Wenona was good friends with Fuerst and his wife, Neola, who was Seneca. But Neola, like other Native performers who were her friends, most certainly separated Wenona the person from Wenona the Indian. As her grandson put it, "Neola would privately roll her eyes" at and spit raspberries behind someone pretending to be an Indian.[38]

To be clear, Wenona would not have led any moral charge against the way Natives were hired for and portrayed in the burgeoning world of film—or Wild West shows, for that matter. Ethnocentricity simply was not a concern in the times she lived, nor did she see herself as a celebrity who should make moral pronouncements that resonated with anybody. And, of course, to do so would run counter to everything she purported to be, anyway.

Wenona agreed with the sentiment of her old love, Jim Kid Willoughby, who wrote "Once a Cowboy" sometime while he was in California. In this song, he presciently lamented film's replacement of the Wild West experience,

> You can have my chaps for I've quit my job
> And here are my spurs and saddle too.
> You can have my gun belt and old Betsy Colt.
> For there ain't a thing on the range to do.

The bellowing heard [*sic*] has strayed away,
And d——d if I know what to do;
Most every puncher that throwed a rope
Has gone to work for a picture show—
The hinges creak in the bunk-house door.
And there ain't no cook like there used to be.
Frying sow-belly and singing a tune,
And the Waddys as mad as they could be.
The bunch grass Susies in the lazy breeze.
And the blossom nod their head now
Where punchers shout whoopee.
But all of 'ems gone with a picture show.
And so I say you can have my chaps
And everything else of my outfit too.
Take my gun and cartridge belt.
There is no place for a buckaroo.
I know the trail from Wyoming up,
I have worked in sunshine, rain and snow.
There is a damn few of us left.
Who in hell invented the picture show.[39]

Wenona also agreed with Edith Tantlinger, who said in a 1920s interview that movies had killed the Wild West show even before the Great War: "Movies had no real cowboys. Supers hired by the day, in chaps and sombrero that a real cowpuncher would not be caught dead in, spoiled the dare-devil spirit of the west. . . . For they have cranked the Wild West out of America."[40] The Tantlingers noted that they had learned a thing or two from acting in the occasional movie, and that the "action" and "spirit" and "color" of the Wild West—itself an imitation of something—would never be captured in film. Incorrectly, they predicted the demise of Hollywood's attempt to capture the West.

But again, the sharpshooter's reasons for not participating in the new world of film are simpler than all this. The limitations and rigors of filmmaking in its infancy, especially for Ince's westerns, meant that there was a lot of standing around for long hours, waiting for film to load and scenes to commence. Also, there would have been no opportunities for Wenona to do rapid shooting, because the storylines typically did not call for it, and following her on a galloping horse while shooting was impossible in those days of the stationary camera.

Thus, in April 1912, Wenona happily traveled to northern California, performing near many of her old stomping grounds with Beasley, the Tantlingers, and the various tribesmen and tribeswomen who did not stay in Inceville. The press still referred to Wenona as the "Sioux girl" in spite of the fact that she was forty-one. Her death-defying acts of shooting from the back of a galloping horse far surpassed any of those attempted by younger performers—anywhere.

No one in the 101 Wild West knew how events unfolding overseas were about to affect them personally and professionally.

Chapter Seven
THE GIRL IN CALIFORNIA

Their rivalry fuels arguments to this day among the
cognoscenti. Suffice it to say, both were remarkably
talented, and both had a take-no-prisoners intensity
toward their artistry with guns and ammunition.

R. L. Wilson, of Oakley and Smith,
Silk and Steel: Women at Arms, 2003

In the spring of 1913, Oglala Sioux war chief Iron Tail jumped from
the Two Bills Show to the Miller 101 Wild West. By this time, Cody's
poor management skills and taste for reckless investment had taken
a toll, and the Two Bills Show was on the verge of disaster. By the
time the Lillie-Cody show closed for good that summer, Joe Miller had
already publicized Iron Tail as part of the 101 family so much that it
was hard to imagine he had ever been elsewhere. The Sioux chief was
also now the face on the Treasury Department's famous "Indian head
buffalo" nickel—something Miller played up in April 1913, at the 101's
first show of the season.

At this time, Wenona, the 101's other famous "Indian," was nursing a temporary hurt—she and Beasley separated when he decided
to move to Europe. Imitating Buffalo Bill, the Miller brothers and
Arlington decided to make the 101 a global extravaganza. The previous winter, they had negotiated a deal with Hans Stosch-Sarrasani,
owner of the "grandest show ever seen in Europe." Based at a six-
thousand-seat arena in Dresden, Germany, the circus featured a broad

range of attractions such as wild-animal acts, tumblers, jugglers, and a complete Wild West show.[1] Stosch-Sarrasani requested the services of some "real Sioux Indians" in the hopes of making his European tour more authentic. The Millers complied by dispatching fifty Oglala Sioux under the stewardship of Beasley.

The cowboy left for Germany on March 5, 1913, with a stopover in Britain for a performance at Crystal Palace, London. How Beasley and Wenona parted is unrecorded, but this was the last time the shooter saw him for at least seven years—maybe ever. While in Europe, the cowboy met Miss Elsie Harvey, a British actress with German citizenship, almost as soon as he landed there. The two married in 1914, and this is likely the reason Beasley was able to stay in Europe with Stosch-Sarrasani and later Circus Orlando, long after his American mates had been expelled. Beasley eventually returned to the United States with his wife, and died in 1926, in relative obscurity.

Almost immediately after Beasley sailed from America, Wenona took up with an Oglala Sioux named William Eagle Shirt—or so the story went. "Some of the best shooting in the 101 Wild West," reported a newspaper in Fort Scott, Kansas, "is accomplished by a Sioux Indian girl, who is known among her people as Princess Wenona, although her real name is Mrs. Com. Eagle Shirt."[2] This pairing played beautifully into a yet another revised biography for Wenona, which was clearly the creative fiction of smaller-town papers trying to fill space—though certainly neither Wenona nor anyone at the 101 refuted it. Mr. and Mrs. Eagle Shirt were, according to this story, childhood sweethearts, and had eloped in their teens: "The wanderings of the pair and the necessity for providing for themselves, developed Princess Wenona's cleverness as a sure-shot, and on her return to the tribe, where once her father had ruled as head chief, she became the champion rifle shot of the tribe." Her shooting, the story concluded, took the crowd to its feet every time.[3]

William "Good Lance" Eagle Shirt was an intriguing man to be paired with. After Tom Ince became principal director for Bison Films in Los Angeles, he hired the twenty-seven-year-old as one of the first Indian actors to play major roles.[4] He was born on a portion of the Great Sioux Reservation in South Dakota that would later become known as the Pine Ridge Reservation—Wenona's purported place of birth.

Eagle Shirt spent his early life on the Great Plains until his family was forced to settle on the reservation in 1889. While living there, he married a woman named Mottie; they had a daughter, Bessie. He joined the Miller Brothers Wild West Show some time around 1910. In 1912, Eagle Shirt was quartered with the other Oglala actors on the Bison lot in Inceville.

The first film in which Eagle Shirt was credited as an actor was *War on the Plains,* an epic two-reeler directed by Ince and released by Bison on February 23, 1912. A milestone in western film history, its scenario was actually written by Eagle Shirt, too. *War on the Plains* also starred Francis Ford, the brother of director John Ford, and famed cowpuncher Art Acord, both regulars in Ince's early films. Eagle Shirt acted in other films, including 1913's *The Heart of an Indian* and 1912's *Battle of the Red Men,* for which he also wrote the scenario. His scores of starring roles included *The Invaders,* made in 1912 for Ince's Kay-Bee film company and directed by Ince and Francis Ford.

As noted above, Eagle Shirt was not really married to Wenona. Their romance was a fire lighted by the film company's press corps with flames stoked by *Billboard,* and neither performer had reason to dispute it. Wenona dutifully signed postcards advertising the two of them as "Wenona & William Eagle Shirt."[5] It is true that Eagle Shirt divorced his first wife, Hattie, around 1911, and would remarry in 1917 or so. But the handsome man stayed in Hollywood when most of the 101, including Wenona, went back on tour in mid-1912. He split his time between southern California and Oklahoma, where the 101 started its own motion picture company. Additionally, the Sioux actor had two small children still on the Pine Ridge reservation in South Dakota—it seems unlikely that Wenona and Eagle Shirt even had so much as had a dalliance.

Between 1912 and 1915, the 101 Ranch Real Wild West wended its way through America, performing in as many cities and towns as possible. Wenona may have crossed paths with her sister, who was performing with a subsidiary of Yankee Robinson's Circus called Texas Bill's Wild West—ironically owned by an Englishman. No doubt, Nellie's handlers took a page from Wenona's book. "Indian Princess Coming," blared papers like the *Hobart Daily Republican:* "Among the Indians with the Texas Bill's Wild West . . . is Princess 'Kiowa,' noted as one of the greatest rifle shots and rope throws in the world. This is her first season on tour. She appears at every season of the Wild West and is delighted with her first trip through civilization."[6] Yankee Robinson's did not bother with a full-fledged biography for Nellie—imitators of Wenona rarely got one—but it did make sure that spectators knew that, just like big sister years earlier, "Kiowa" knew English fluently, and would be glad to engage in conversation with ladies visiting its Indian Camp.

From the beginning of the 1909 season until the advent of the Great War in Europe, writes Wallis, the 101 Ranch remained a steady income producer for the Millers. Profits ranged from a low $47,000 in 1909 to a high of $200,000 in 1915—equivalent to more than $4 million today. Revenue spiked in 1913, after the Two Bills Show filed for bankruptcy in July, and Buffalo Bill and Pawnee Bill left the circuit forever.[7] In August, all three Miller brothers attended the Buffalo Bill sale in Denver, where they purchased seventy-eight of his best show horses for pennies on the dollar, and most of his arena stock, wardrobe and costumes, a lighting plant, and a good amount of other capital.[8]

Because of these acquisitions and good ticket sales wherever they went the Miller brothers decided that, in spite of their losses in Europe, they would push forward with plans for the 1915 season. As Wallis explains, they threw caution to the wind and put out two 101 Ranch Wild West shows. One of them was a traveling production that opened on April 10 at Hot Springs, Arkansas. This show highlighted the horse and cowboy feats learned on the 101 Ranch at Bliss.

To be sure, the extravaganza was still hair-raising, with the usual violent bronco-busting and buffalo stampedes. It had the typical parades of Cossacks and Mexicans, and cowboys and cowgirls "dressed as they appear in real life or the arena." This branch of the Wild West Show featured a former cowboy named Jess Willard, the "Pottawatomie Giant," a boxer who had just beaten Jack Johnson in Havana, Cuba, and taken the heavyweight champion title of the world.[9]

The 101's primary show, however, made its way to San Francisco, where on February 20, 1915, it opened the Panama-Pacific International Exposition. It was held to commemorate the opening of the Panama Canal in 1914, which had brought the city closer commercially to the Atlantic ports of North and South America, Exposition boosters told Joe Miller that it was expected to draw more than thirteen million visitors during its yearlong run. This number turned out to be nineteen million, in about ten months' time. The fair featured eleven exhibition palaces showcasing objects from every corner of the globe, more than fifteen hundred sculptures commissioned from artists all over the world, sixty-five acres of amusement concessions, and an aviation field. Fifty California counties, forty-eight states, and twenty-one countries mounted displays in the exposition's grand pavilions.[10]

Wild West performances were planned for an arena at "Rainbow City," which was built beside the Presidio, once a garrison for Spanish soldiers and now a sprawling U.S. military reservation. The arena was at the terminus of the "Joy Zone," the amusement Midway of the fair—there were also zones for science, education, and technology, and ethnological exhibits. One of the most prominently featured acts of the Joy Zone was, of course, Wenona.

The "Princess" was so long and well entrenched in her persona now, at age forty-four, that people remembered her as a Sioux orphan growing up in California. *Sunset Magazine* writer Frances Groff, when penning her in-depth article about the Exposition in 1915, mentioned that she got to catch up with her friends Eagle Eye and Wenona. "The Princess Wenona," she wrote, "is a pleasant-faced, sweet-mannered, soft-voiced woman who would live in a tepee if she had a million dollars and who wants to be in the show game until she passes on."[11] Groff intimated that Wenona's appearance at the Exposition was a homecoming of sorts, since she had made her first public appearance at nearby Woodward's Gardens.

It would have been hard for Groff to "remember" otherwise. San Francisco's press corps was determined to embrace its prodigal Sioux daughter, and simultaneously, assist Exposition boosters in "feminizing" the fair. Newspapers mentioned Wenona's crack shooting in passing, along with the other exotic offerings at the Exposition, but all this was completely overshadowed by a *San Francisco Chronicle* story that newspapers nationwide immediately lapped up: "The adoption of a little white child by Princess Wenona, an Indian squaw who gives some crack rifle shooting demonstrations at the '101 Ranch' on the Joy Zone of the exposition, has aroused a storm of protest that threatens to bring the Indian life of the little youngster to a speedy termination." Several people had made complaints to Secretary M. J. White of San Francisco Society for Prevention of Cruelty to Children."[12] Furthermore, reported the *Chronicle,* notice was sent to the 101 that the child must be returned to its mother, allegedly an old friend of Wenona's on whom she took pity.

Hundreds of newspapers across the United States printed the same version of the story, along with a large photo of Wenona smiling while holding a cranky-looking one-and-a-half-year-old, of indeterminate gender: "Princess Wenona and her foster white child—Fulfilling an old vow of friendship made many years ago, 'Princess' Wenona, a Sioux squaw who is exhibiting her wonderful rifle marksmanship on the Zone at the Panama exposition, has adopted the child of Lillian Clayton. Mrs. Clayton had known the squaw as a girl. Sick, without money and discouraged, she recently went to the exposition to find work. There she met the squaw, who proved her willingness to help the friend of many years ago by taking the child to raise while the mother went to the hospital."[13]

Oddly, Secretary White's action seems to have come before the flurry of syndicated reports of Wenona's adoption of the "babe." This suggests that perhaps there was a kernel of truth to the story, and the 101's public relations machine quickly played it to the hilt. Years later, when the *Ponca City (Okla.) News* was discussing Wenona's death and funeral, it lamented that she had no known relatives, at least in that part of the country, and that "A son has not been heard from for several years." This could have referred to some tot brought to the Ranch for a short time.[14]

If Wenona brought a child to Oklahoma, it really was a temporary act of kindness or fascination, because Wenona had never shown any interest in caretaking beyond certain animals. Whether or not the markswoman really tried to adopt a child mattered much less than the impression that she had. It softened her image a bit, and gave the illusion that she was younger than she was. Also, phrases found in the syndicated article prompted the idea of the "civilizing" force of whites, which was especially present in the Exposition's imperialistic motifs. For instance, she was observed "crooning a strange lullaby and pressing her own brown cheek against the white baby in her arms." And:

"pleasure seekers have seen this woman with her heritage of stoicism give away to raptures of endearment."

On a grander level, Wenona-as-mother was a perfect companion story for the feminine, virtuous patina that Exposition officials were trying to lend their city this year. While the Exposition was officially a celebration of the opening of the Panama Canal, it was widely regarded as an opportunity to demonstrate the city's resilience in the wake of a devastating 1906 earthquake, and its rehabilitation into world-class status.[15]

As early as 1910, San Francisco's business elite had pledged four million dollars to the exhibition, and thanks in large part to efforts of the newspaper magnate William Randolph Hearst, the San Francisco Police Commission enacted strict ordinances that shut down prostitution, saloon dancing, and females working or drinking in saloons at all.

The *San Francisco Examiner* explained this crusade as a way to shut down the market of "immoral and vulgar pleasure" and replace it with "a great market for wholesome and decent fun."[16] To say that Wenona was an unattached female who needed to be made "wholesome" is a stretch, but the alleged adoption was a windfall for 101 Ranch and Exposition public relations workers—to not play it up would be a missed opportunity. There was already a widely circulated press release about the 101 cowgirls—who were just as daring and competent as their male counterparts—adding a much-needed "feminine touch" to the exhibition.

The 101 troupe packed up on June 14, 1915, and got ready to move on. For about a month, the Exposition had been paying the 101 $3,000 a week directly, so it could offer free tickets to orphans and poor patrons. Like any other show, it began to wane, so the Panama-Pacific Exposition replaced the Wild West with Colonel Cummins's reenactment of the Seige of the Alamo, and with "Custer's Last Charge" as an after-show.

The main section of the 101 troupe left for Erie, Pennsylvania, to join the road version of the 101, which still had Jess Willard as its main attraction. Many of the ropers and cowboys stayed on to work for Cummins, including Bee Ho's brother Weaver Gray, Skeeter Bill and his wife Dorothy Morrell, and Pedro Leon, who earlier this year had lassoed an ailing sea lion out of the surf in Santa Monica, and veterinarian E. J. Webber, who had a penchant for marrying young women in the various cities the 101 visited. Forty Mexicans and an equal number of Native Americans stayed with Cummins, too.[17]

Wenona went off on her own for a few months. She headlined at the Hippodrome and Orpheum in San Francisco over the summer, and in the Los Angeles Hippodrome in the fall. "If the Princess Winona [*sic*] were in Europe at the present time," said the *Los Angeles Times,* "there would be bidders aplenty for her services among the warring countries. She 'knocks the spots out' of almost everything that is presented on the Hippodrome stage."[18] For a few weeks beginning December 11, 1915, Wenona was a featured attraction at Los Angeles' Prosperity Carnival and Indoor Fair, set up at the Old Boston Store building in downtown. She brought a "miniature Wild West" with her, which probably consisted of some trained horses, but most certainly included her beloved piebald pony, Rabbit.

For the first time in her career, Wenona's presence was overshadowed by other acts—novelties, rather—such as one featuring Prince Ludwig, the thirty-one inch tall "aristocratic resident of Midget City," and others with trained cats and "Moorish girls" portraying exotic dances from the Far East. The crack shooter might have blanched at the grand picture of her and Rabbit in the *Los Angeles Times* because it was slapped together with one of Jane Greene, contestant for Carnival Queen.[19]

Boosters of San Diego's Panama–California Exhibition made slightly more noise about Wenona's attendance there in the spring of 1916. The *Evening Tribune* reminded its readers that Wenona used to be a household name in California, as Lillian F. Smith, the California Girl. "She made records in the state with a 22-cal. rifle that have never been beaten, and which she is able to repeat at the present day."[20]

San Diego's performance run marked the last time the California Girl was in her home state.

Chapter Eight
SUNLIGHT IN OKLAHOMA

Riding on her broncho, she shoots with such dexterity
and skill from the most difficult angles and positions,
that it staggers the human imagination.
Pittsburgh Daily Post, about Wenona, July 2, 1916

"Princess Wenona, a few lines from you would be appreciated,"
wrote "Whistling Annie," *Billboard*'s gossip columnist on
October 28, 1916. The shooter's name had been missing from newsprint while she was pondering which touring company to join. But
after leaving San Diego, Wenona joined Pawnee Bill's Wild West again,
avoiding the uncertainty of the 101 Ranch's show, which was going
through some interesting changes.

Although the 1915 season was one of its most prosperous ones, with
a net profit of more than $200,000, the Miller brothers knew it was a
fluke. Michael Wallis notes that they credited the season's substantial
financial success to the increase in foreign money entering the United
States in exchange for war supplies; more disposable cash became
available to the public, who used it on shows and other leisure activities.

Jess Willard, the boxer, left the 101 at the end of the 1915 season
tour to headline at the Sells-Floto circus. Suspicious of unstable conditions around the globe, Joe Miller recognized the importance of finding
another major celebrity name for the 1916 season. He found it in the form
of "a living metaphor for the way generations of Americans imagined the
Wild West"—William F. "Buffalo Bill" Cody, a former fierce competitor.[1]

Day after day, the old Colonel, once on his horse, rode out as proudly as ever. He never missed a parade or performance that season, and even shot glass balls from the saddle every time he was called up.

Cody and Joe Miller redesigned their Wild West. It was now called "Buffalo Bill and 101 Ranch Wild West Combined, with the Military Pageant [of] Preparedness." The term "preparedness" had become a popular catchword by 1916, as more and more Americans found it difficult to follow President Wilson's neutrality stance in the face of global warfare.

For the 101, this meant that the show became more of a military spectacle, and less of a frontier-conquering diorama. Cody and Miller convinced the United States War Department that regular army troops were needed for the program, and the army immediately saw the recruiting value of exposing large audiences to a show made up of 101 Ranch riders, Buffalo Bill Cody, and "an army of Uncle Sam's gallant defenders of Old Glory."[2]

Was the addition of Cody the reason Wenona decided not to rejoin the 101 show that year? Maybe. Buffalo Bill had given the shooter her national and international celebrity decades earlier, as he had scores of others over his lifetime. But she could not have forgotten how he deserted her for the Butlers. Moreover, Wenona, who had always made every single shot count, would have been appalled by the "booming of field artillery and the crack of carbines and revolver shots" unleashed by veteran cavalrymen in a bizarre hybrid of frontier and modern warfare.

Gordon Lillie, on the other hand, offered Wenona her usual salary to join his tried-and-true Pioneer Days, a scaled-down version of his shows of years past. Pawnee's producers created moveable scenery that could be set up in any real small town to mimic an 1870s Oklahoma Territory village. "The cowboys, cowgirls, Indians and Mexicans are there," wrote *Billboard*, "giving the usual exhibitions of shooting, bucking horse riding, lariat throwing, etc."[3] Most importantly for performers like Wenona and bucking horse champ Lulu Parr, who had also joined, each scene was specifically tailored to their specialties.

The year 1916 proved to be a strange one for the world of Wild Wests in general, and for Wenona-Lillian personally. In May, Chief Iron Tail, her one-time 101 cohort, became sick on a passenger train somewhere after leaving Fort Wayne, Indiana, and died on May 29, shortly after he arrived in Chicago. On December 9, Wenona's first love, Jim

"Kid" Willoughby passed away. Oddly enough, it was from a quick bout of pneumonia, and not from the horrendous fall he took over a two-hundred-foot cliff near Los Angeles, which had laid him up for eighteen weeks. "I got five big holes in my head, the back cords of my neck torn loose from my skull, five ribs broke, my right knee dislocated, my nose broke, and my lower jaw fractured," he wrote a friend in Cheyenne, but he had "growed back" and was looking forward to working again.[4] Willoughby was a crew member on the iconic movie *Birth of a Nation* shortly before he died.

All three Miller brothers spent most of the summer of 1916 in and out of hospitals with influenza. Their inability to promote the show aggressively, coupled with inclement weather and an virulent epidemic of polio around Ponca City, caused crowds to dwindle for the 101's Wild West.

And toward the end of 1916, in spite of his recent 101 performances and his insistence to the contrary, Colonel Buffalo Bill Cody was dying. A clipping from a North Platte newspaper dated December 23 announced that Cody, who had been very ill for several days in Denver, "at one time being reported near death," was improving. But those in the Wild West circuit, particularly those in the 101, knew better. The man who had once leaped on and off a bronc, racing at full speed, did not even have the strength to pull himself into the saddle of a gentle, standing mount.[5] Those in the business knew that the creator of re-creation had only weeks to live. He died on January 10, 1917.

Wenona dutifully performed for Pawnee Bill's "Pioneer Days" in 1916. It was a crowded lineup. Lillie had recently discovered and signed Canadian "bronc buster" Leonard Stroud. In addition to Parr, he introduced female "cowpunch" Babe Willets, and one Nellie Burgess, "a Mexican," joined as a trick rider. Taking advantage of General Pancho Villa's attack on New Mexico in March 1916, Lillie hired Mexicans who had allegedly served under Villa to help re-create the raid and the subsequent American response.

But Wenona could not regain the publicity toehold she once enjoyed with Pawnee Bill. If a spotlight needed to be placed on a female from his show, Gordon Lillie made sure it was squarely on his wife, May. Lillie had fully intended to showcase Wenona as in seasons past, but now he was absent from the day-to-day operations of his live performances, distracted by personal issues. In 1916, he and May adopted a child and named him Billy. Following in the footsteps of his neighbors the Miller Brothers, Gordon also began to diversify his investments, opening an oil refinery in Yale, Indian Territory, Oklahoma, and raising cattle. But besides raising their son, the most important thing in the lives of the Lillies was the conservation of buffalo. The result of Pawnee Bill's distraction would be to introduce Wenona to a new mate.

In the fall of 1879, the Pawnees had made their last buffalo hunt, and Gordon Lillie accompanied them and captured four young ones. It was then and there that the impresario made up his mind to preserve this magnificent beast for posterity. In the mid-1880s, after they married and moved to their land on Blue Hawk Peak in Osage County, Oklahoma, the Lillies began breeding these four buffalo with hand-picked mates orphaned from other herds. By 1914, primarily because of May's skill in running a ranch, the couple owned more than two hundred head of buffalo. They were used in Lillie and Cody's film ventures, but also in yearly hunts, which culled out sick and aging animals whose meat was sold to prominent buyers all over the nation. The money raised and the publicity served to advertise the plight of the American buffalo, and the need for conservation.

Someone else was keenly interested in Pawnee Bill's buffalo herds, too—someone who would become one of Wenona's longest relationships. "His chief fame," wrote the *Perry (Oklahoma) Journal* of Emil Lenders, "rests on his ability to paint a buffalo and [he] is credited with being the only artist being able to make the hair really stand out on the animal." The buffalo was his primary lure, but by 1916 Lenders was well established as the preeminent painter of wolves, Indians, and wild horses.

Lenders, prepossessing with his trademark long flowing hair, put his heart and soul into his work, writes Michael Wallis. To know his subjects, he routinely traveled around the nation with Wild West shows, and mingled with their various Indian tribes. He learned some Indian dialects and he was supposedly an honorary member of at least five clans.[6]

This passion for authenticity is evident in the painstaking notes the artist took during his travels with natives during the first decades of the twentieth century. His foreword to the notes read, "All references to Indians mean those I saw in the buffalo and fighting days [the

America's Best Female Sharpshooter

1880s], which are far different personages from what we have today, influenced by the white race who, like all half civilized people, took all of the vices and few of the virtues of the white man's civilization. I came into contact with some old Indians whose life history would make a dime novel look like a nursery story."[7]

Born Emil von Lendershausen in 1864 to German parents in either London or Berlin, he always told friends that Native American Indians had fascinated him since he was a little boy, and early on was determined to travel to the United States. He may have attended a court school in southern Germany, and he claimed to have studied with Karl von Piloty, the most successful academic painter in Germany at that time. Despite his mother's disapproval, Lenders attended the Berlin Art School. He also tried to become a stage actor in his teens, much to the dismay of his family, who wanted him to pursue something more practical.

Unable to reconcile his parents' expectations with his own, Lenders sailed to the United States in 1887, and three years later, married a widowed German in Chicago. This marriage was short-lived for some reason, and he made his way to Philadelphia, where he soon found work painting the pets of upscale patrons. In December 1895, he married Miss Eva Day of Philadelphia, whom he may have met in a local dramatic production, and in November of the following year, the couple had a daughter. Sadly, the baby died at age eleven months. Another daughter, Eva Rita, was born to the couple in August 1898. In addition to painting and breeding dachshunds, Lenders was an active city council member. Still, he felt confined in the city, and yearned to see the wide-open plains and western sunlight he read about. Soon, the artist was leaving Pennsylvania on longer and longer sojourns west, returning with sketches and paintings of Pawnee, Sac and Fox, Osage and Sioux, Comanche, Ponca, and many other tribes.

This did not sit well with Eva. She was alone much of the time with a young child, and often when Emil did return, he brought members of the tribes he had painted. Her Quaker upbringing allowed her to have no problem with the fact that her husband welcomed people of color into their home. Rather, her irritation was that Emil seemed to identify more and more as one of them—this ran counter to her religion's resistance to "fakery," one of the reasons she stopped participating in theatrical productions, and most certainly the reason she refused to go with him to that theatrical incubator, the 101 Ranch, when he started to visit there regularly.

Ironically, it was Eva Lenders who introduced her husband to showman Pawnee Bill, whose wife she knew from their shared Quaker background in Philadelphia. Nonetheless, no one looked askance at Eva's absence the weekend of December 16, 1910, when Lenders attended the Lillies' monstrous housewarming parties. Gordon and May celebrated the completion of their new palatial home at Blue Hawk Peak, a hilly spot overlooking a bend in the Black Bear River in Pawnee, Oklahoma.

At this housewarming party, Lenders found himself in an "inner circle" of unique men and women—Pawnee Chief White Eagle, Joe Miller, old-time boomers, ranchers, farmers, and businessmen. There were other important western artists there, such as Edward Willard Deming, Charles Schreyvogle, and Henry H. Cross, all masters of painting the disappearing frontier. Buffalo Bill was given the distinction of hunting down and shooting an unruly bull that was upending the Lillies' herd, accompanied by the entire party and select Osage and Pawnee Indians.

Lenders, earlier this year, had sold an unprecedented number of Native American artifacts he had gathered since the end of the nineteenth century. John Pierpont Morgan paid the artist $30,000 for his collection of thousands of items, including extremely rare buffalo hide shields, costumes, and war relics from Apache, Sioux, Cheyenne, Kiowa, Blackfeet, Cree, Pawnee and other tribes. This money, coupled with his earnings from real estate ventures back in Philadelphia, made Lenders fairly well-off, if not rich. Thus, he started thinking about putting permanent roots down in Oklahoma.

"I found sunlight in Oklahoma," Lenders was fond of saying. He also found a home at the 101 Ranch. The Millers' prairie empire, Wallis writes, provided Lenders with the subjects he was looking for as an artist—cowboys and cowgirls, herds of bison, cattle and horses, wild game, and several Indian tribes dwelling nearby.[8] He was consumed with preserving the West the way it once was, especially the buffalo, and determined to paint the grand animals for posterity.

Lenders and Wenona met at Cummins' Indian Congress at the Pan-American Exhibition, but at that time the shooter was involved with Hafley, and Lenders was more interested in meeting Chiricahua

Apache chief Geronimo. As Lenders tells the story, he found the chief in a talkative mood one day, and asked him "if he was ever sorry about all the people he had killed in his life." Geronimo answered him by way of sign language: only once, when he "caught a young Mexican in Arizona, stripped him to the skin, and tied him with feet up and head down to a pole or sapling, his head being directly over an anthill, and then rode on and left him."[9] Fifteen years later at the 101, Lenders and Wenona met again.

Through 1916, Lenders continued to travel back and forth between Ponca City and Philadelphia, even fulfilling his alderman duties in the latter. But by the end of the year, he was in Oklahoma nearly full-time, much to the chagrin of his wife and teenaged child.

In April 1917, with the announcement of the United States' entry into WWI, the 101 Ranch's younger residents and performers waited nervously to see if they would have to leave for service. Despite this anxiety, and the black cloud of Cody's death still hanging low, a paycheck was a paycheck, and anyone who could went out with Pawnee Bill's Pioneer Days. Wenona gamely and ably performed, especially at Luna Park, Coney Island.

Still, the Sioux pretender was tired and bored. At forty-six, Wenona was already about ten years older than most seasoned cowboys and cowgirls residing on the Ranch, and also those traveling with Pawnee Bill's outfit. She loved her horses and shooting—her eyesight was still particularly good, given her age and occupational hazards—but hated getting up so early in the morning and sharing cramped living quarters on the road. When she returned to her tiny cottage on the 101 grounds at the end of the 1917 season, she and Lenders may have commiserated about the aches and pains of traveling.

Brothers H. R. and Irving J. Polack had approached Wenona while she was in Pittsburgh with Pawnee Bill, in the fall of 1917. These men, once owners of a vaudeville and tabloid agency, and then a traveling carnival, sought an act that would marry the successful elements of Wild West shows with a more contained one-ring format. They thought Wenona and her command of animals big and small would be a perfect headliner for their "20 Big Shows" outfit, and offered her a handsome salary.

The "princess" needed a manager, and Lenders was happy to oblige. The artist placed an advertisement in *Billboard*'s March 9, 1918 issue, which called for trick riders, ropers, bucking horse riders, high school riders, Indians, and feature western acts; also canvas men, light men, and property men, to be a part of Princess Wenona's Western Show, to open in the South and run thirty weeks from the end of March. At some point, the Polacks added a "mind-reading mule" to the act. "The show will be a model one," Lenders said, "with lots of new ideas, everything brand new and no money will be spared to make the outfit perfect to the smallest detail."[10]

Polack Bros. 20 Big Shows and Wenona's new western congregation opened in Salisbury, North Carolina to the usual fluffy acclaim given to smaller-region events, earning "the most phenomenal business ever recorded for a town of 20,000 population." *Billboard* exclaimed: "L. W. Lenders [*sic*], featuring Princess Wenona, the famous horseback rifle and pistol shot, has a high-class Wild West show."

The show closed after a successful three months' engagement at Marlin Park, in Pottsville, Pennsylvania, on August 29. Because the federal government had taken control of the railroads during World War I, lines were often cancelled or changed at the last minute, or not operating at all. So Wenona and Lenders's show had to be moved to winter quarters by motor trucks. Riding horseback, "Princess" Wenona and two male employees drove the stock necessary for the fair engagements from Pottsville to the Philadelphia County Fair grounds, a distance of 140 miles, counting detours, and sometimes over the rough mountain trails, "a feat of endurance for the little Indian woman on her little pony."[11] The trip took two and a half days. Wenona arrived on the fair grounds early Monday morning and did her horseback shooting act the same afternoon.

Because of worsening railroad conditions, the couple had to cancel her southern circuit of fairs. Consequently, Lenders ordered sufficient trucks and trailers to go out the next season independent of the railroads. In all likelihood, he purchased some cars and equipment from Frank Hafley, who was trying to remain solvent after purchasing his "Diamond D Ranch," four hundred acres near Ridgway, Colorado. An advertisement for the railway car *Mamie Francis* describes the kind of accommodations Wenona was accustomed to: "Private end, with state room and drawing room, closets etc.; also eight lower and upper berths for Performers, with toilet and wash room, kitchen and range and dishes, dish racks, etc.; pantry off kitchen can be used for dining room, three-tier ice chest on platform, four possum bellies, water tanks for 500 gallons water, two heating systems, Steam and Baker hot water system. Car is 75 feet over all, steel wheels, 8-inch channel beam from draw head to draw head, steel platform; pass M. C. M. on any road."[12] The difference between the days when Wenona might have shared a car like this with Frank or even with Wayne Beasley was that she and Emil would most certainly have had to offset the $2,000 cost by stuffing every performer they could in the car.

Wenona was certainly glad to have a partner who watched her back. On November 10, while she and all the performers were participating in a "peace parade" in Somerton, Pennsylvania, burglars smashed open a storeroom at the Wild West's winter quarters. The men savagely killed the watchdog on hand, and took everything of value, including two gold-plated rifles that the Winchester Arms Company had given Wenona, a gold-plated target-pistol presented to her by Smith & Wesson, a finely carved leather saddle with a silver plaque that was gifted to Lenders by William Cody, and many other valuable and sentimental items. Worse, the thieves drove away with their loot in Wenona's private touring car. When Lenders returned to the grounds at 10 P.M. and discovered the theft, he contacted a friend of his who was chief of police, who wired every law-enforcement official within sixty miles, and the burglars were ultimately apprehended in New Jersey the following morning.[13] Had the crooks damaged her belongings or managed to sell them, it would have been ruinous—there was no such thing as insurance for Wild West outfits.

It is not clear what attracted Lenders to Wenona, besides the thrill and ease of traveling with someone else who could not care less if he tramped off for a day or two, exploring the cities to which they traveled. To be sure, both had failed at least once with traditional marriages and were never going to be ones who were comfortable with societal norms. An undated entry from one of Lenders's diaries clearly shows his feelings toward what he perceived as "typical" white females, "There is no doubt but that some enterprising squaws filled the body of a stripped prisoner of war with pitch pine splinters and set 'em fire. Even their white sisters would be willing to do far worse to their friends if they were not under the protection of the law, and figuratively speaking

they stick every day their tongue pine splinters in their friends meanwhile smiling at them benevolently and patting them on the back and
setting the other pine splinters on fire."[14] Wenona and Lenders may
simply have been attracted to each other, but perhaps they also got
along so well because they were used to living unconventional lives.

Wenona and Lenders liked to visit Indian reservations when they
were near them at their stops. Lenders would visit with tribal elders,
and the shooter would visit schools, entertaining the kids and handing
out free tickets to the Native American students. The Polack brothers
secured a fairly lucrative series of dates in Ontario, Canada, and the
Great Lakes region of the United States during August 1919, and while
in Brantford, Ontario, Wenona entertained some two hundred children of the Mohawk tribe. The show was steadily growing—*Billboard*
noted that it had grown from five horses to eighteen, that "Manager
Lenders" was always on the lookout for anything that would strengthen
or improve the attraction, and that the two would enjoy a bright future
together.[15] The next month, while in Erie, Pennsylvania, Lenders took
the liberty of purchasing two well-trained snow-white horses with
money Wenona had earned in an exceptionally popular Detroit show.

Still, it surprised few that Wenona and Lenders suddenly opted
out of continuing their show, despite talks of a contract with Con T.
Kennedy. The markswoman was nearing fifty years of age, and had
been performing rigorously much longer than most human beings
could ever have withstood. Lenders was at least fifty-five years old,
and wanted to grow old in Oklahoma. The couple sold some of their
show accoutrement to Honest Bill's Wild West, and rented a small
house in Bliss, a 101 Ranch town in Noble County. The two referred to
themselves as a married couple in the 1920 census, but bigamously, as
Emil was still wedded to Eva.

"What do the queen of the sawdust ring and the well known painter
of western horses do when they settle down to vacation time?" asked
the *Joplin Globe* on December 4, 1921, "They raise chickens, forty
acres of them." Wenona had purchased the poultry farm about two
years earlier, when "she and her husband decided that life for them was
the farm life," and desired to make this permanent.[16] Indeed, in 1922,
they managed to get the 101 Ranch Trust to grant them twenty acres
on land south of Bliss.[17] Like so many other performers and ranchers

America's Best Female Sharpshooter

and oilmen, they were living on land swindled from the Ponca tribe by the Miller brothers. If Emil Lenders once thought a great deal about the concept of Europeans taking land away from native dwellers, he felt no compunction about it here and now. In an undated note from the turn of the twentieth century, he had written,

> We stole every inch of land we have from the Indians. The white man was always a step ahead of the Indian. First came the conquistadores and the Indian arrows dropped off them, for their shirts were made in the blacksmith's shop.
>
> Then other Europeans came with guns. Mr. Indian might have gotten one by-and-by, but then he would lack the powder. At last the Indian got a flint lock gun and powder to load it with, took them about twenty minutes—the white man came on the stage with the breach-loader. After the Indian gets a breach-loader, the pale face comes around with a repeater. Anyway, it was no fun for the Indian to fight the white man for so many of them were bald headed.[18]

A lengthy federal investigation of the Millers started in the early 1920s; eventually, a grand jury returned forty-nine criminal indictments against the brothers for defrauding the Poncas of large tracts of allotted lands between 1917 and 1920.[19]

Wenona and Lenders entitled their purchase "Thunderbird Ranch." Lenders made this his studio, and Wenona tended to Rabbit and her other horses, rabbits, and livestock. They also cultivated dozens of beehives—Wenona sold eggs and honey at "company town" stores at the main 101 Ranch property. The couple's attempt at this mini-utopia would later become the center of an ugly legal battle.

Despite the fact that this was to be a retirement of sorts, the two heretofore itinerants quickly found that ranching could be difficult. During the week of April 9, 1922, rainfall was so heavy and continuous that it eventually broke a dam fifteen miles northeast in Ponca City, causing a massive flood on Thunderbird. The water level in the ranch's stream rose twenty-five feet above its usual watermark, and caught the apiary department first, sending hives of bees bouncing up and down the current. Boards stapled to the bottom of the hives kept them afloat, but naturally, this incited rebellion in the bees. Lenders and another employee were stung head to toe trying to rescue them, which they succeeded in doing, although they spent a couple of painful and sleepless days resuscitating some of the bees over oil stoves. Meanwhile, the flood also swept through the brooder house, which had a capacity for six thousand chicks, and drowned three thousand, three-week-old Leghorns. Sixteen barrels of white turkey nests, all with eggs, floated away.[20]

In spite of this, and more minor setbacks, the couple revived their chicken farm, and had a thriving fruit orchard with five hundred peach trees, five hundred blackberry plants, and five thousand grape vines.[21] They raised and then sold a herd of valuable Swiss goats to a neighboring ranch. Lenders painted some of his best works here, such as "Evenly Matched," which depicted a duel between two buffalo bulls, and "Indians in Camp at 101 Ranch." Wenona was content to make new friends at the 101, and cared not one bit that one Mrs. Marjorie Doxstader of Minnesota was making headlines as a vaudeville singer in the 1920s, using Wenona's moniker and elements of her biography. Wenona may have felt that Doxstader posed no publicity threat because her act was limited to vocals.

The former "Sioux princess" also took up writing. Fifty-six years old, she was arthritic and could not possibly be expected to do work around the Ranch that required heavy lifting or hours of standing, although she still helped direct others on how to break horses once in awhile. She bartered for food and animal supplies at the Ranch by providing some memories and short stories for *The 101 Magazine,* a publication Joe Miller started in 1923. Miller was determined that his newsletter would deal only with "facts as actually seen, experienced, and retold by the old time cow punchers and frontiersmen themselves," and usually Wenona's vignettes had a kernel of truth to them, if only the fact she was actually at the event she was writing about. All of her stories reflect the time and place in which she lived, such as this recollection of a rodeo she attended in Kansas in April 1896:

> As it always happens when a bunch of real cow hands get together, there will be one of the boys who has to produce the fun for the rest . . . he always has a nickname. This fellow I am telling about got his nickname on a cow ranch where there was

a Chinese cook. One day the boss wanted Ed Small to come to the office, so he sent the chink out to find him. After being gone an hour, here came the cook all out of breath, saying: 'Me looka high low—no catcha boy.' So from that day to this he is still 'High-lo.'

The story continues with some usual stereotypes of nonwhites being the butt of a joke. High-lo got caught up in a poker game with some cowboys, and when someone jokingly banged on the door of the bunk house and yelled, "Open the door in the name of the law," then pushed open the door, they saw the whites remained but "a broken window showed what became of High-lo. . . . He might be running yet—altho I saw him in Marland not long ago, with a look as wild as ever."[22]

Some of Wenona's stories could be construed as the simple, meandering thoughts of an aging woman, but they were more than that. For years, she had talked of writing her memoirs, and some columns that appeared to be minutiae were her way of recollecting when time permitted. This was not a publication that could be taken too seriously, but sometimes Wenona's writings reflected both her enterprising spirit and also some childlike naïveté:

I was wearing a very fine muskrat coat and cap and Mr. Brooks [assistant show manager] asked me where in the world I had been able to get such a coat with such fine skins, all made from the Bilberry Fair Grounds in Pennsylvania. . . . I noticed a small branch or brook running through the center field. The idea came to put out a few traps and see what they would catch. The first night to my surprise, the catch amounted to eleven muskrats. Then I went at it in earnest, catching about a hundred that winter. Among them were three wonderful black skins which I sold for $35.00 apiece. I made the other skins into the coat which Mr. Brooks has admired so much. Some who read this may not believe the tale of the coat, but if such is the case, ask Mr. Brooks.[23]

On November 3, 1926, the world received word that Annie Oakley had died in Greenville, Ohio, at the home of a relative. She had been ill for about a year, and had been ordered by her doctor to abandon writing her already voluminous memoirs. In his weekly Sunday column, which reached thirty-five million readers, Will Rogers took pains to make sure his friend Oakley was embedded in posterity as the number one rifle shot the world had ever known: "She was the reigning sensation of America and Europe during all the heyday of Buffalo Bill's Wild West show. She was their star. Her picture was on more billboards than a modern Gloria Swanson. It was Annie Oakley, the greatest woman rifle shot the world has ever produced. Nobody took her place. There was only one."[24]

History might have had a different lens with which to view Annie Oakley and Lillian Frances Smith's relationship if Oakley's health had improved in 1925, for earlier that year, she had turned down a "flattering offer" to appear with the Miller brothers' 101 Ranch Wild West Show. "Ill health," *Billboard* reported, "caused Miss Oakley to abandon thoughts of further trouping."[25] Wenona could not have gone on the road with the Wild West due to her own virtual retirement, but there is no question they would have crossed paths. The question remains, would they have buried any hatchet and talked as two famous markswomen, and compared stories and points of view? Or would they simply have thrown a veiled barb or two, and then ignored each other, as they had done the prior forty-five years?

Two weeks later, a much smaller news item appeared in the papers. The Central Press noted that Emil Lenders took a trip to Chicago, where his "locks attracted merriment," and thus, he got his first haircut in sixty-two years. An accompanying photo shows him with his trademark handlebar moustache and a shorn head. As a result, the story wrote, "Lenders went home with less than he brought."[26] This was not exactly true. He brought home a girlfriend, in the form of Miss Katherine Carrico Vigas.

Vigas, then forty-one years old, looked a bit like a naturally scrubbed Mary Pickford, with strawberry-blonde hair. She was a gifted photographer who lived near Lenders and Lillian in Bliss, Oklahoma. Raised about a hundred miles outside of Chicago, Vigas moved to Wichita, Kansas as a young adult, where she partnered with photographer Jack Goldberg. The purpose of this trip to Chicago just prior to the holidays of 1926 was, according to Lenders later, so that he could meet with Eva and work on their marriage, but it may also have been so that

America's Best Female Sharpshooter

Katherine could introduce Lenders to her father, who lived nearby. If her father was skeptical of the pairing, he had every right to be: his daughter was sleeping with a man who still had a mistress in Lillian, and was, of course, still married to Eva.

Whenever she could get away, Katherine would leave the boring bread-and-butter job of family portraiture and drop down to Ponca City, just a couple of hours by rail, and take photos of any Pawnee Bill or Miller 101 doings. Finally, she purchased a studio of her own in Enid, Oklahoma, just an hour east of the 101. It was here at the Ranch that Lenders and Vigas met, two artists somehow drawn to each other. For awhile, Lenders even kept an apartment in Oklahoma City, where the couple would rendezvous. It is not clear whether Wenona had any problem with this.

She may not have known about Katherine yet, but Eva Lenders had finally had enough of Wenona. On July 19, 1927, Eva filed for divorce on grounds of cruelty, abandonment, and alienation of the affections of their daughter—although their daughter was now grown and married. Mrs. Lenders charged that her husband left them for good while they were on vacation in Atlantic City in July 1918; Emil rather flimsily countercharged that it was wife and daughter who abandoned him, and furthermore, that Eva had been taking visits from a neighborhood lothario named Holt Hamilton. Eva shot back that her husband had been living with "a Princess Winona," and he wanted a divorce as well so he could marry her.[27]

The couple split their sizeable real estate holdings and finally divorced in the summer of 1927. But, of course, Emil Lenders did not marry Wenona, but rather, set up a household with Katherine Vigas. The couple moved to an apartment in Oklahoma City, and eventually married, in July 1929. From the few extant letters between Wenona and Lenders around this time, it appears that they parted on friendly terms. In December 1928, Emil wrote to ask if she could send along a prized saddle she was storing for him, and added that he was very sorry to hear about "poor old Rabbit," who had passed away a couple of months before.

Wenona, meanwhile, decided to write her life's story in earnest, as many had asked her to do over the years. With Rabbit gone, she decided it was time to let someone more able take care of Thunderbird

Ranch, and she leased it out. The Millers let her move into one of the tiny cabins they owned on the Salt Fork River, which were originally built for tourists who came from all over the world to visit the Ranch in its heyday.

Alas, the woman was not meant to be a writer. Within the confines of the few years she wrote, her surviving writings seem to veer from stories of the "good old days" of the wild west and vaudeville, to more reflective, possibly drink-inspired sketches, such as "A Thought":

> "Jack and Jill went up the hill, to get a pail of water. Jack fell down and broke his crown, and Jill came tumbling after." Now what a silly thing for Jill to do, to come tumbling after Jack, but that is the way with a man and a maide, he falls—and she follows after—that is if she loves him. How many Jacks and Jills are in this old world of ours, that keep climbing up, and get nearly to the top, and then come tumbling down. Some never care to try to make the grade again, so they keep on slipping lower, and lower—until they are lost forever.

For other stories, Wenona may have cherry-picked from the various religions of friends on the Ranch, or possibly from Masonic tenets she learned over the course of her vaudeville years:

> But—if Love comes along and looking down, sees them in the dark waters of dispair, reaches out a hand, lifts them up and places their feet once more on the ladder of Fame, bringing them into the light of God, He in His wonderful wisdom points the way upward and onward, showing them that there is always hope where there is life, promising them nothing but his forgiveness as a reward for their repentance, glorifying the life to come in such an understanding way, that they have but one wish, and that is to go higher up each day, that one day they may sit at the Masters feet, and have everlasting life—basking in the sunshine of His smile.[28]

Wenona's hopeful contemplation was certainly a departure from her usual plucky irreverence, possibly signaling a change in her health.

Memoir-writing is a quiet, individual pursuit. Wenona was distracted by all the interesting characters who also found refuge at the

Ranch, some with very colorful lives like her own. One of her closest friends there was actress Jane Howard Woodend, who led a double life for a decade or so. Jane, or "Jennie," was born in 1876, and grew up under much more gilded circumstances than Wenona, although maybe not happier ones. Woodend's grandfather was a banking scion in New York City, and left her mother a sizeable fortune, which she inherited at age nineteen when her mother died. She soon fell in love with physician William E. Woodend, who already had a taste for a life beyond his means when they married in 1898. He wasted no time convincing Jane to buy him a seat on the New York Stock Exchange.

For a few years, their lives were perfect. The couple indulged their love of all good things—particularly horses. The Woodend stables became the talk of New York. For one Chicago show alone, the couple took with them twenty-five horses, forty-five carriages, traps, drags, carts, and a retinue of servants. Dr. Woodend beat out Reginald Vanderbilt for a top prize at a national horse show at Madison Square Garden in 1903.

And then it all crashed. Clients accused Dr. Woodend of not purchasing their stock certificates with thousands of dollars they had placed in his care. He had apparently been spending clients' money for personal items, and although Jane tried to hide him from deputies, he was finally arrested on May 3, 1904. The equestrienne soon learned that all of their properties had been mortgaged way beyond any possibility of payment, and creditors seized all of their belongings and horses.

Desperately, Jane Woodend tried to earn money by taking a small part in a play for the New York Academy of Music, called *Crackers,* which included a scene with live horses. A loyal friend of her husband was the producer, and felt sorry for her—although she did have enough beauty and grace not to embarrass the production. "Mrs. Woodend has never acted before," remarked the *Tampa Tribune,* but "is confident that she will succeed by her efforts and help to repair the fallen fortunes of her husband."[29] But the couple was tens of thousands of dollars in personal debt that could never be paid off with even the most brilliant of acting careers, and moreover, Jane fell ill after a few months and could not continue her run.

And so, after watching her husband run through the little money she had saved for basic necessities, as well as the money of her enfeebled brother, Jane had no choice but to somehow make a living with horses. In 1908, she joined the 101 Ranch Wild West as a trick rider for the opening and closing acts. No one among the social elite of Manhattan knew of her double life, until she badly sprained her ankle in May of 1911 at a Brooklyn show, and the press put it together when a doctor of her social set was seen visiting her apartment. Somewhat relieved that her secret was out, Woodend permanently split from her husband and headed to Oklahoma.

Like Wenona, Jane found refuge at the 101 Ranch. Her friend, cowboy Tom Mix, had enticed her and her husband to visit the Ranch in happier days, and the fresh air had done wonders for her health. She applied for any position having to do with equines, and got one as a fence rider.

Jane's new job had little in common with jumping graceful hurdles at Madison Square Garden. She started out before daybreak, equipped with a coil of barbed wire and an outfit of pinchers and pliers to manipulate the wire. She would trot along miles of fence until she came to a spot that was broken, and with her tools, mend the breach. It was not uncommon for this tiny woman to cover fifty miles or more a day, with no company save for her spotted horse and the occasional steer. Winter was even more rigorous because she was required to carry a pickax and break up ice chunks so the cows could drink. For this, the Ranch paid her thirty dollars a month.

Later, Woodend took her place among the regular show cowgirls, if only in the background. In her album at the Gilcrease are photos of her palling around with Wenona, Martha Allen Schultz (also a close friend of Wenona's), Tillie Baldwin, Prairie Rose Henderson, Bessie Herberg and others. Woodend also acquired some chickens, so her brother, whom she cared for, could manage them and contribute to their finances. Visitors to the Ranch would sometimes try to spot Jane in her fancy, leopard-skin coat—a remnant of her wealthier days that was now the only substantial clothing she had against the cold. Wenona often helped Jane with the chickens, and in exchange, received a bird here and there to cook, and eventually, some brood hens. They spent many evenings talking about the "good old days."

Wenona's next closest confidante was Martha Posenke Allen Schultz, married to 101 Ranch cowboy and arena director Clarence

Otto Schultz. She may have gotten to know Wenona through Lenders, given that her husband and Lenders socialized with others of German heritage on the Ranch. During the interwar years, the 101 loaned Clarence to Circus Sarrasani in Dresden, Germany, which exchanged performers with the Miller Bros. 101, mostly so it could take advantage of the Millers' contract with the Pine Ridge Agency for Native American actors. Schultz's main function as director of Sarrasani was to make sure the Sioux were treated well and paid on time, but also to make sure they did not run away to other European circuses offering them twice their salary.[30] Martha may have acted as a den mother of sorts to the Indian women. A family member recalled that later, at the Chicago World's Fair in 1933, she tried to dissuade the Indians from using the flush toilets to wash their clothing, whether by choice or necessity.

Like so many others on the Ranch, this husband-wife team was childless. Martha came to the 101 Ranch in 1914, seeking employment as an exhibition rider; she and Clarence married two years later, and perfected a knife-throwing act they performed between managerial duties when traveling. Wenona and Martha became close—Mrs. Schultz was named in the shooter's notification portion in her will, with just a handful of others. Wenona was a big sister of sorts to her, showing her how to manage the less sophisticated environs of Noble. Likely she taught Martha the proper way to visit the outhouse, which was with a pistol. This advice was validated one night not long after Martha had moved to Oklahoma. She thought to check out the seating area before doing her business, and found a rattlesnake coiled around the hole. She calmly shot the snake, and went ahead with matters at hand.[31]

Wenona also befriended the husband-wife team that owned a grocery serving the 101 Ranch, where she sold her chicken eggs. Arthur and Jessie Rynearson had married in Kansas, where Arthur worked for Boeing making seaplane parts. He did not have a college degree, but he was a gifted tinkerer and self-taught scientist. When work with Boeing dried up, the Rynearsons moved to Bliss, Oklahoma, where Arthur held several positions, including that of mail carrier. Jessie taught a Methodist Sunday school class in a little schoolhouse across the street—there was no church available. Eventually, the couple purchased a storefront, and stocked it with everything a community could need: dry goods, produce, and medicines.[32]

The Rynearsons were an exceptionally hospitable couple; it is obvious why Wenona was drawn to them. They were respectful of people of all socioeconomic and ethnic backgrounds, including blacks and Native Americans. Their daughter, Lucille, recalled that in a community where the "N word" was used as commonly as water, her parents expressly forbade the use of it in their store or at home.[33] Bill Pickett, a black man famous as the 101's "bulldogger" cowboy, recalled that Rynearson would often go to the Bliss Cafe, buy him a good dinner, and bring it to the store's back room so he could eat it. "It was the only way a Negro could get a hot meal in Bliss at that time," wrote a Pickett biographer in 1977.[34]

Arthur Rynearson became a pharmacist—he could not afford to study for a medical degree in his younger years—because he was distressed at how Indians were treated both in his native Kansas and particularly in northern Oklahoma, where they were often sent to quacks and given diluted or fake medicine, or ignored completely. This Arthur tried to remedy at his store. He even outfitted cars and homes for performers and other ranch folks who had physical disabilities—a concept way ahead of its time. Wenona—poor by design or choice the last five years of her life—also received medical attention from the Rynearsons.

Most importantly, the former shooter found true friendship with this couple. They embraced the concept of independent womanhood, even discouraging their daughter from marrying until later in life, and teaching her how to drive and take apart and reassemble a car. Without question, they counseled Wenona to part ways with Emil Lenders and helped her move her things into her cottage. If they did not see her for a few days in a row, Jessie would go to check on her and make sure she was all right.

Wenona's personal finances toward the close of the third decade of the twentieth century were streamlined, to put it politely. Like so many other show business people, she had spent a great deal of what she earned simply to keep going on the road, and had squirreled away virtually nothing for her last years. This was years before Social Security and other safety nets for older Americans. She had no legal or romantic partner to lean on—she was the antithesis of Annie Oakley, who with Frank Butler had retired in comfort and security and left half a million dollars from their estate to various relatives.

Because she already lived without the trappings of a conventional retirement, Wenona was likely ignorant of her landlords' financial troubles during the last few years of her life. Indeed, from outward appearances, it seemed everything was the same. The 101 still had thousands of acres planted with wheat, corn, oats, and forage as far as the eye could see. There were schools, churches, miles of roads, countless orchards and mills for the fruit grown in them, a dude ranch, oil refineries, an ice plant, a dairy plant, packing plants, laundries, and a cafe, not to mention the endless trails as far as the eye could see, and miles of Salt Fork River tributaries to explore. The "White House," the Miller mansion, still stood in all its grandeur. The 101 Ranch Store still stocked everything from "a needle to a Ford car," and serviced customers within a fifty-mile radius of the Ranch.[35]

But things were changing. The Millers had revived their Wild West show in 1925, hiring "California Frank" Hafley and Colonel Zack Mulhall as arena directors, along with proven cowboy and cowgirl performers such as Bill Pickett, Mexican Joe Barrera, Reine Hafley Shelton, Tad Lucas, Stack Lee, and Milt and Mildred Hinkle. But, although the outfit was booked in twenty-nine states and Canada during that season, the show lost money. The Millers had had to contend with intense rivalry from other circus interests, new governmental regulations, rising costs of advertising, train accidents, and lawsuits. As Wallis explains, they also continually faced adverse weather, ranging from frigid temperatures at the start of the season to heat waves later in the year, not to mention catastrophic cyclones, rains, and windstorms in some places. Generally, this revived show was marked by misfortune, poor management, and labor litigation, and would never return a profit again, let alone gross the $800,000 it earned between 1908 and 1916, when Princess Wenona was a fixture.

The balance sheets for the Wild West show were only part of a much larger problem. Ernest W. Marland, who had built an oil empire with the Millers on leased Ponca lands, had overextended himself and the Marland Oil Company, borrowing enormous sums from Wall Street bankers to maintain his extravagant lifestyle and enlarge his petroleum operations. In 1928, the price of crude oil dropped just as the company's oil production saturated the market. The banks called in their loans, took over the board of directors, and Marland lost his company, which eventually merged with Continental Oil Company.[36]

Correspondingly, the Miller brothers' oil fortunes decreased, exacerbating their already existing problems.

Some in the industry predicted this overproduction of oil long before Wall Street availed itself to Marland, mostly because it was Marland who was causing it. On July 30, 1927, the *San Francisco Chronicle* had pointed out that Marland's concern about "reckless extraction" from West Coast wells was disingenuous, and could be alleviated if he would deign to shut down his own southern California holdings.

Again, Wenona had no specific interest in these things, but she most certainly experienced the same shocking portent of times to come as her friends and neighbors did on October 21, 1927. Early that morning, Joe Miller calmly settled a dispute between two show roustabouts, and then drove to the ranch store to pick up some groceries. He chatted with other shoppers, loaded the boxes into his automobile, and left for his residence. He waved at some cowboys visiting in front of the store and touched the brim of his hat. It was ten o'clock in the morning, and the last time anyone saw this employer of thousands alive.[37] Joe's cousin stopped by his place that afternoon, and found him dead next to his idling car in the garage. The family speculated that he had a heart attack and was overcome by carbon monoxide fumes as he lay unconscious.

At the Colonel's funeral on October 26, Princess Wenona mourned alongside scores of noted plainsmen, Indians, cowboys, cowgirls, Russian Cossacks, circus performers, and oilmen. Schools in Ponca City and neighboring communities were dismissed so children could attend the service. Oklahoma Governor Henry S. Johnston, an old family friend and legal advisor to the Millers, wept openly at the service. A large group of Indians appeared, according to Wallis, consisting mostly of Poncas. Led by Horse Chief Eagle and Crazy Bear, they stood in mourning blankets beside the coffin and then, one at a time, each quietly spoke to Joe in the Ponca language, which he had learned as a young boy. "As the funeral procession wended its way to the family plot near Ponca City," recalled Joe's daughter, Alice Miller Harth, "those of us who were sensitive to the thing that was happening realized we were seeing the beginning of the end to an era." The things that they had known so well and taken for granted, she wrote, could not survive in a changed world. They were fast becoming an anachronism.[38]

Zack Miller stopped by Wenona's home on occasion to chat, but probably gave no hint of the burdens that were piling up on his desk and in his heart—both he and George continued to put their best face forward. In 1928, each performance of the 101 Wild West had proved a financial failure, and Zack turned more of his attention to the cattle business they had in Florida while George responded by plunging them even deeper into the oil business, heavily mortgaging the Millers' holdings in Louisiana and elsewhere, hoping to making a killing to pay off the show's deficits.[39] The markswoman knew that as long as any Miller brothers were alive, she would have a place to live.

Sometime in the spring of 1927, Wenona fell violently ill with a case of food poisoning—not uncommon for people who slaughtered and cooked their own food at this time. She stayed in a friend's bed for several weeks, and though she recovered from this infection, she shortly afterward fell ill with "dropsy," edema in the legs, and other effects of congestive heart failure.[40]

In spite of her failing health and lack of money, Wenona was still a familiar sight in Marland and Ponca City. She came into town often the last couple of years of her life in an "old buggy" pulled by a nag, usually followed by several of her adopted stray dogs. She often visited with Frank Wallisch, a talented Austrian baker, and his wife Mamie; perhaps they gave her discounted bread goods at the end of the day. The news of George Miller's horrible death in a car accident on February 2, 1929, must have come as a huge blow—only Zack was left of these three men who created the entire world Wenona had lived in for half of her life.

Around the same time as the stock market crash of October 1929, Wenona's body slowed considerably. She was arthritic, as most Wild West performers were if they reached retirement age, especially in the shoulders and the ankles. She was most likely deaf because of her lifetime of shooting, and though she could still shoot a squirrel at two hundred feet well into her fifties, Wenona's peripheral eyesight was probably fading as well.[41] Her heart was shutting down, either because of an undetected virus or perhaps a congenital defect.

After Christmas, Wenona developed double-pneumonia, and never recovered. Lungs covered with layers of black soot, expelled by her guns over the decades, exacerbated her cough. Her arms, feet, and lower abdomen began to swell uncontrollably, and she could barely speak. January 17, 1930, was then Oklahoma's coldest day in recorded history, and no one checked to make sure Wenona had enough wood alcohol and firewood for her little stove—the only source of heat in her little cottage. Within days, Wenona entered the Ponca City Hospital, where the Sisters of St. Joseph at least made her feel comfortable but knew she would not be leaving their charge.

There, she passed away quietly on February 3rd. She was fifty-nine years old, the same age as her mother when she died, also of heart failure.

The "Princess" left a will with trusted friend Arthur Rynearson, who faithfully executed her wishes for a simple burial in her Indian clothes. She asked that a hundred dollars from her estate be donated to the Salvation Army, and that her clothing be given to Mary Newton, the wife of a 101 teamster and a woman who was good to her. She left her jewelry to friend Elsie Robertson, and her guns, medals, and show clothing to be disposed of by Rynearson.

On Wednesday, February 5, Wenona's body lay in state at the mortuary for all who had known her during the last fifteen years to pay their respects. A short service was given at the First Christian Church of Ponca City, led by Reverend G. Frank Sanders, who had officiated at the memorials of Joe and George Miller. A prayer of Wenona's choosing was said at her service:

> God, let me live each lovely day
> So I may know that come what may
> I've done my best to live the way
> You want me to.
> Forgive me if I do not pray
> The ultra sanctimonious way
> In church on Sabbath day
> As Christians do.
> Just let me know if I should stray
> That I may stop along the way
> At any time of night or day
> And talk to you.[42]

This poem, which some papers said Wenona had written, was actually composed by entertainer Elsie Janis, but the sentiments exactly fit those of the markswoman. One of her final requests was that she be buried under her real and maiden name of Lillian Smith, and Rynearson made sure this was done. She had created a savings account, evidently for the purpose of defraying her burial expenses, which came to about $300, and Arthur paid them in full right after her service.

Zack Miller was away from the ranch, so his cousin W. A. Brooks helped with her funeral arrangements. Brooks, writes Wallis, along with four cowboys and a local newspaper reporter acted as pallbearers. "It was the worst possible time for a burial," he noted, "After days of snow, sleet, and freezing rain, the ground was frozen as hard as stone and the gravediggers cussed and moaned."[43] Lillian had no relatives at her funeral but there were a few friends from the Ranch.

The death certificate noted Lillian Smith as "Widowed," which was probably the best guess as to her status as anyone could make. She donated her most prized possessions to the Oklahoma State Historical Society: a beaded surcingle, a beaded blanket, one pair of gold-plated spurs, an ermine-trimmed buckskin dress, and some photographs. She also gave them all the guns in her possession at that time: four Winchester carbine rifles, .44–40-caliber; two gold-plated Winchester rifles, .22-caliber; one gold-plated Smith & Wesson revolver, .38-caliber; and a gold-plated Smith & Wesson pistol, .22-caliber. Additionally, she left a bulletproof vest, one she had kept from Casimir Zeglen, and a fancy beaded one. Arthur Rynearson took a deliberate and precise inventory of her less valuable, household items. This list showed how simply Lillian had lived her last few years. Among her last and only possessions were a typewriter, two old trunks, a gun trunk, three brooder lamps to keep chickens warm, one cream separator, a small oil stove, a few dishes, and a basket with her beadwork in it. She had about $800 in her bank account, which Rynearson used to pay off various debts.

Newspaper obituaries nationwide dutifully and falsely reported Lillian as the daughter of a Sioux chief, and Rynearson wrote a handful of people she had asked him to notify when "Our Father calls me home." These included Ada Somerville Gray, Bee Ho's wife, sharpshooter friend Alf Rieckhoff, and "California Frank" Hafley, by then living in Colorado. Her far-flung bunch of friends also included Martha Schultz, at this time working in Dresden, Germany; Mr. and Mrs. Fred

Cook of Santa Barbara, stable keepers and longtime friends from her home state; and Ruth Campbell, a woman in her eighties who had run a rather bawdy boardinghouse in Louisville for more than forty years, where Lillian no doubt stayed the many times she toured through. Ethel May Shorey, an actress friend from Massachusetts she had met during her vaudeville days, was notified as well.

Newspapers across the United States printed a few lines of obituary for Lillian. Most reminded readers that she had once performed with Buffalo Bill and met with Queen Victoria. Her fame as the exceptional teen shot was largely forgotten, and the intricacies of her career were ignored. The big story of the day was crippling unemployment across the United States.

Still, many papers some found room to mention one or all of her unbroken records. They were:

- Breaking glass balls thrown in the air using a .22 rifle: 323 balls without a miss; 495 of 500 thrown; hitting 100 balls in 80 seconds.
- From the back of a running horse: broke 71 of 72 balls thrown in the air.
- Using a single loading .22 rifle: hit 300 swinging balls in 14 minutes, 33 seconds.
- Using four Winchester repeating rifles, .22-caliber, for three hours daily, hit 72,800 swinging balls over six days.
- Made 24 of 25 8-inch bull's-eyes at 200 yards.

"Times have changed and the expert marksman is neither so common nor so important as a generation ago," added the *Miami Herald* added in assessing Lillian Smith's career. And though the paper was alluding to changing times, it was correct in ending with the note that Princess Wenona would never have a successor.[44]

AFTERWORD
Recoil

I n 1994, Jerry Murphey and other members of the 101 Ranch Old Timers Association started looking in a Ponca City, Oklahoma, cemetery for the grave of Princess Wenona, who had asked to be buried under her birth name—Lillian Smith. Longtime *Daily Oklahoman* reporter Michael McNutt wrote that Murphey's endeavor was made more difficult by the fact that no appropriate marker appeared in the Odd Fellows cemetery in which she was allegedly put to rest.

In 1999, the searchers' efforts paid off. They found a site they believed to be Smith's, based on an entry and internment grid. When digging for the memorial's foundation, workers found a small concrete block six inches below the ground with the inscription "Wenona, P '30." According to Murphey's wife, a grave next to it had been dug the following year, and Lillian's stone was covered over.[1]

Truthfully, there was no one to keep her memory alive. Her main corps of friends—those with whom she had forged the strongest ties at the 101 Wild West back in 1910—were deceased or had long scattered to other parts of the United States. Frank, Mamie, and Reine Hafley enjoyed a brilliant rodeo career together until the mid-1930s, after which Reine went out with her own family. Since 1918, the Hafleys had wintered on their ranch in Ridgway, Ouray County, Colorado. They purchased this sprawling property from two of the infamous Marlow brothers, a gang of five who straddled both sides of the law. In her diary, Mamie wrote that the couple found out about Wenona's death in their local paper on February 5. She also wrote that on the following day, the "Col," her husband, "cried about Wenona."[2] Charles Franklin Hafley succumbed to cancer on October 16, 1940, and Mamie died from cancer ten years later.

Fanny "Nurse" Liesy stayed in occasional contact with Wenona, but for the most part, she had her hands full taking care of the Hafleys.

She was completely devoted to the family—she cosigned the deed to the Ridgway ranch house and made at least part of the down payment. She was governess, nurse, and playmate to Reine through the latter's early teens, and remained the grand dame of the household until she passed away there in 1946, at age eighty-seven.

Bee Ho and Ada Somerville Gray had been on the vaudeville circuit since the early 1920s, performing death-defying knife-throwing tricks and roping with the likes of Will Rogers, with Ada doing her trained horse specialties. In addition, Bee Ho acted and rode in a handful of silent films including Erich von Stroheim's 1924 epic *Greed*, for which he was hired to throw a knife during a pivotal saloon altercation scene. About the time Wenona began to decline, he was operating his own Wild West tent show, but was forced to cease operations due to the Great Depression. After Ada's death in 1941, he struggled to keep an able assistant. He had something of a second run when he acquired and trained a young coyote he named "Chink" to yodel with perfect pitch while he sang and played banjo, and he was a radio personality on variety shows, performing with the likes of Fred Stone and Bing Crosby. Bee Ho, who was once described by newspapers as "America's most famous cowboy," died on August 3, 1951, penniless and essentially forgotten, much like his friend Wenona.

This obscurity also describes the death of Jane Woodend, who was born with a silver spoon in her mouth and was equally blessed with talent. She hardly missed a day of work since she moved to the Ranch permanently and not even when her brother was discovered frozen to death four years earlier, having collapsed in some shallow water. Woodend died in March 1938, with just a few dollars to her name and no relatives to mourn her.

After breaking up with Emil Lenders, Wenona harbored no resentment toward him. Neither did she bear ill will toward his close friend, Gordon Lillie. But despite their history together at the Pawnee Bill Wild West and their close proximity—Lillie's sprawling ranch abutted the 101—Wenona had no inclination to make the bumpy trip to see him, and they had little in common anyway. Gordon and his wife, May, were still mourning the loss of their son, Billy, who had accidentally hanged himself in 1925. At the time of Wenona's death, Gordon was busy running "Pawnee Bill's Old Town," two miles west of his ranch, a tourist attraction featuring log cabins, tepees, saloons, and other curiosities from the Old West. Six years later, May tragically died in an automobile accident, in which her husband was driving. Gordon was heartbroken until the day he died in 1942, at age eighty-one. Unfortunately, Old Town burned to the ground in 1944, along with some of the finest objects of Indian art and artifacts of the Old West.

Emil Lenders died in 1934, in Oklahoma City. Years later, his wife, Carrico, attempted to sell a gas lease on Thunderbird Ranch lands and discovered that her husband had not only kept up a friendship with Wenona until her death but also had never really cauterized his legal obligations with the shooter. There was some question as to who owned the Thunderbird Ranch at the time of Wenona's death, and who owned several of Lenders's paintings. Carrico Lenders argued that Arthur Rynearson, as executor of Wenona's estate, had improperly given away these paintings and owed her thousands of dollars.

The courts disagreed with the second Mrs. Lenders. They acknowledged that Carrico had a valid claim to the Thunderbird lands, because she produced a contract between Wenona and Emil that allowed one or the other to full ownership if he or she paid off the majority of the mortgage. Emil had done so, but let Wenona live there as long as she pleased, and she did come and go until her death. Without expressly saying so, Rynearson, through his attorney, intimated that Lenders had left Wenona without the means to a comfortable end to her life. In her probate file, Rynearson noted that a contract between Lenders and Wenona had conveniently showed up at his office after her death. According to this contract, their land could belong to Lenders since he was going to be responsible for paying off the mortgage. However, Rynearson wrote, Lenders had abandoned the poultry business and Wenona had to use her cash to pay expenses. That left her without the money to pay off the mortgage, so she lost the Thunderbird.

As for the valuable paintings—one of which was a life-sized portrait of the shooter—the County of Perry, Oklahoma, concurred with Rynearson that at least two paintings were expressly given to Rynearson's daughter by Emil himself, and that the remaining three were Wenona's to bequeath through her estate. The court also agreed that the number of items in Wenona's possession had been agreed upon by Wenona and Emil and attested to by Rynearson, a trusted friend. Interestingly, Lenders's portrait of Wenona was left unfinished, and so was the elaborate studio on Thunderbird, for which he had spent a great deal of time and money—probably Lillian's money.

In her final years, Wenona was either completely comfortable with the fluidity and ambiguity of her partnership with Lenders—after all, her whole life and almost all of her relationships were chaotic—or she was too tired to care. Arthur Rynearson, however, cared very much. In his final deposition of Carrico's suit, this man of few words managed to simultaneously convey his thoughts about the painter's ego in life, and his irritation about Carrico's treatment of Lillian's character in death: "[I] experienced a radiant sense of JOY for having attended the close of the GYPSY like career of 'Princess Wenona' and the last entanglement of a 'WORLDS MASTER ARTIST' whose master pieces embodied the 'SOUL' of America and the 'AMERICAN' as God Made It, and HIM."[3] Arthur Rynearson died in 1963, four years after his wife, Jessie.

According to her will and estate papers, Lillian Smith had no known heirs. Nellie was not named. Nellie, whoever she really was, was likely "Mountain Nell," who was billed as the "Champion Rifle Shot of the World" for Yankee Robinson's Circus until the end of 1916, when management dropped Wild West acts from the show and turned it largely into a traveling menagerie. No record for Nellie after that has been found.

Brother Charles Smith was a farmer and stockkeeper in Los Banos, California, until his death decades earlier in 1902. A Los Banos resident recalled that it was his talent for calling ducks that caused his demise. "When he would call, the chords [sic] in his throat would become strained. Eventually they swelled up so much they killed him."[4] This neighbor had probably witnessed Lillian's brother suffering from the effects of throat cancer, or another ailment that would enlarge his neck. Descendants of Charles's stepdaughter, Lois Irene Wilkins, have always been told they were somehow related to Annie Oakley.[5]

In August 1999, the 101 Ranch Old Timers and other sponsors unveiled a handsome stone monument at Lillian's gravesite in Ponca City Odd Fellows Cemetery. The four-foot-tall black marble headstone features the image of Princess Wenona, along with an inscription of her record-breaking accomplishments as a trick shot artist and her association with the 101 Ranch. Her birth and death dates match up exactly as February 3, incorrectly possibly for some posthumous flair that Wenona would have appreciated.

The rivalry between Lillian Smith and Annie Oakley makes for a good story. The antagonism between the two—as sporadic as it was and limited mostly to the Buffalo Bill Wild West—is almost always the first thing that historians write when discussing them together. Oakley, reflected Pawnee Bill historian Anna Davis, helped to create the stereotype of the prairie beauty, helped by the fact that her promotional materials sort of downplayed any masculine associations with her actions. She still managed to maintain the standards of what was deemed ladylike. Not Lillian Smith. She bragged and wore flashy clothes and she liked men. Smith felt at home with the cowboys and the Native Americans with the show, and this really flew in the face of Oakley's conservative social behavior.

With just a few paragraphs of innuendo and double entendres, the Butlers managed to—unwittingly—paint Lillian as a fat, wanton alcoholic for posterity. If, in fact, Smith drank to excess on occasion, she would not be the first or last Wild West actor to do so. Given that the shooter performed death-defying stunts on a horse until she was at least fifty years old with no issues—and with guns, no less—we can assume that drinking was not a problem during her career.

The Smith-Oakley rivalry even seeped into a 2002 legal analysis of the latter's libel suit against William Randolph Hearst nearly a century earlier. In this treatise, published in an *American Bar Association* journal, the authors identify Maud Fontannielo, a burlesque performer, as Lillian Smith. Fontannielo did act under the assumed identity of Lillie Cody, purportedly a relative of the Colonel. Fontannielo was arrested in 1903 for stealing money for cocaine.[6] Newspaper magnate William Randolph Hearst twisted her lie one step further and allowed his papers to charge that Maud was Annie Oakley, and had been using drugs for years, and was now in prison. It did not help that at court, Maud claimed she was the most famous rifle shot in the world, and had cracked under the weight of show business life. But she was not Annie Oakley, or Lillian Smith either.

This kind of blatant and horribly unfair yellow journalism obviously took a terrible toll on the real Annie Oakley. She famously sued

William Randolph Hearst for libel and won. Lillian Smith had absolutely nothing to do with the situation, but even three-quarters of a century after both womens' deaths, her name is still intertwined with desperation, substance abuse, and lying.

Lillian Smith and Annie Oakley paved the way for other women by presenting shooting as mass entertainment. The truth is, America had long been fascinated by women toting guns, but until the mid-1880s when Smith and Oakley broke into national headlines, stories tended to be framed within the context of pioneer women, such as those popularized in William W. Fowler's popular 1878 book about mothers lulling their babies to sleep with muskets by their sides, or about women who bit musket balls into pieces in order to kill more Indians. There were also those women shooters featured in dime novels, who could fire rounds with the best of their male counterparts. But these females—Belle Starr and Calamity Jane, for example—"clearly preferred to embrace the wilderness rather than stamp it out."[7] Smith and Oakley, on the other hand, reenacted the civilization of the frontier through their Wild West shows and vaudeville appearances. Part of this was because they were born half a generation after dime-novel star heroines, but also because they styled themselves as "the good gals," Oakley by being the athletic Victorian icon, and Smith by being the "tamed Indian."

Smith and Oakley were also exceptional because both had very long careers—roughly forty-five years apiece. They both had been children who shot as a means to feed their families, and both successfully transitioned to the heights of exhibition shooting in their teens, using shotgun, rifle, and pistol. Smith and Oakley both headlined the vaudeville and Wild West circuits, and both stopped making public appearances in 1922.

The similarities stop there. Oakley knew how to frame her talents within the context of what America and even the rest of the world expected of a female contender in the sporting world. She vociferously encouraged women to learn how to shoot, and she did this often. During World War I, she offered to recruit and train a regiment of women sharpshooters. "I have been teaching women to shoot for many years, at Wentworth in summer and Pinehurst in winter, without compensation, because I had an ideal for my sex. I have wanted them to be capable of protecting their homes," she declared to a reporter in 1919, and similarly many other times. (As well, Edith Tantlinger offered to raise a "regiment of women sharpshooters" when America was on the verge of conflict with Mexico in 1914.) Lillian's leadership in this regard did not last, for the very simple reason that she just did not care about making an indelible imprint in the world of female sports and shooting in general as much as making sure she had immediate opportunities to shoot. The closest she ever got to shaping public discourse was being the subject of suffrage jokes, such as the one made by the *Daily Alta California*, which said of her skill as a teenager: "If her sisters generally adopt her system [of shooting] they will not be long denied the right of voting."[8]

Lillian merely wanted to shoot, and to make enough money to do so. She was not thrifty like Oakley and others, who saved for their families and their retirement. She never sought roots anywhere so much as she tried to have a roof over her head, which she was able to do by forming relationships with men who would keep her protected yet still showcase her talents—all while still maintaining her autonomy.

The Olympics did not add women's shooting competitions until 1984. Perhaps if they had done so a hundred years earlier, Smith and Oakley could have settled the matter of superiority once and for all—and maybe invited other females to join their ranks. There was a time when Lillian Smith could have trained this next generation of performers, but instead she spent her last years trying to create the stable family life she never had, exchanging food and labor with other orphaned entertainers and 101 Ranch inhabitants, with memories of being the true California Girl to keep her warm.

APPENDIX
Lillian's Guns

At the time of her death, Lillian had only a few of her guns in her possession. According to an inventory of her estate, she had two "well worn" gold-plated Winchester 1890 rifles; a gold-plated .22-caliber Smith & Wesson revolver; and a gold-plated .38-caliber Smith & Wesson revolver. As with most celebrity shooters, she probably had had many other guns that were gifts from welcoming committees, admirers, or gunmakers. For example, Marlin Firearms sent her a gold-mounted .22-caliber rifle in 1903 and Lillian explained that though she had high hopes for the model—"I think that they [the Marlins] will beat the Winchester as far as the action goes"—she could not tell until she had used it. It appears it was not to her liking because newspaper and photographic accounts show she continued with Winchester.[1]

Decades after her death, these guns were in the wind, dispersed among private collectors, but collectors Ruth and Jerry L. Murphey managed to pull some back together, along with a few of her other pieces, such as another Winchester, Model 1873. The handguns were custom made for her in 1901, and the rifles have some elaborate carvings of her name on them, along with some alterations that allowed her to shoot from horseback.

Because Lillian was a shooter for so many decades and was so versatile, it is hard to classify what kind of weaponry she favored at any given time. It is possible, however, to make some good guesses. Until she joined Buffalo Bill's Wild West in 1886, Lillian was fairly faithful to her Ballard 7.5-pound .22-caliber with its rimfire cartridge. The Ballard single-shot was patented in 1861 and manufactured by various companies until 1875, when its production was turned over to John Marlin. Collectors agree that the Marlin-Ballard rifles manufactured in the mid-1870s until 1891 are some of the finest single-shot rifles ever made, perfect for hunting small game, and it is likely Levi Smith gave his daughter his old one in favor of one of these newer Marlins.

From time to time, in the early 1880s, the girl shooter also mentioned owning a little Henry rifle. In 1866, this gun, which had been used extensively during the Civil War, was passed over for regular army use because it was not able to handle the new breed of high-powered cartridges favored by the military. Again, Lillian probably inherited this rifle from a male family member. With the war over, a new "improved Henry" went into production. The resulting Model 1866, produced by the Winchester Repeating Arms Company, would become the first Winchester rifle. Nicknamed "The Yellow Boy" due to the color of its bronze alloy frame, the model fired the same .44-caliber rimfire cartridges as the old Henry, but with an improved closed-tube magazine and loading gate allowing for cartridge loading on the right side of the receiver.[2]

This Henry model was soon followed by the Winchester 1873 design, a breakthrough rifle that allowed shooters to carry a single kind of ammunition. Its powerful .44-40 centerfire cartridge could chamber in a cowboy's Colt sidearm, making it more practical when traveling on horseback. The reliability, firepower, and popularity of the 1873 rifle earned it the slogan "The gun that won the West." Carried by everyone from trappers and mountain men to ordinary cowboys, the lever-action Winchester rifle became the iconic armament of westward expansion. Buffalo Bill Cody wrote in a letter to Winchester: "Allow me to say that I have tried and used nearly every kind of gun made in the United States, and for general hunting, or Indian fighting, I pronounce your improved Winchester the boss."[3] Lillian used at least one of these during her hunting trip to the Northwest, too. Like Annie Oakley and many others, Lillian also relied upon single-shot pistols, revolvers, repeating rifles like the Winchesters, Stevens, and Colt Lightnings and 12- and 16-gauge shotguns to entertain her audiences, depending on whether they were indoors or out.

There were a lot of improvements in ammunition during Lillian's theatrical years as well. In 1895, Walt Lindsley, in conjunction with King Powder Company in Cincinnati, invented a smokeless powder recipe, which the Peters Cartridge Company in Kings Mill (also in Ohio) immediately purchased. These smokeless cartridges greatly improved rifle performance and reliability, and also made performances much cleaner, especially in a crowded venue. Also, Peters and other bullet makers improved cartridges that contained shot but were molded for handguns, rifles, or carbine rifles. This was to protect the audience. William Cody is often criticized in history books for using these shot-wrapped bullets to give the impression that he hit more targets with a rifle than would normally be possible, but the fact is, safety was a more important factor than accuracy. Shooters like Cody, Smith, and Oakley had thousands upon thousands of hours of practice under their belts, bolstering their natural shooting proficiencies. There is no doubt they could hit just about any target they wished, but they could not control where a missed cartridge would end up. For example, when Cody was right next door to the World's Fair in the middle of Chicago in 1893, he used shot cartridges so an errant one would not hit someone perhaps thousands of feet away in another tent or sidewalk.

Wild West show performers used a variety of guns. Firearms historian David Kennedy notes that people in the extravaganzas would have used any weapon they liked—anything from a .22-caliber rifle to a .45-caliber Colt or .44-caliber Smith & Wesson to a wide variety of different carbines and rifle made by Winchester, Marlin, and any other manufacturer. Many guns had the same capabilities as many others, but differed in how they fit best with the shooter. Firearms might have been modified to fit a performer's physical stature, or as often was the case with handguns, might have been set with a special set of hand grips.[4] A modification could be made on the inside the gun as well. For example, May Lillie had one of her Smith & Wesson pistols modified from a .32-caliber to a .22-caliber—the weight and the feel of the .32 felt good in her small hands, but she liked the performance of a .22 chamber and thus had a slimming tube put in the larger-caliber gun.

Just as she did not keep many firsthand records of her life, Smith did not keep track of her many guns, and did not seek or gain as many endorsements as aggressively as Oakley and others. Without seeing those guns or at least serial numbers, it is impossible to know what kind of personal preferences or modifications she may have had. Hafley brought several Colt .45 single-action revolvers to his relationship with Lillian; he used them almost exclusively during his California sheriff days. The Wenona & Frank duo used Smith & Wesson .38 Police Specials during at least their first two years together, 1898 and 1899, and probably through 1904.

Similarly, it is difficult to know exactly what stock of guns Smith kept during her Wild West heyday—roughly 1904 to 1917. On horseback, Smith would have used her carbine rifles, with a 20-inch barrel and a shorter stock rather than the usual 24-inch barrel and full stock. The shorter stock and barrel moved the gun's center of gravity gun to the rear, allowing the gun to move around a little bit easier as she was trying to acquire her target or turn the point to a shot. When using a revolver on horseback, she used a single-action Colt Army, which was very popular among 101 Ranch performers.[5]

Smith and Oakley were truly ambidextrous—they could fire just as easily from their left hand as they could with their right, and they could effortlessly handle two firearms at the same time. Howard Bliss recalled his surprise at Lillian's adroitness with this rifle at such a young age: "I had not thought it possible before this, that a single loader could be fired so rapidly, and can hardly understand it yet as I look back at it, that she could go through all the motions so smoothly, as I stood and watched her it looked very simple and easy." He noticed that she could hit a bull's-eye at thirty-two feet with the Ballard, twenty-five times a minute, with seconds to spare. "It seemed to me, without any exaggeration, that the gun gave out a steady stream of fire from the first shot to the end of the twenty-five cartridges."[6]

Appendix

NOTES

Introduction

1. "There are said to be many attractive cowgirls . . . ," *San Jose Evening News*, April 9, 1912, 8.

2. The most comprehensive biography to date for Lillian is a chapter by Michael Wallis in his *The Real Wild West: the 101 Ranch and the Creation of the American West*. He describes her meteoric rise to fame by way of the Buffalo Bill Wild West and later vaudeville, her penchant for marriage, and her last years, reclusiveness, and alcoholism at the 101 Ranch. Throughout the golden age of Wild West shows, writes Wallis, when there were plenty of expert marksmen, no one could compare with Lillian-Wenona. Michael Wallis, *Real Wild West*, 309–16.

3. Warren, *Buffalo Bill's America*, 239.

4. Yost, *Buffalo Bill*, 168.

5. Most derogatory information about Lillian-Wenona has been sourced from Phoebe Ann Moses, better known as Annie Oakley, and from those writing about Oakley. In her definitive biography *Annie Oakley*, historian Shirl Kasper discusses the tensions between Smith and Oakley in Buffalo Bill Cody's 1886–87 Wild West tour, both in America and Europe. Glenda Riley, in her *Life and Legacy of Annie Oakley*, similarly describes the women's wrestling over the spotlight at this time.

Over time, these observations became definitive statements about Smith, who is now rarely thought of at all except dismissively as a one-time rival to Oakley, or perhaps as a footnote in the stories of Wild West icons Gordon Lillie (Pawnee Bill), 101 Ranch businessman Joe Miller, or of course, William Frederick Cody.

6. Weston, "Buffalo Bill's Champion Girl Shot: Lillian Smith of Corralitos . . . ," *Aptos Almanac*, 12.

7. Shirley, "Four Lives of Princess Wenona," *Old West* (Spring 1991), 14–19.

8. Wallis, *Real Wild West*, 315.

9. Shirley, "*Lillian Smith*: Bill Cody's 'California Girl,'" *Real West*, 13.

10. Browder, *Slippery Characters*, 67.

11. Dalton, *Under the Black Flag*, 1914.

Chapter 1

1. Biographical entry in *Buffalo Bill's Wild West . . . An Illustrated Treatise*, 49. Other contemporary sources cite similar versions of the mountain lion shooting.

2. *Santa Cruz Weekly Sentinel*, September 11, 1880, 3.

3. *Sporting Life*, April 22, 1885, 10.

4. Browder, *Ethnic Impersonators*, 69.

5. "Princess Wenona a Graduate of Carlisle Indian School," *Elkhart (Ind.) Daily Review*, June 28, 1911, 1.

6. Ibid.

7. Ann Gidley Rowley, "Quakers and Their Meeting House At Apponegansett," paper read at meeting of the Old Dartmouth Historical Society, August 14, 1940, www.whalingmuseum.org.

8. Sawyer, *Moving On*, 2004. See, specifically, "Story of the Crow Emigrant Train." Unfortunately, the page numbers in this edition are not consistent.

9. Quoted by Chappel, "Early History of Mono County," 244–48.

10. Great Register of California, 1876.

11. Sawyer, *One Man Show*, 165.

12. Igler, *Industrial Cowboys*, 53–54.

13. Sawyer, *Moving On*, 65.

14. Eventually, Miller and Lux took a controlling interest in the corporation and built what is now known as the Central California Irrigation District, connecting the Sacramento and San Joaquin River deltas with the San Francisco Bay and Pacific Ocean.

15. See Igler's comprehensive book, *Industrial Cowboys*.

16. See Igler's chapter "Laboring on the Land," *Industrial Cowboys*.

17. Sawyer, *Moving On*, 75.

18. For example, see J. E. Newsome, "Hunting with Animal Blinds," 20–22.

19. Charles Sawyer, *One Man Show*, 165, 182.

20. "One Hundred and Forty Geese in Two Shots," *Sacramento Daily Record-Union*, January 29, 1877, 3. The *Record* added a preamble: "The *Merced Express* caps all the goose stories with this one."

21. Transcription of memoirs of William Knight and other Merced pioneer families, courtesy Ralph Milliken Museum of Los Banos, Calif.

22. Transcript of interview with Los Banos pioneer William Riley Knight, courtesy Ralph Milliken Museum.

23. Sawyer, *One Man Show*, 214.

24. *San Francisco Chronicle*, January 6, 1878, 7.

25. Ibid., May 24, 1878, 1.

26. "Outdoor Amusements," *Sacramento Daily Record-Union*, August 30, 1879, 4.

27. "A Feminine William Tell. Marksmen Unwilling to Test Her Prowess," *San Francisco Chronicle*, February 24, 1885, 5.

28. Ibid.

29. Wallis, *Real Wild West*, 309.

30. The 1870 U.S. census clearly states their true names, ages, and birth states.

31. Betty Lewis, "Lillian Smith was Watsonville's homegrown sharpshooter."

"That Was Watsonville" column, *Watsonville (Calif.) Register-Pajaronian*, September 30, 2004.

32. *Sacramento Daily Record-Union*, June 20, 1881, 4.

33. "Sharp shooting: Remarkable Marksmanship by a Ten-Year-Old Girl," *Daily Alta California*, reprinted from the *Watsonville Pajaronian*, June 17, 1881. Exactly who the Austin Brothers were is lost to history, but one was likely Charlie Austin, who was an expert at using his Winchester to shoot potatoes out of the fingers of his assistant, or to extinguish cigarette butts with a bullet.

34. "Sharp shooting: Remarkable Marksmanship by a Ten-Year-Old Girl," *Daily Alta California*, repeated from the *Watsonville Pajaronian*, June 17, 1881. The rifle referred to here is a .22-caliber Ballard, which Smith preferred until she reached adolescence.

35. "Whip & Spur," *Wheeling Register*, June 25, 1881.

36. Peter Hartlaub, "Woodward's Gardens Comes to Life in a Book," *San Francisco Chronicle*, October 30, 2012, available at http://www.sfgate.com/default/article/Woodward-s-Gardens-comes-to-life-in-book-3990569.php.

37. Given what we know about Lillian's father, it is strange that he did not try to exploit the fact that she was technically nine years old earlier in the summer. Presumably, the papers simply rounded up, since the birth date was so close.

38. *San Francisco Chronicle*, July 25, 1881, 3.

39. *Buffalo Bill's Wild West . . . An Illustrated Treatise*, 49.

40. Bliss, *Wing and Glass Ball Shooting*, 33.

41. Ibid., 33–34.

42. *Daily Alta California*, March 23, 1885, 1.

43. Ibid.; see also "Featherless Flyers," *Daily Alta California*, April 6, 1885, 1; "Pigeon Shooting," ibid., April 13, 1885, 8; and "Fleet Flyers," ibid., April 19, 1885, 1.

44. "Pigeon Shooting," ibid., June 1, 1885, 1. John Kerrigan might have proved a formidable match for Lillian in ensuing years, were it not for the distraction of horrible events in the next six months, in which his wife mutilated their landlady with a razor, thinking she was having an affair with Kerrigan. The sharpshooter eventually procured a pardon for his wife, after she spent ten years at San Quentin Prison.

45. *New Bedford Standard*, via the *Boston Post*, June 25, 1881, 4.

46. For example, see "A Girl Who Can Shoot," *Chicago Tribune*, May 24, 1886, 9.

47. Kasper, *Annie Oakley*, 11.

48. Ibid., 12–13.

49. Riley, *Life and Legacy of Annie Oakley*, 23–24.

50. Kasper, *Annie Oakley*, 12.

51. *New York Sun*, September 7, 1884, 5.

52. "Little Miss Smith," *Santa Cruz Surf*, February 25, 1884, clipping file of Pajaro Valley Historical Association.

53. Ibid.

54. With this invention, glass spheres filled with feathers could be ejected en masse, much like clay pigeons today.

55. *American Field*, August 23, 1884.

56. "A Challenge," *Santa Cruz Surf*, July 18, 1884.

57. *Breeder and Sportsman*, March 8, 1884.

58. *San Francisco Chronicle*, January 27, 1885, 3.

59. Ibid., April 2, 1885, 3.

Chapter 2

1. Nellie Yost writes an extremely detailed account of Cody both on- and off-stage: *Buffalo Bill*, 165–68.

2. Letter to A. Hoell and Co., Baltimore, April 7, 1886. Currently in possession of http://www.snyderstreasures.com/pages/finecollectibles.htm. Levi Smith apparently had big plans for Lillian even before Cody came to California. On January 23, 1886, the *Merced Express* touted her superior skill and claimed she was set for a tour of the United States and Europe.

3. Yost, *Buffalo Bill*, 167.

4. "Buffalo Bill," *Omaha Bee*, April 17, 1886, 8. Lillian's age may have simply been a mistake here, or Cody may have rounded up so as to appear a little more scrupulous.

5. Yost, *Buffalo Bill*, 167.

6. *St. Louis Republican*, May 14, 1886, 2.

7. For discussion of Oakley's real birth name, see Shirl Kasper's *Annie Oakley*, ch. 3.

8. Kasper, *Annie Oakley*, 5.

9. Ibid., 7.

10. Ibid., 9.

11. See the biography of Frank Butler on *American Experience*'s "Annie Oakley" site: pbs.org/wgbh/americanexperience/features/biography/oakley-butler/.

12. Quoted in Kasper, *Annie Oakley*, 27.

13. *Breeder and Sportsman*, April 9, 1887, 230.

14. Riley, *Life and Legacy of Annie Oakley*, 35–37.

15. Oakley, *My Life*, chapter 7.

16. "They" refers to Cody and Nate Salsbury, promoter and financial partner in the Wild West show. Quote appeared in *Reading (Pa.) Times*, November 29, 1926, 7. Thanks to the Garst Museum in Greenville, Ohio, for help in authenticating it.

17. Shirley, "Bill Cody's 'California Girl,'" 46–76.

18. Letter dated June 12, 1904, written from Troy, New York, Jerry and Ruth Murphey Collection. Wenona's choice of Rieckhoff as a confidante is interesting. To be sure, he was a talented shooter, but he was followed by notoriety and limited employability since he had been arrested in 1895 for fatally missing his target and hitting assistant's breastplate.

19. See, for example, *New York Sun*, May 17, 1886, 6. The young shooter may have looked back on this event with some embarrassment in later years, as she could not have then known the depths of Cody's legal struggles with Doc Carver, and that both took turns trying to lure the other out in public in order to serve lawsuits.

20. *San Francisco Chronicle*, July 6, 1886, 3.

21. "Indians at Erastina: Successful Opening of Buffalo Bill's 'Wild West' Show," *New York Times*, June 26, 1886, 2.

22. *New York Herald*, June 26, 1886, 10.

23. Transcript in *Cincinnati Enquirer*, August 13, 1887, 11. The original source, *London Topical Times*, cannot be found.

24. Ibid.

25. The earliest known transcript of this interview was printed in the summer of 1887 by London's *Topical Times* (n.d.) and reprinted with variations in American papers. This version appeared in the *Santa Cruz Sentinel* on October 8, 1887.

26. *Santa Cruz Sentinel*, October 18, 1887, 3.

27. "'Jim the Kid's' Bride," *New York Herald*, October 3, 1886, 11.

28. "Jim Kid's Alleged Bride," *Boston Daily Globe*, October 5, 1886, 3.

29. "Wild Life in Madison Square Garden," *New York Tribune*, November 25, 1886, 5. For a vivid description of "A Drama of Civilization," of both its technical feats and its reflection of moral ambiguity in U.S. history, see Warren, *Buffalo Bill's America*, chapter 10.

30. Reddin, *Wild West Shows*, 84–86; Yost, *Buffalo Bill*, 180–81.

31. Twain quoted in Russell, *Lives and Legends of Buffalo Bill*, 321

32. Manifest, "S. S. Nebraska," Buffalo Bill Center of the West; "Good-Bye to Buffalo Bill," *New York Times*, March 31, 1887, 8; Yost, *Buffalo Bill*, 185, and "Buffalo Bill's Goodbye," *New York Times*, April 1, 1887, 8.

33. Kasper, *Annie Oakley*, 70.

34. Ibid., 71.

35. Yost, *Buffalo Bill*, 191.

36. The Queen's attendance was a boon for future sales, but on this particular day, Cody's financial backers may have shivered, as security measures required that most of the arena be kept clear of a paying public.

37. Queen Victoria Diaries, Royal Archives, Windsor Castle, UK.

38. For an in-depth discussion of Victoria's possible views of Native Americans at the Wild West, see Moses, *Wild West Shows and the Images of American Indians*, 1996.

39. *Illustrated London News*, May 9, 1887.

40. *Rifle*, n.d. Reprinted in the *Christchurch Star*, New Zealand, April 12, 1887, 3.

41. From Cody's updated autobiography, titled *Story of the Wild West and Camp-Fire Chats*, although John Burke almost certainly wrote or edited some or all of this.

42. Kasper, *Annie Oakley*, 82–86.

43. *Breeder and Sportsman*, June 23, 1887, 54.

44. Ibid., September 3, 1887, 151.

45. Ibid., September 17, 1887, 182.

46. *American Field*, December 10, 1887.

47. McMurtry, *Colonel and Little Missie*, 149.

48. *Sacramento Daily Record-Union*, August 27, 1887, 2.

49. Kasper, *Annie Oakley*, 86.

50. Ibid., 87.

51. "Memories of Annie Oakley," *Pinehurst (N.C.) Outlook*, February 3, 1917, 4.

52. *St. James Evening Review and Gazette*, July 20, 1887, 5.

53. *London Evening News*, July 20, 1887, 2.

54. Wilder, *The People I've Smiled With*, 108.

55. "Buffalo Bill and His Show Repeat the Triumphs of Last Year," *New York Times*, May 31, 1888, 8.

Chapter 3

1. *Breeder and Sportsman*, June 4, 1887, 358; "Miss Lillian Smith," ibid., January 26, 1889, 54.

2. Kasper, *Annie Oakley*, 100–101. It should be added here that, according to Kasper, Annie may have demanded Lillian Smith's departure as part of her agreement to return to Cody's show in 1889.

3. Ibid., 257.

4. "Miss Lillian Smith," *Sacramento Sunday Union*, August 4, 1889, 1.

5. "Summer Sojourners," *Sacramento Daily Record-Union*, August 26, 1889, 1.

6. This Bill Cook's identity is lost to time, if he existed at all.

7. Letter from C. L. Daily, Neuilly, France, 22nd/89, Western History Collection, Denver Public Library. Although the month is not noted, it can be assumed it was written sometime between latter May and July, given that BBWW set up in the former month, and that both documents needed to cross the ocean in order for the news to reach California papers in August.

8. "A Letter from Jim Kid," *Cheyenne Leader*, July 30, 1889, 1.

9. See description of a nineteenth-century shooting gallery in "Expert Marksmen: Sketches in a Shooting Gallery," *San Francisco Sunday Chronicle*, May 5, 1889.

10. Smalley, "'Our Lady Sportsmen,'" 360.

11. Ibid., 359.

12. *San Francisco Bulletin*, May 24, 1890, 4.

13. "Lillian F. Smith," *Salem Evening Capital Journal*, September 13, 1890, 3.

14. *Idaho Statesman*, April 22, 1891, 5.

15. *Dalles Daily Chronicle*, May 20, 1891, 3.

16. See, for example, *Portland Oregonian*, April 5, 1891, 8.

17. Portions of the San Joaquin River swell with floods at certain times of the year, which sounds counterintuitive for sailing long distances, but the condition makes it easier to do so. Lillian was most likely waiting for this opportune (and safer) time.

18. *San Francisco Call*, June 10, 1892, 2.

19. "Girl in a Small Boat: Lillian Smith Journeying Down the San Joaquin," *Chicago Daily Inter Ocean*, June 19, 1892, section 2.

20. One account of her trip is "One of the Smiths," *San Francisco Call*, July 17, 1892, 3.

21. Interview with Los Banos resident William M. Wiley, May 25, 1955, transcript courtesy Ralph Milliken Museum. For an example of the Latta trip, see "Inland Boat Near End," *San Francisco Chronicle*, June 30, 1948, 14.

22. *San Francisco Call*, July 17, 1892, 1.

23. Ibid., March 27, 1894, 4.

24. Ibid., August 28, 1894, 7.

25. For example, see "At the Playhouses," *Los Angeles Times*, December 3, 1895, 6.

26. "Sex Against Sex," *Los Angeles Times*, December 25, 1895.

27. "City Briefs," ibid., January 1, 1896, 40.

28. *New York Clipper*, November 5, 1897.

29. *Fresno Republican*, August 1, 1897, 2.

Chapter 4

1. *General Index to Compiled Service Records of Volunteer Soldiers Who Served During the War with Spain*, Microfilm publication M871, 126 rolls, ARC ID: 654543, Records of the Adjutant General's Office, 1780s–1917, Record Group 94, National Archives at Washington, D.C.

2. E-mail to author from Tom Shelton, June 13, 2014.

3. See Kasper, *Annie Oakley*, 195.

4. Ibid., 169.

5. Thanks to Roy Jinks, historian for Smith & Wesson Firearms, for checking their voluminous records. There is nothing in those records to support or refute the Hawaiian story.

6. Lillian Smith to Alf Rieckhoff, October 10, 1900, Jerry and Ruth Murphey Collection.

7. Another widely accepted theory for the Butlers' altered wedding date is that the later date better coincided with Annie's change of birth date during her Buffalo Bill rivalry with Lillian Smith.

8. *Arizola (Ariz.) Oasis*, April 28, 1900, 7.

9. *Tombstone Prospector*, November 18, 1899, 4; *Phoenix Republican*, November 24, 1900, 6.

10. Lillian Smith to Alf Rieckhoff, October 10, 1900, Jerry and Ruth Murphey Collection.

11. Document dated "189—," presumably so a desk editor could fill in "8" or "9." Jerry and Ruth Murphey Collection.

12. Wallis, *Real Wild West*, 313.

13. Ephemeral file, Jerry and Ruth Murphey Collection.

14. Program transcript, *American Experience*'s "Annie Oakley" site, http://www.pbs.org/wgbh/americanexperience/features/transcript/oakley-transcript/.

15. Wenona to unknown friends. n.d., 1902, Western History Collection, Denver Public Library.

16. "Frank and Wenona," *National Police Gazette*, July 27, 1901, 6.

17. Cummins, *Historical Biography*. For more on Cummins, see Parezo and Fowler, *Anthropology Goes to the Fair*, and Moses, *Wild West Shows and the Images of American Indians*.

18. Advertisement, "Biograph: Wenona and Frank: Greatest of All Rifle Shooting Specialties," *Philadelphia Inquirer*, December 22, 1901, 2.

19. "Indian Congress Celebrities: Geronimo, Wenona and Calamity Jane on the Midway," *Watertown (N.Y.) Daily Times*, September 3, 1901, 7.

20. Undated clipping from *New York Police Gazette* in Jerry and Ruth Murphey Collection, but most certainly from 1901.

21. "Indian Lore: Princess Wenona," *101 Magazine*, November 1926, 19.

22. Pan-American Exhibition Scrapbook Collection, vol. 14, 241. See http://www.nyheritage.org/collections/pan-american-exposition-scrapbooks.

23. Ibid., vol. 12, 12.

24. Ibid., vol. 14, 20.

25. Ibid., vol. 18, 39. Like many clippings in this invaluable collection, this one has no date, but in context must be August 27, 1901, since it refers to Cody's opening on the 26th.

26. Ibid., vol. 14, 105.

27. See "Wenona a Wonder," ibid., August 24, 1901, vol. 17, 164.

28. "Shooting Humbugs," ibid., vol. 30, September 5, 1901, 406.

29. Pan-American Exhibition Scrapbook Collection, vol. 17, 164.

30. "Annie Oakley Protests," *American Rifleman*, July 25, 1901, 288.

31. *Buffalo Courier*, September 22, 1901, 27.

32. Pan-American Exhibition Scrapbook Collection, vol. 21, 43.

33. Ibid., 43, 47.

34. See, for example, ibid., September 25, 1901, vol. 21, 28.

35. See "Wonderful Wenona," ibid., vol. 21, 146.

36. Pell, Buel, and Boyd, *McKinley and Men of Our Times*, 202.

37. McLaird, *Calamity Jane*, 196.

38. Pan-American Exhibition Scrapbook Collection, vol. 23, 163. The gentleman described the couple's street outfits: "Wenona was gotten up in a marvelous costume of many colors with a long trail which nearly tripped her up, and the dashing cowboy in his cutaway and red necktie looked like a very ordinary individual with none of the Wild and Wooly Western air about him."

39. See *Los Angeles Herald*, November 19, 1903, 8.

40. "Jacket Turned Bullet at Distance of Five Paces," *Denver Post*, December 1, 1903, 7.

41. Rieckhoff correspondence, Jerry and Ruth Murphey Collection.

42. Lillian to Alf Rieckhoff, February 7, 1903, Jerry and Ruth Murphey Collection.

43. Quoted in Wilson, *Silk and Steel*, 162.

44. Wenona to Alf Rieckhoff, November 28, 1902, Jerry and Ruth Murphey Collection.

45. Wilson, *Silk and Steel*, 164–65.

46. Elizabeth Toepperwein was the first woman in the United States to qualify as a national marksman with the military rifle and the first woman to break one hundred straight targets at trapshooting, a feat she repeated more than two hundred times, often with a twelve-gauge Winchester model 97 pump gun.

47. Keith-Albee Manager Reports, September 2, 1902–September 3, 1903, 109, 134, 165, Keith-Albee Vaudeville Collection.

48. For discussion of salaries and conditions for vaudeville performers during the twentieth and twenty-first centuries in America, see Wertheim, *Vaudeville Wars*.

49. *Chicago Tribune*, May 31, 1903, 42.

50. Lillian Smith to Alf Rieckhoff, June 12, 1904, Jerry and Ruth Murphey Collection.

51. Lillian Smith to Alf Rieckhoff, January 7, 1906, Jerry and Ruth Murphey Collection.

52. "Cupid Plays Prank," *Richmond Planet*, September 24, 1904, 2. "We-no-aye-te" does not translate the same as "We-no-nah" in Sioux, but it worked for the purposes of a highly fictional newspaper account.

Chapter 5

1. Historian Philip Deloria, paraphrased in Laura Browder's *Slippery Characters*, 65–66.

2. "A Girl Who Was Raised with a Rifle," *New York World*, June 24, 1906, Jerry and Ruth Murphey Collection.

3. *Harrisburg Independent*, June 7, 1904, 3.

4. "Pawnee Bill's Show," Washington, D.C., *Evening Star*, June 2, 1904, 3.

5. "Princess Wenona's Pony 'Piebald' Dies at Age 25," *Ponca City (Okla.) News*, October 28, 1928.

6. "Marvelous Marksmanship," *Ottawa (Kans.) Evening Herald*, September 16, 1905, 2.

7. "Princess Wenona Was Hurt," *Iola (Kans.) Register*, September 23, 1905, 7; "Show Woman Killed," *Chanute (Kans.) Sun*, September 23, 1905, 1; *Sun* (Ottawa, Kans.), September 22, 1905, 5.

8. *New York Clipper*, December 16, 1905, 1113.

9. Wenona to Robert H. Hartley, March 10, 1904, Western History Collection, Denver Public Library.

10. Frank and Wenona to Robert H. Hartley and wife Marie, February 9, 1904; April 4, 1904; May 30, 1904; November 14, 1904; November 22, 1904, Western History Collection, Denver Public Library.

11. See 101 Ranch Old Timers' Association website: http://www.101ranchota .com/history.html. For a comprehensive source about the 101 Ranch, see Wallis, *Real Wild West.*

12. "A Famous Resort Is 101 Ranch," *Show World,* June 29, 1907.

13. Ritter quoted in newsletter, www.101ranchota.com/history.html. L. C. Moses notes that this could easily have been called Geronimo's first buffalo hunt, too. Bedonkohe Apache Indians were not exposed to many buffalo in northern Mexico, Arizona or New Mexico.

14. *Billboard,* March 16, 1907. James Bailey, of later Barnum & Bailey circus fame, died in 1906, leaving Cody without a managing partner. At seventy years old, Buffalo Bill was exhausted, and anxious and distracted over his financial troubles. Lillie immediately began machinations to buy the Bailey heirs' third-part ownership in Cody's Wild West. He was not successful in doing this until 1908, but was distracted by this possibility until then and not seriously considering suitors like Frank Hafley.

15. *Atlanta Constitution,* July 9, 1907, 10.

16. "And Now the Exposition at Jamestown," *New York Times,* April 21, 1901, 1.

17. Ruiter, "Jamestown Ter-Centennial Exposition of 1907," *Encyclopedia Virginia,* http://www.encyclopediavirginia.org/Jamestown_Ter-Centennial_ Exposition_of_1907.

18. Deloria, *Indians in Unexpected Places,* 56; Fields, "Circuits of Spectacle," 446.

19. Moses, *Wild West Shows,* 183; Fields, "Circuits of Spectacle," 446.

20. Ibid.

21. Wallis, *Real Wild West,* 294.

22. *Billboard,* March 28, 1908, 25.

Chapter 6

1. Parascandola, "America's Playground," *Ultimate History Project,* http:// www.ultimatehistoryproject.com/coney-island.html.

2. *Billboard,* May 30, 1908, 23.

3. "Samson's Entertaining Ways," *Omaha Bee,* October 4, 1908, 4.

4. Untitled, undated clipping, Jerry and Ruth Murphey Collection.

5. Wallis, *Real Wild West,* 303–4.

6. "Splendid Midway Fair Attractions," *Augusta (Ga.) Chronicle,* October 27, 1909, 10.

7. Ibid. The Extreme Cowboy Racing Association allows for a fifty-five mile-per-hour top speed for a shooter in a breakaway. In an arena of unknown depth, forty miles per hour is a more conservative estimate.

8. *Billboard,* June 18, 1910, 59.

9. Records of Clark Gray, grandnephew of Bee Ho Gray and author of *Legendary Life of Bee Ho Gray*.

10. Interview transcripts, e-mails dated January 15, 2015, and July 16, 2016, from Thomas Shelton, grandson of Mamie and Frank Hafley.

11. "Wind Has Fun with a Circus," *New York Sun*, July 18, 1906, 1.

12. Princess Wenona to Joe Miller, December 29, 1910, box 1, folder 8, Miller Brothers 101 Ranch Collection, Western History Collection.

13. Roth, "101 Ranch Wild West Show, 1904–1932," vol. 43 (1965): 416–31.

14. Joe Miller to Edward Arlington, January 4, 1911, box 1, folder 8, Miller Brothers 101 Ranch Collection, Western History Collection.

15. See "Death of a Girl Was Freely Predicted," *New Castle (Pa.) News*, April 18, 1911, 10.

16. Wallis, *Real Wild West*, 356–57.

17. Ibid., 357.

18. Ibid., 358.

19. Ibid., 308 and 340.

20. Edith Tantlinger Diary no. 3, Edith and D. Vernon Tantlinger Collection, Western History Collections.

21. For example, (Boise) *Idaho Statesman*, June 16, 1912, 2.

22. "'Buffalo Bill' Needed," *Santa Monica Daily Outlook*, January 16, 1912, 8.

23. Wallis, *Real Wild West*, 359.

24. "Indian Girl a Real Heroine," *Santa Monica Daily Outlook*, December 18, 1911, 1.

25. "Wild West Will Soon Be Here," *Santa Monica Daily Outlook*, November 13, 1911, 8; "Final Roundup at Praeger Park Tonight," *Los Angeles Times*, November 13, 1911.

26. Wallis, *Real Wild West*, 389.

27. "Real Injuns in War Paint in This Show," *Los Angeles Times*, November 10, 1911, 119.

28. "Novel Wild West Show," ibid., November 9, 1911, 118 and "Wild West as It Really Was," ibid., November 12, 1911, V23.

29. *San Francisco Chronicle*, April 20, 1912, 1.

30. *Variety*, August 23, 1912, 14.

31. See *Charlotte Observer*, October 22, 1911, 7.

32. *Variety*, August 23, 1912, 14.

33. Wallis, *Real Wild West*, 366.

34. The Miller Brothers 101 Ranch owned the land (about 18,000 acres of seacoast land in Santa Ynez Canyon and the surrounding hills) where Universal Pictures was eventually established.

35. "Indians No Longer Shy at Camera, Like 'Movie' Posing," *Fort Worth Star Telegram*, September 28, 1913, 10.

36. Postcard, Alfred and Mae Rieckhoff to Wenona, January 25, 1928. Jerry and Ruth Murphey Collection.

37. See Luther Standing Bear's *My People the Sioux*, 283–85.

38. Transcription of interview with Raymond "Littlewolf" Spendley, February 1, 2015, in possession of the author.

39. E-mails from Philip Sheldon to author, August 7, 2014–April 15, 2016.

40. Wallis, *Real Wild West*, 434.

Chapter 7

1. Wallis, *Real Wild West*, 398.

2. *Fort Scott (Kans.) Monitor*, September 23, 1913, 6.

3. For example, see *Macon Daily Chronicle*, September 13, 3.

4. As Wallis discusses in his *Wild West* chapter "Inceville," the blatant racism of the time was a key factor in the decision not to award starring roles to Indians. Beyond bigotry, he writes, the quandary of giving Indians better billing was further exacerbated because—except for the traditional dances and ceremonials—playacting was not part of the culture of most Indian tribes. Their main contribution to early westerns came from the air of authenticity their very presence brought to the screen. It was Vern Tantlinger who began recruiting Oglalas from Pine Ridge for the Miller Brothers' 101 Ranch Wild West show in 1909.

5. Undated 101 Ranch correspondence, Jerry and Ruth Murphey Collection.

6. *Hobart (Okla.) Daily Republican*, September 11, 1912, 1.

7. Wallis, *Real Wild West*, 339.

8. Ibid., 399.

9. Willard was rumored to have made about $150,000 from a six-month tour with the 101 in the second half of 1915. He quit in December to focus on boxing only, and held the champion heavyweight title until he was soundly beaten by Jack Dempsey in 1919.

10. "Upcoming Exhibitions," California Historical Society, http://www.californiahistoricalsociety.org/exhibitions/upcoming_exhibitions.html.

11. Groff, "Exposition Moths," 148.

12. *San Francisco Chronicle*, April 14, 1915, 4.

13. For example, *Rockford (Ill.) Daily Register Gazette*, April 29, 1915, 6.

14. Transcript of article dated February 3, 1930. Jerry and Ruth Murphey Collection.

15. For detailed discussion of gender, sexuality, and morality imbued in the Panama-Pacific Exposition, see Sides, *Erotic City*, and Markwyn, *Empress San Francisco*.

16. Sides, *Erotic City*, 23.

17. *San Francisco Chronicle*, July 1, 1915, 5.

18. *Los Angeles Times*, October 15, 1915, II6.

19. Ibid., December 11, 1915, II2.

20. "New Shows Join Isthmus: Woman Rifle Shot," *San Diego Evening Tribune*, March 21, 1916; "Wenona," ibid., April 7, 1916, 9.

Chapter 8

1. Wallis, *Real Wild West*, 455.

2. Ibid., 456–57.

3. *Billboard*, July 18, 1916.

4. Transcription of a letter from Willoughby, which appeared in the *Wyoming Semi-Weekly Tribune*, January 22, 1915.

5. Yost, *Buffalo Bill*, 398–400.

6. Wallis, *Real Wild West*, 314–15.

7. Lenders, "Random Notes of the Old West," 23.

8. Wallis, *Real Wild West*, 315.

9. Lenders, "Random Notes of the Old West," 165.

10. "Princess Wenona's Show," *Billboard*, March 23, 1918, 64.

11. *Billboard*, April 20, 1918, 39.

12. Ibid., September 21, 1918, 25.

13. "Winter Quarters Robbed," *Billboard*, November 30, 1918, 57.

14. Lenders, "Random Notes of the Old West," 68.

15. *Billboard*, August 23, 1919, 46.

16. *Joplin Globe*, December 4, 1921, 7.

17. Wallis, *Real Wild West*, 315.

18. Lenders, "Random Notes of the Old West."

19. Wallis, *Real Wild West*, 473.

20. See "Save Bees in High Flood Waters," *Tulsa World*, April 13, 1922, 5.

21. *Daily Ardmoreite* (Ardmore, Okla.), October 12, 1924, 27.

22. Princess Waynona, "An Incident of the West," Jerry and Ruth Murphey Collection.

23. Princess Waynona, "The Tale of a Coat," Jerry and Ruth Murphey Collection.

24. Will Rogers quoted in Kasper, *Annie Oakley*, 239–40.

25. Ibid., 237.

26. *Springfield (Ill.) Republican*, November 12, 1926, 1.

27. *Perry Daily (Okla.) Journal*, June 26, 1928, 1.

28. "Work as Writer Begun by Princess Wenona at Marland Home," *Ponca City (Okla.) News*, May 12, 1929.

29. *Tampa Tribune*, August 24, 1904, 1.

30. For an in-depth understanding of Germany's historical fascination with the American natives, see Penny's *Kindred by Choice*.

31. Interview with Joseph Ruet, grandnephew of Martha Allen Posenke Schultz, November 9, 2014.

32. Interview with Patricia Sayre, great-granddaughter of Arthur and Jessie Rynearson, June 25, 2014, transcript in possession of the author. Special thanks to Kay Bauman, great-granddaughter of Jessie Rynearson, for providing memories of Rynearson niece Ottie Brown Rury DeYong.

33. Interview with Patricia Sayre.

34. Haines, *Bill Pickett, Bulldogger*, 71–72.

35. The best description of the 101 at this time and any other can be found in Wallis, *Real Wild West*.

36. Soon after renamed Conoco.

37. Wallis, *Real Wild West*, 502.

38. Ibid., 504.

39. Ibid., 505.

40. This friend tried to collect his expenses related to his care of Wenona after she died and her estate was posted in local papers. His request was deemed a "fraud," but given what we know of Wenona's heart condition, it is entirely likely that this occurred and she neglected to pay her friend for medicines and loss of work during his family's care for her.

41. She may have started experiencing these long-term effects of shooting years before. Reine Hafley remembered going with her mother and stepfather to get supplies at the 101 Ranch store around 1923, when she was twelve. At first, the family figured Wenona snubbed them for some reason, since she did not wave or say hello. Reine could not help herself—she was very fond of Aunt Wenona—and jumped in front of her. Wenona was startled a bit, and then hugged and chatted with the child. Reine remembered that was the last time she saw the markswoman.

42. This poem by Elsie Janis was syndicated in newspapers such as the *Pittsburgh Daily Post*, May 5, 1925, 6.

43. Wallis, *Real Wild West*, 316.

44. *Miami (Fla.) Herald*, February 11, 1930, 6.

Afterword

1. McNutt, "Riflewoman's Grave Found in Ponca City," *Daily Oklahoman*, August 21, 1999.

2. Mamie Francis Hafley diaries, courtesy Shelton family. Transcription in possession of the author.

3. Court Documents from Wenona Estate, Noble County Courthouse, Gilcrease Museum, Tulsa, Okla.

4. Transcription of interview with James Huston, July 13, 1926, Ralph Milliken Museum Archives.

5. E-mail from Dr. Matthew Hayward, April 18, 2015, in possession of the author.

6. Julin and Wallace, "Who's that Crack Shot Trouser Thief?," 1–7. For other viewpoints of this litigation and its primary participants, see Kuntz, *A Pair of Shootists* and Soodalter, "Annie Oakley vs. Hearst's Worst."

7. Browder, *Her Best Shot*, 82.

8. *Daily Alta California*, January 21, 1884, 2.

Appendix

1. Lillian Smith to Alf Rieckhoff, November 22, 1903. Jerry and Ruth Murphey Collection.

2. Phelps, "Best of the West: The Winchester Rifle."

3. Boorman, *History of Winchester Firearms*, 44.

4. "Historic Firearms," narrated by Anna Davis and Erin Brown, *Pawnee Bill Ranch Podcast*, January 1, 2013. Transcript of podcast available at http://www .okhistory.org/sites/pbtranscript1.php.

5. Special thanks to David Kennedy, of the Cherokee Strip Regional Heritage Center, and Paul Szymaszek, Colt Firearms Historian, for taking my questions about weaponry used at the Wild West shows.

6. Bliss, *Wing and Glass Ball Shooting*, 34.

BIBLIOGRAPHY

Archival Sources

"California Great Registers, 1866–1910." County clerk offices, California. Available at http://familysearch.org. Accessed June 14, 2016.

Circus Historical Society. www.circushistory.org.

Edith and D. Vernon Tantlinger Collection. Western History Collections. University of Oklahoma Libraries.

Garst Museum. National Annie Oakley Center. Greenville, Ohio.

General Index to Compiled Service Records of Volunteer Soldiers Who Served during the War with Spain. National Archives and Records Administration, Washington, D.C.

Jerry and Ruth Murphey Collection. Gilcrease Museum. University of Tulsa.

Keith-Albee Vaudeville Theater Collection. Special Collections. University of Iowa Libraries.

King's County Clerk–Recorder's Office. Hanford, Calif.

Libraries and Archives of the Autry. Autry Museum of the American West. Los Angeles.

Library of Congress. Washington, D.C.

Massachusetts Town and Vital Records, 1620–1988. Available at ancestry.com.

McCracken Research Library. Buffalo Bill Center of the West. Cody, Wyo.

Merced County Clerk–Recorder's Office. Merced, Calif.

Michael Wallis Manuscript Collection. Oklahoma Center for Poets and Writers Manuscript Collections. Oklahoma State University–Tulsa Library.

Miller Brothers 101 Ranch Collection. Western History Collections. University of Oklahoma Libraries.

National Cowgirl Museum and Hall of Fame. Fort Worth, Tex.

Oklahoma Historical Society. Oklahoma City.

Oklahoma State Department of Health. Oklahoma City.

Pajaro Valley Historical Association. Watsonville, Calif.

Pan-American Exhibition Scrapbook Collection. New York Heritage Digital Collections. Buffalo and Erie County Library. Available at www.newyorkheritage .org.

Queen Victoria Diaries. Royal Archives. Windsor, UK.

Ralph Leroy Milliken Museum. Los Banos, Calif.

Record of Deaths, City and County of San Francisco. San Francisco Genealogy. Available at www.sfgenealogy.com/sf/index.htm.

San Joaquin County Recorder's Office. Stockton, Calif.

Shelton Family Rodeo Archives. Private family collection. Tilden, Tex.

Western History Collection. Denver Public Library.

Periodicals

American Field. August 23, 1884; December 10, 1887.

"Annie Oakley Protests." *American Rifleman.* July 25, 1901, 288.

Billboard. March 16, 1907; May 30, 1908; June 18, 1910; March 23, April 20, November 30, 1918; August 23, 1919.

Breeder and Sportsman. March 8, 1884; April 9, June 23, September 3 and 17, 1887; January 26, 1889.

Chappel, Maxine. "Early History of Mono County." *California Historical Society Quarterly* 26 (September 1947): 244–48.

Fields, Alison. "Circuits of Spectacle: The Miller Brothers' 101 Ranch Real Wild West." *American Indian Quarterly* 36 (Fall 2012): 443–64.

Groff, Frances A. "Exposition Moths." *Sunset,* 148.

"Indian Lore: Princess Wenona." *101 Magazine.* November 1926.

Julin, Thomas R., and D. Patricia Wallace, "Who's That Crack-Shot Trouser Thief?" *Litigation* 25 (Summer 2002).

Lenders, Emil W. "Random Notes of the Old West." *Central States Archaeological Journal* 15 (January 1968).

Newsome, J. E., "Hunting with Animal Blinds in Merced County." *California Fish and Game.* January 1926, 20–22.

Phelps, Steven. "Best of the West: The Winchester Rifle, the Gun That Won the West." *Cowboys and Indians.* June 2013.

Riley, Glenda. "Annie Oakley: Creating the Cowgirl." *Montana: The Magazine of Western History* 45 (Summer 1995): 32–47.

Russell, Ona. "What's in a Name Anyway?: The Calamity of Calamity Jane." *American Studies* 35 (Fall 1994): 21–38.

Ruth, Barbara Williams. "The 101 Ranch Wild West Show, 1904–1932." *The Chronicles of Oklahoma* 43: 416–31.

Shirley, Glenn. "Bill Cody's California Girl." *Real West.*

Show World. June 29, 1907. Available at www.circushistory.org/showworld/whowworld1907.htm.

Smalley, Andrea. "'Our Lady Sportsmen': Gender, Class, and Conservation in Sport Hunting Magazines, 1873–1920." *Journal of the Gilded Age and Progressive Era* 4 (October 2005): 355–80.

Soodalter, Ron. "Annie Oakley vs. Hearst's Worst." *Wild West.* February 2015.

Sporting Life. April 22, 1885, 10.

Variety. August 23, 1912.

Books

Bliss, H. C. *Wing and Glass Ball Shooting.* Philadelphia: Franklin News, 1886.

Boisseau, T. J., and Abigail M. Markwyn, ed. *Gendering the Fair: Histories of Women and Gender at the World's Fairs.* Urbana: University of Illinois Press, 2010.

Boorman, Dean K. *The History of Winchester Firearms.* Guilford, Conn.: Globe Pequot, 2001.

Browder, Laura. *Her Best Shot: Women and Guns in America.* Chapel Hill: University of North Carolina Press, 2008.

————. *Slippery Characters: Ethnic Impersonators and American Identities.* Chapel Hill: University of North Carolina Press, 2000.

Buffalo Bill's Wild West, America's National Entertainment, An Illustrated Treatise of Historical Facts and Sketches London: Allen, Scott, 1887.

Cody, William F. *Story of the Wild West and Camp-Fire Chats.* Philadelphia: Historical Publishing, 1891.

Cody, William F. *The Life of Hon. William F. Cody, Known as Buffalo Bill.* Edited and with an introduction by Frank Christianson. Lincoln: University of Nebraska Press, 2001.

Collings, Ellsworth, and Alma Miller England. *The 101 Ranch* (Norman: University of Oklahoma Press, 1971).

Cummins, Frederick T. *Historical Biography and Libretto of the Indian Congress.* Buffalo: n.p., 1901.

Dalton, Kit. *Under the Black Flag.* Memphis, Tenn.: Lockard Publishing Company, 1914.

Deloria, Philip J. *Indians in Unexpected Places.* Lawrence: University Press of Kansas, 2004.

Gray, Clark. *The Legendary Life of Bee Ho Gray.* Houston: John M. Hardy Publishing, 2014.

Haines, Bailey C. *Bill Pickett, Bulldogger: The Biography of a Black Cowboy.* Norman: University of Oklahoma Press, 1977.

Igler, David. *Industrial Cowboys: Miller & Lux and the Transformation of the Far West: 1850–1920.* Berkeley: University of California Press, 2001.

Kuntz, Jerry. *A Pair of Shootists: The Wild West Story of S. F. Cody and Maud Lee.* Norman: University of Oklahoma Press, 2010.

Markwyn, Abigail. *Empress San Francisco: The Pacific Rim, the Great West, and California at the Panama-Pacific International Exposition.* Lincoln: University of Nebraska Press, 2014.

McLaird, James D. *Calamity Jane: The Woman and the Legend.* Norman: University of Oklahoma Press, 2005.

McMurtry, Larry. *The Colonel and Little Missie: Buffalo Bill, Annie Oakley, and the Beginnings of Superstardom in America.* New York: Simon and Schuster, 2006.

Moses, L. G. *Wild West Shows and the Images of American Indians, 1883–1933*. Albuquerque: University of New Mexico Press, 1996.

Oakley, Annie, Toni E. Seiler, and Marilyn Robbins. *The Autobiography of Annie Oakley*. Greenville, Ohio: Darke County Historical Society, 2006.

Parezo, Nancy J., and Don D. Fowler. *Anthropology Goes to the Fair: The Louisiana Purchase Exposition*. Lincoln: University of Nebraska Press, 2007.

Pell, Edward Leigh, James W. Buel, and James P. Boyd. *McKinley and Men of Our Times; Together with the Great Questions with Which They Have Been Identified and Which Are Still Pressing for Solution*. St. Louis: Historical Society of America, 1901.

Penny, H. Glenn. *Kindred by Choice: Germans and American Indians Since 1800*. Chapel Hill: University of North Carolina Press, 2013.

Reddin, Paul. *Wild West Shows*. Champaign: University of Illinois Press, 1999.

Riley, Glenda. *The Life and Legacy of Annie Oakley*. Norman: University of Oklahoma Press, 2002.

Russell, Don. *The Lives and Legends of Buffalo Bill*. Norman: University of Oklahoma Press, 1960.

Sawyer, Charles, ed. *Moving On: A Compilation of "The Plains Over," "Story of the Emigrant Train of 1865," and "Then We Came to California."* Los Banos, Calif.: Ralph Milliken Museum Society in association with Loose Change Publications, 2004.

———. *One Man Show: Henry Miller in the San Joaquin*. Los Banos, Calif.: Ralph Milliken Museum Society, 2003.

Sides, Josh. *Erotic City: Sexual Revolutions and the Making of Modern San Francisco*. New York: Oxford University Press, 2009.

Standing Bear, Luther. *My People the Sioux*. Lincoln: University of Nebraska Press, 1975.

Wallis, Michael. *The Real Wild West: The 101 Ranch and the Creation of the American West*. New York: St. Martin's Press, 1999.

Warren, Louis S. *Buffalo Bill's America: William Cody and the Wild West Show*. New York: Alfred A. Knopf, 2005.

Wertheim, Arthur Frank. *Vaudeville Wars: How Keith-Albee and Orpheum Circuits Controlled the Big Time and Its Performers*. New York: Palgrave Macmillan, 2006.

Wilder, Marshall P. *The People I've Smiled With: Recollections of a Merry Little Life*. New York: Werner, 1899.

Wilson, R. L. *Silk and Steel: Women at Arms*. New York: Random House, 2003.

Yost, Nellie Snyder. *Buffalo Bill: His Family, Friends, Fame, Failures and Fortune*. Chicago: Swallow Press, 1979.

Author Interviews

The records of these interviews are in the author's possession.

Burton, Rod, grandnephew of "Oklahoma Dan" Sistrunk. June 2, June 5, and November 17, 2014.

Duttle, Terry, step-great-granddaughter of Carrico Vigas Lenders. February 5–8, 2015.

Gray, Clark, grandnephew of Bee Ho Gray. June 9, 2014–January 1, 2015.

Hodge, Sara, great-granddaughter of Emil Lenders. May 26 and June 23, 2014.

Ruet, Joseph, grandnephew of Martha Allen Posenke Schultz. November 9 and December 9, 2014.

Sayre, Patricia, great-granddaughter of Arthur Rynearson. June 8, 2014–December 31, 2015.

Sheldon, Philip, grandnephew of James "Kid" Willoughby. October 3, 2014–December 31, 2015.

Shelton, Thomas, grandson of Mamie Francis Hafley and step-grandson of "California Frank" Hafley. June 23, 2014–December 31, 2015.

Small, Martha, great-granddaughter of Emil Lenders. June 28, 2015.

Spendley, Raymond Littlewolf, grandson of Neola and George Fuerst. January 29 and February 3, 2015.

INDEX

Page references in *italics* denote illustrations.

Exposition (St. Louis, 1904), 88, *97*, 118; Panama-California Exhibition (San Diego, 1915), 142; Panama-Pacific International Exhibition (San Francisco, 1915), 138–42; Pan-American Exposition (Buffalo, 1901), 73–84, *97*, 148; World's Columbian Exposition (Chicago, 1893), 63, 77

Wyoming, 36, 125, 133

Yankee Robinson Circus, 137, 138, 172
Yokuts, 18–19
Yosemite Valley, Calif., 15, 61
Yost, Nellie, 4, 44, 184n1

Zeglen, Casimir, 84–85, 167